ORIGIN AND GROWTH

OF

RELIGION

ORIGIN AND GROWTH

OF

RELIGION

AS ILLUSTRATED BY THE RELIGIONS OF INDIA.

F. MAX MULLER, M. A.

GYAN

Published by

GYAN

Gyan Publishing House
5, Ansari Road
Daryaganj, New Delhi-110002
Phone: 011-47034999, 9811692060
E-mail: books@gyanbooks.com

Distribution Network
gyanbooks.com
India, USA, Canada, UK, Australia, France

ISBN: 978-81-212-8782-1 (PB)
First Published, 1879

2nd Impression 2023

Printed at: Gyan Press, Delhi.

ORIGIN AND GROWTH OF RELIGION
Author: F. Max Muller

THE HIBBERT LECTURES.

LECTURES

ON THE

ORIGIN AND GROWTH

OF

RELIGION

AS ILLUSTRATED BY THE RELIGIONS OF INDIA.

DELIVERED IN THE CHAPTER HOUSE, WESTMINSTER ABBEY, IN APRIL, MAY, AND JUNE, 1878.

BY

F. MAX MÜLLER, M. A.

NEW YORK:
CHARLES SCRIBNER'S SONS.
1879.

To

HER WHOSE DEAR MEMORY

ENCOURAGED, DIRECTED, AND SUPPORTED ME

IN WRITING THESE LECTURES,

They are now dedicated,

AS A MEMORIAL

OF A FATHER'S LOVE.

PREFACE.

The Hibbert Trustees, having requested the publication of these lectures, desire to state some of the circumstances which led to their delivery.

The Founder of the Trust, Mr. Robert Hibbert, who died in 1849, bequeathed a sum of money with directions that the income should be applied in a manner indicated in general terms by him, but with large latitude of interpretation to the Trustees. The particulars are stated in a Memoir of Mr. Hibbert printed in 1874.[1]

For many years the Trustees appropriated their funds almost entirely to the higher culture of students for the Christian ministry, thus carrying out the instruction to adopt such scheme as they "in their uncontrolled discretion from time to time" should deem "most conducive to the spread of Christianity in its most simple and intelligible form, and to the unfettered exercise of private judgment in matters of religion."

In succeeding years other applications of the fund have been suggested to the Trustees, some of which have been adopted. One of the latest has been the institution of a Hibbert Lecture on a plan similar to that of the "Bampton" and "Congregational" Lectures. This proposal, conveyed in a letter which is

[1] Memoir of Robert Hibbert, Esq., Founder of the Hibbert Trust, with a sketch of its history, by Jerom Murch, one of the Trustees.

appended to the present statement, was made by a few eminent divines and laymen belonging to different churches, but united in a common desire for the "really capable and honest treatment of unsettled problems in theology."

After much deliberation the Trustees considered that if they could secure the assistance of suitable Lecturers, they would be promoting the object of the Testator, by courses on the various historical religions of the world. They were so fortunate as to obtain the consent of Professor Max Müller to begin the series, and to take as his subject the religions of India. They were also greatly indebted to the Dean of Westminster, who procured for them from the Board of Works the use of the Chapter House of the Abbey. On the announcement of the Lectures, there was great difficulty in meeting the numerous applications for tickets, which was only overcome by the kind consent of Professor Max Müller to deliver each lecture twice.

Encouraged by the success of this first course, the Trustees have arranged for a second. It will be undertaken by M. le Page Renouf, Her Majesty's Inspector of Schools, and the subject will be the Religions of Egypt; the time proposed is between Easter and Whitsuntide of next year.

J. M.

CRANWELLS, BATH, *October* 5, 1878

MEMORIAL FOR THE FOUNDATION OF A HIBBERT LECTURE.

To the Hibbert Trustees:

Gentlemen, — We, the undersigned, beg to draw your attention to the following statement: —

From the fact that all the chief divinity schools of this country are still laid under traditional restraint, from which other branches of inquiry have long been emancipated, the discussion of theological questions is habitually affected by ecclesiastical interests and party predilections, and fails to receive the intellectual respect and confidence which are readily accorded to learning and research in any other field. There is no reason why competent knowledge and critical skill, if encouraged to exercise themselves in the disinterested pursuit of truth, should be less fruitful in religious than in social and physical ideas; nor can it be doubted that an audience is ready to welcome any really capable and honest treatment of unsettled problems in theology. The time, we think, is come, when a distinct provision for the free consideration of such problems by scholars qualified to handle them may be expected to yield important results. Notwithstanding the traditional restraints which in England have interfered with an unprejudiced treatment of the theory and history of religion, a rich literature has poured in from the liberal schools of Germany and Holland, and has more or less trained and quickened the mind of the present generation, so that there cannot now be wanting qualified laborers in that reorganization of religious thought which is now taking place in our midst. Change of sentiment and feeling cannot be simply imported from abroad: till they pass through the minds of such men they have no local coloring and take no natural growth; and to modify English opinion and institutions there is need of English scholars. That need we think your encouragement can do something to supply. Such institutions as the Bampton Lecture at the University of Oxford, and the younger foundation of the Congregational Lecture among one branch of orthodox Nonconformists, have done much to direct the public mind to certain well-defined views of Christianity. We believe that a similar institution might prove of high service in promoting independence of judgment combined with religious reverence by exhibiting clearly from time to time some of the most important results of recent study in the great fields of philosophy, of Biblical criticism, and comparative theology.

We venture, therefore, to ask you to consider the expediency of establishing a "Lecture" under the name of the "Hibbert Lecture," or any other designation that may seem appropriate. A course, consisting of not fewer than six lectures, might be delivered every two or three years in London, or in the chief towns of Great Britain in rotation. After delivery, the course should be published under the direction of the managers of the lecture; and thus by degrees the issues of unfettered inquiry would be placed in a compact form before the educated public.

(Signed)

JAMES MARTINEAU.	ROBERT WALLACE.
ARTHUR P. STANLEY.	LEWIS CAMPBELL.
JOHN H. THOM.	JOHN CAIRD.
CHARLES WICKSTEED.	WILLIAM GASKELL.
WILLIAM B. CARPENTER.	CHARLES BEARD.
F. MAX MÜLLER.	T. K. CHEYNE.
GEORGE W. COX.	A. H. SAYCE.
J. MUIR.	RUSSELL MARTINEAU.
JOHN TULLOCH.	JAMES DRUMMOND.

TABLE OF CONTENTS.

LECTURE I.

THE PERCEPTION OF THE INFINITE.

PAGE

Problem of the origin of religion 1
Strauss: Have we still any religion 2
Antiquity of religion 3
Science of religion 5
Difference between ancient and modern belief . . . 8
Definitions of religion 9
Etymological meaning of religion 10
Historial aspect of religion 12
Definitions of religion by Kant and Fichte . . . 13
Religion, with or without worship 15
Definition of Schleiermacher (dependence), and of Hegel (freedom) 18
Comte and Feuerbach 19
Difficulty of defining religion 20
Specific characteristic of religion 20
Religion as a subjective faculty for the apprehension of the infinite 21
The three functions of sense, reason, and faith . . . 24
The meaning of infinite 26
Can the finite apprehend the infinite 28
Conditions accepted on both sides 29
Apprehension of the infinite 33
1. The infinitely great 33
2. The infinitely small 36
Growth of the idea of the infinite 40
No finite without an infinite 43

LECTURE II.

IS FETISHISM A PRIMITIVE FORM OF RELIGION?

	PAGE
The first impulse to the perception of the infinite	50
Mana, a Melanesian name for the infinite	51
Fetishism, the original form of all religion	53
De Brosses, the inventor of fetishism	54
Origin of the name of fetish	58
Wrong extension of the name fetish	60
Usefulness of the study of savage tribes	62
Frequent retrogression in religion	64
Difficulty of studying the religion of savages	65
Language of savages	67
Numerals of savages	69
No history among savages	70
No morals among savages	74
Religion universal among savages	76
Study of the religion of literary nations	77
Study of the religion of savages	83
Influence of public opinion on travelers	88
Absence of recognized authorities among savages	89
Authority of priests	90
Unwillingness of savages to talk of religion	91
Wide extension of the meaning of fetish	94
Antecedents of fetishism	95
Ubiquity of fetishism	98
No religion consists of fetishism only	101
Higher elements in African religion. Waitz	102
Zoölatry	109
Psycholatry	112
Many-sidedness of African religion	113
Supposed psychological necessity of fetishism	115
Whence the supernatural predicate of a fetish	117
Accidental origin of fetishism	118
Are savages like children	119
The four steps	121
Fetishism not a primary form of religion	122

LECTURE III.

THE ANCIENT LITERATURE OF INDIA, SO FAR AS IT SUPPLIES MATERIALS FOR THE STUDY OF THE ORIGIN OF RELIGION.

	PAGE
Usefulness of the study of literary religions	124
Growth of religious ideas in Judaism, Zoroastrianism, etc.	125
Growth of religion in India	127
Right position of the Veda in the science of religion	128
Discovery of Sanskrit literature	129
Buddhism the frontier between ancient and modern literature in India	129
The Veda proclaimed as revealed	132
Historical character of the Vedic language	138
The four strata of Vedic literature	140
I. Sutra period, 500 B. C.	140
II. Brâhmana period, 600–800 B. C.	144
III. Mantra period, 800–1000 B. C.	145
IV. *Kh*andas period, 1000–1010 B. C.	144
The Veda handed down by oral tradition	148
Postscript to the third lecture	153

LECTURE IV.

THE WORSHIP OF TANGIBLE, SEMI-TANGIBLE, AND INTANGIBLE OBJECTS.

Evidence of religion never entirely sensuous	162
External revelation	163
Internal revelation	164
The senses and their evidence	166
The meaning of manifest	167
Division of sense-objects into tangible and semi-tangible	168
Trees	169
Mountains	169
Rivers	170
The Earth	171
Semi-tangible objects	172
Intangible objects	173

PAGE
Testimonies of the ancients as to the character of their gods . . . 174
Testimony of the Veda . . . 175
Testimony of the undivided Aryan language . . . 176
Origin of language . . . 177
Early concepts . . . 179
Everything named as active . . . 180
Active does not mean human . . . 181
Grammatical gender . . . 182
Auxiliary verbs . . . 184
AS, to breathe . . . 185
BHÛ, to grow . . . 185
VAS, to dwell . . . 185
Primitive expression . . . 186
Likeness, originally conceived as negation . . . 187
Standing epithets . . . 188
Tangible objects among the Vedic deities . . . 191
Semi-tangible objects among the Vedic deities . . . 192
Fire . . . 198
The Sun . . . 200
The Dawn . . . 201
Audible objects among the Vedic deities . . . 202
Thunder . . . 202
Wind . . . 203
Marutas, the storm-gods . . . 203
The Rain and the Rainer . . . 204
Vedic pantheon . . . 205
The Devas . . . 206
The visible and the invisible . . . 207

LECTURE V.

THE IDEAS OF INFINITY AND LAW.

Nihil in fide quod non ante fuerit in sensu . . . 210
Theogony of the Veda . . . 216
The infinite in its earliest conception . . . 217
Aditi, the infinite . . . 218
Aditi not a modern deity . . . 220
Natural origin of Aditi . . . 220

	PAGE
Darkness and sin	222
Immortality	223
Other religious ideas in the Veda	224
The idea of law	226
The Sanskrit *Ri*ta	229
The original meaning of *Ri*ta	230
Story of Saramâ	232
*Ri*ta, the sacrifice	235
The development of *Ri*ta	236
Difficulty of translating	236
Was *Ri*ta a common Aryan concept	237
*Ri*ta is Asha in Zend	240

LECTURE VI.

ON HENOTHEISM, POLYTHEISM, MONOTHEISM, AND ATHEISM.

Is monotheism a primitive form of religion	245
The science of language and the science of religion	246
The predicate of God	249
The new materials supplied by the Veda	250
Henotheism	250
The Sun in his natural aspects	251
The Sun as a supernatural power	255
The Sun in a secondary position	260
The Sky as Dyaus, or the Illuminator	265
Struggle for supremacy between Dyaus and Indra	268
Hymn to Indra, as a supreme god	270
Hymn to Varu*n*a as a supreme god	273
Henotheism, the dialectic period of religion	275
The supremacy of different Devas	276
Further development of henotheism	278
Tendency towards monotheism	281
Visvakarman, the maker of all things	282
Pra*g*âpati, the lord of creatures	284
Tendency towards atheism	287
Faith in Indra, doubts about Indra	289
Difference between honest and vulgar atheism	292

LECTURE VII.

PHILOSOPHY AND RELIGION.

	PAGE
Collapse of the gods	299
The object of divine appellation	300
Neuter names higher than masculine or feminine	301
Âtman, the subjective self	302
Âtman, the objective self	303
The philosophy of the Upanishads	306
Pra*g*âpati and Indra	307
Yâ*g*navalkya and Maitreyî	316
Yama and Na*k*iketas	320
Religion of the Upanishads	325
Evolution in Vedic religion	327
The four castes	329
The four stages or Â*s*ramas	330
First stage, Studentship	331
Second stage, Married Life	333
Third stage, Retirement	336
Life in the forest	341
The end	346
Phases of religious thought	349
Retrospect	359
INDEX	365

I.

THE PERCEPTION OF THE INFINITE.

THE PROBLEM OF THE ORIGIN OF RELIGION.

How is it that we have a religion? This is a question which has not been asked for the first time in these latter days, but it is, nevertheless, a question which sounds startling even to ears that have been hardened by the din of many battles, fought for the conquest of truth. How it is that we exist, how it is that we perceive, how it is that we form concepts, how it is that we compare precepts and concepts, add and subtract, multiply and divide them — all these are problems with which everybody is more or less familiar, from the days in which he first opened the pages of Plato or Aristotle, of Hume or Kant. Sensation, perception, imagination, reasoning, everything in fact which exists in our own consciousness, has had to defend the right and reason of its existence; but the question, Why we believe, why we are, or imagine we are conscious of things which we can neither perceive with our senses, nor conceive with our reason — a question, it would seem more natural to ask than any other — has but seldom received, even from the greatest philosophers, that attention which it seems so fully to deserve.

STRAUSS: HAVE WE STILL ANY RELIGION?

What can be less satisfactory than the manner in which this problem has lately been pushed into the foreground of popular controversy? Strauss, in many respects a most acute reasoner, puts before us in his last work, "The Old and the New Faith," the question, "Have we still any religion?" To a challenge put in this form, the only answer that could be given would be an appeal to statistics; and here we should soon be told that, out of a hundred thousand people, there is hardly one who professes to be without religion. If another answer was wanted, the question ought to have been put in a different form. Strauss ought before all things to have told us clearly what he himself understands by religion. He ought to have defined religion both in its psychological and historical development. But what does he do instead? He simply takes the old definition which Schleiermacher gave of religion, viz., that it consists in a feeling of absolute dependence, and he supplements it by a definition of Feuerbach's, that the essence of all religion is covetousness, which manifests itself in prayer, sacrifice, and faith. He then concludes, because there is less of prayer, crossing, and attending mass in our days than in the Middle Ages, that, therefore, there is little left of real piety and religion. I have used, as much as possible, Strauss's own words.

But where has Strauss or anybody else proved that true religion manifests itself in prayer, crossing, and attending mass only, and that all who do not pray, who do not cross themselves, and who do not attend mass, have no longer any religion at all, and no belief in God? If we read on, we are almost tempted to admit that M. Renan was right in saying that those poor Germans try very hard to be irreligious and atheistical, but never succeed. Strauss says: "The world is to us the workshop of the Rational and the Good. That on which we feel ourselves absolutely dependent is by no means a brute power, before which we must bow in silent resignation. It is order and law, reason and goodness, to which we surrender ourselves with loving confidence. In our inmost nature we feel a kinship between ourselves and that on which we depend. In our dependence we are free, and pride and humility, joy and resignation, are mingled together in our feeling for all that exists."

If that is not religion, how is it to be called? The whole argument of Strauss amounts, in fact, to this. He retains religion as the feeling of dependence, in the full sense assigned to it by Schleiermacher, but he rejects the element added by Feuerbach, namely, the motive of covetousness, as both untrue and unworthy of religion. Strauss himself is so completely in the dark as to the true essence of religion, that when, at the end of the second chapter of his book, he asks himself whether he still has a religion, he can only answer, "Yes or No, according as you understand it."

Yes, but this is the very point which ought to have been determined first, namely, what we ought to understand by religion. And here I answer that in order to understand what religion is, we must first of all see what it has been, and how it has come to be what it is.

ANTIQUITY OF RELIGION.

Religion is not a new invention. It is, if not as old as the world, at least as old as the world we know. As soon almost as we know anything of the thoughts and feelings of man, we find him in possession of religion, or rather possessed by religion. The oldest literary documents are almost everywhere religious. "Our earth," as Herder[1] says, "owes the seeds of all higher culture to religious tradition, whether literary or oral." Even if we go beyond the age of literature, if we explore the deepest levels of human thought, we can discover, in the crude ore which was made to supply the earliest coins or counters of the human mind, the presence of religious ingredients. Before the Aryan languages separated — and who is to tell how many thousand years before the first hymn of the Veda or the first line of Homer that ethnic schism may have happened? — there existed in them an expression for light, and from it, from the root *div*, to shine, the adjective *deva* had been formed, meaning originally "bright." Afterwards this word *deva* was applied, as a comprehensive designation, to all the bright powers of the morning and the spring, as opposed to all the dark powers of the night and the winter; but when we meet with it for the first time in the oldest literary documents, it is already so far removed from this its primitive etymological meaning, that in the Veda there are but few passages where we can with certainty translate it still by "bright." The bright dawn is addressed in the Veda as *devî ushas*, but it must remain doubtful whether the old poets still felt in that address the etymological meaning of brightness, or whether we ought not to translate *deva* in the Veda, as *deus* in Latin, by God, however difficult we may find it to connect any definite meaning with such a translation. Still, what

[1] Herder, *Ideen zur Geschichte der Menschheit*, 9. Buch, p. 130 (ed. Brockhaus).

we know for certain is, that *deva* came to mean "god," because it originally meant "bright," and we cannot doubt that something beyond the meaning of brightness had attached itself to the word *deva* before the ancestors of the Indians and Italians broke up from their common home.

Thus, whether we descend to the lowest roots of our own intellectual growth, or ascend to the loftiest heights of modern speculation, everywhere we find religion as a power that conquers, and conquers even those who think that they have conquered it.

SCIENCE OF RELIGION.

Such a power did not escape the keen-eyed philosophers of ancient Greece. They, to whom the world of thought seems to have been as serene and transparent as the air which revealed the sea, the shore, and the sky of Athens, were startled at a very early time by the presence of religion, as by the appearance of a phantom which they could not explain. Here was the beginning of the science of religion, which is not, as has often been said, a science of to-day or of yesterday. The theory on the origin of religion put forward by Feuerbach in his work "On the Essence of Christianity," which sounds to us like the last note of modern despair, was anticipated more than two thousand years ago by the philosophers of Greece. With Feuerbach religion is a radical evil, inherent in mankind — the sick heart of man is the source of all religion, and of all misery. With Herakleitos, in the sixth century B. C., religion is a disease, though a sacred disease.[1] Such a saying, whatever we may

[1] See *Heracliti Ephesii Reliquiæ*, ed. Bywater, p. 57, l. 18, from *Vita Heracliti e Diogene Laertio*, ix. 1. Mr. Bywater places the saying τὴν

think of its truth, shows, at all events, that religion and the origin of religious ideas had formed the subject of deep and anxious thought at the very beginning of what we call the history of philosophy.

I doubt, however, whether there was in the sayings of Herakleitos the same hostile spirit against all religion as that which pervades the writings of Feuerbach. The idea that to believe is meritorious was not an ancient Greek idea, and therefore to doubt was not yet regarded as a crime, except where it interfered with public institutions. There was, no doubt, an orthodox party in Greece, but we can hardly say that it was fanatical;[1] nay, it is extremely difficult to understand at what time it acquired its power and whence it took its coherence.[2]

Herakleitos certainly blames those who follow singers (ἀοιδοί),[3] and whose teacher is the crowd, who pray to idols, as if they were to gossip with the walls of houses, not knowing what gods and heroes really are. Epikouros does the same. But, unlike Epikouros, Herakleitos nowhere denies the existence of invisible Gods or of the One Divine. Only when he saw people believing in what the singers, such as

τε οἴησιν ἱερὰν νόσον ἔλεγε, among the Spuria, p. 51. It seems to me to have the full, massive, and noble ring of Herakleitos. It is true that οἴησις means rather opinion and prejudice in general than religious belief; but to the philosophical mind of Herakleitos the latter is a subdivision only of the former. Opinion in general might be called a disease, but hardly a sacred disease, nor can sacred disease be taken here either in the sense of great and fearful disease, or in the technical sense of epilepsy. If I am wrong, I share my error with one of the best Greek scholars and mythologists, for Welcker takes the words of Herakleitos in the same sense in which I have taken them. They are sometimes ascribed to Epikouros; anyhow they belong to the oldest wisdom of Greece.

[1] Lange, *Geschichte des Materialismus*, i. 4.

[2] See E. Curtius, *Über die Bedeutung von Delphi für die Griechische Cultur*, Festrede am 22 Februar, 1878.

[3] *Heracliti Reliquiæ*, cxi., cxxvi.

Homer, and Hesiod, told them about Zeus and Hera, about Hermes and Aphrodite, he seems to have marveled; and the only explanation which he could find of so strange a phenomenon was, that it arose from an affection of the mind, which the physician might try to heal, whensoever it showed itself, but which he could never hope to stamp out altogether.

In a certain sense, therefore, the science of religion is as little a modern invention as religion itself. Wherever there is human life, there is religion, and wherever there is religion, the question whence it came cannot be long suppressed. When children once begin to ask questions, they ask the why and the wherefore of everything, religion not excepted; nay, I believe that the first problems of what we call philosophy were suggested by religion.

It has sometimes been asked why Thales should be called a philosopher, and should keep his place on the first page of every history of philosophy. Many a school-boy may have wondered why to say that water was the beginning of all things should be called philosophy. And yet, childish as that saying may sound to us, it was anything but childish at the time of Thales. It was the first bold denial that the gods had made the world; it was the first open protest against the religion of the crowd — a protest that had to be repeated again and again before the Greeks could be convinced that such thinkers as Herakleitos (Reliquiæ, xx.) and Xenophanes had at least as good a right to speak of the gods or of God as Homer and other itinerant singers.

No doubt, at that early time, what was alone important was to show that what was believed by the crowd was purely fanciful. To ask how those fanciful opinions of the crowd had arisen, was a problem belonging to a later age. Still, even that problem was not entirely absent from the minds of the earliest thinkers of Greece; for no one could have given the answer ascribed to Herakleitos who had not asked himself the question which we ask ourselves to-day: What, then, is the origin of religion? or, to put it into more modern language, How is it that we believe, that we accept what, as we are told by enemy and friend, cannot be supplied to us by our senses or established by our reason?

DIFFERENCE BETWEEN ANCIENT AND MODERN BELIEF.

It may be said that, when Herakleitos pondered on οἴησις, or belief, he meant something very different from what we mean by religion. No doubt he did; for if there is a word that has changed from century to century, and has a different aspect in every country in which it is used — nay, which conveys peculiar shades of meaning, as it is used by every man, woman, or child — it is religion. In our ordinary language we use religion in at least three different senses; first, as the object of belief; secondly, as the power of belief; thirdly, as the manifestation of belief, whether in acts of worship or in acts of real piety.

The same uncertainty prevails in other languages. It would be difficult to translate our word religion into Greek or Sanskrit; nay, even in Latin, *religio* does by no means cover all that religion comprehends in English. We need not be surprised, therefore, at the frequent misunderstandings, and consequent wranglings, between those who write on religion, without at least having made so much clear to themselves and others, whether by religion they mean religious dogma, religious faith, or religious acts.

I have dwelt on this point in order to show you that it is not from mere pedantry if, at the very outset of these lectures, I insist on the necessity of giving a definition of religion, before we attempt another step in our journey that is to lead us as near as possible to the hidden sources of our faith.

DEFINITIONS OF RELIGION.

It was, I think, a very good old custom never to enter upon the discussion of any scientific problem without giving beforehand definitions of the principal terms that had to be employed. A book on logic or grammar generally opened with the question, What is logic? What is grammar? No one would write on minerals without first explaining what he meant by a mineral, or on art without defining, as well as he might, his idea of art. No doubt it was often as troublesome for the author to give such preliminary definitions as it seemed useless to the reader, who was generally quite incapable of appreciating in the beginning their full value. Thus it happened that the rule of giving verbal definitions came to be looked upon after a time as useless and obsolete. Some authors actually took credit for no longer giving these verbal definitions, and it soon became the fashion to say that the only true and complete definition of what was meant by logic or grammar, by law or religion, was contained in the books themselves which treated of these subjects.

But what has been the result? Endless misunderstandings and controversies, which might have been avoided in many cases, if both sides had clearly defined what they did, and what they did not understand by certain words.

With regard to religion, it is no doubt extremely difficult to give a definition. The word rose to the surface thousands of years ago; it was retained while what was meant by it went on changing from century to century, and it is now often applied to the very opposite of what it was originally intended to signify.

ETYMOLOGICAL MEANING OF RELIGIO.

It is useless with words of this kind to appeal to their etymological meaning. The etymological meaning of a word is always extremely important, both psychologically and historically, because it indicates the exact point from which certain ideas started. But to know the small source of a river is very different from knowing the whole course of it; and to know the etymology of a word is very different from being able to trace it through all the eddies and cataracts through which it has been tossed and tumbled, before it became what it is now.

Besides, as with rivers, so with words, it is by no means easy to put our finger on the exact spot from whence they bubble forth. The Romans themselves felt doubtful as to the original meaning of *religio*. Cicero, as is well known, derived it from *re-legere*, to gather up again, to take up, to consider, to ponder — opposed to *nec-ligere*, to neglect; while others derived it from *re-ligare*, to fasten, to hold back. I belief myself that Cicero's etymology is the right one; but if *religio* [1] meant originally attention, regard, rev-

[1] Rĕligio, if it was derived from *rĕ-legere*, would have meant originally gathering again, taking up again, considering carefully. Thus *dī-ligo*

erence, it is quite clear that it did not continue long to retain that simple meaning.

meant originally to gather, to take up from among other things; then to esteem, to love. *Negligo* (nec-lego) meant not to take up, to leave unnoticed, to neglect. *Intelligo* meant to gather together with other things, to connect together, to arrange, classify, understand.

Rĕlego occurs in the sense of taking back, gathering up (Ovid. Met. 8. 173): Janua difficilis filo est inventa relecto, "The difficult door was found by the thread [of Ariadne], which was gathered up again." It is frequently used in the sense of travelling over the same ground: Egressi relegunt campos (Val. Fl. 8. 121). In this meaning Cicero thinks that it was used, when applied to religion: Qui omnia quæ ad cultum deorum pertinerent diligenter retractarent et tamquam relegerent, sunt dicti religiosi ex relegendo, ut eleganter ex eligendo, tamquam a diligendo diligenter, ex intelligendo intelligenter: his enim in verbis omnibus inest vis legendi eadem quæ in religioso (Cic. de Nat. Deor. 2, 28, 72), "People were called religious from relegere, because they went over again, as it were, and reconsidered carefully whatever referred to the worship of gods."

Relegere would therefore have meant originally much the same as respicere, revereri, which, from meaning to look back, came to mean to respect.

An ancient author quoted by Gellius (4. 9) makes a distinction between *religiosus*, which he uses in the sense of superstitious, and *religens*. "Religentem esse oportet," he says, "religiosum nefas:" it is right to be reverent, wrong to be religious, *i. e.* superstitious. The difficulty that rēligio has retained its long ē, being also written sometimes relligio (from redligio), is not even mentioned by Cicero. Lucretius uses both rēduco and rēlatum with a long e.

Religio, used subjectively, meant conscientiousness, reverence, awe, and was not originally restricted to reverence for the gods. Thus we read: Religione jurisjurandi ac metu deorum in testimoniis dicendis commoveri, "to be moved in giving evidence by the reverence for an oath, and by the fear of the gods" (C. Font. 9. 20). Very soon, however, it became more and more restricted to reverence for the gods and divine things. People began to speak of a man's religion, meaning his piety, his faith in the gods, his observance of ceremonies, till at last an entire system of faith was called religiones or religio.

The other derivation of religio is supported by high authorities, such as Servius, Lactantius, St. Augustin, who derive it from *religare*, to bind up, to fasten, to moor. From this point of view *religio* would have meant originally what binds us, holds us back. I doubt whether with Pott (Etym. Forsch. i. p. 201) we can say that such a derivation is impossible. No doubt a noun like *religio* cannot be derived direct from a verb of the first conjugation, such as *religare*. That would give us *religatio*, just as *obligare* gives us *obligatio*. But verbs of the first conjugation are themselves derivatives, and many of them exist by the side of words derived from their more simple roots. Thus, by the side of *opinari* we have

HISTORICAL ASPECT OF RELIGION.

It must be clear that when we have to use words which have had a long history of their own, we can neither use them in their primitive etymological meaning, nor can we use them at one and the same time in all the senses through which they have passed. It is utterly useless to say, for instance, that religion meant this, and did not mean that; that it meant faith or worship, or morality or ecstatic vision, and that it did not mean fear or hope, or surmise, or reverence of the gods. Religion may mean all this; perhaps at one time or other the name was used in every one of these meanings; but who has a right to say that religion shall at present or in future have one of these meanings, and one only? The mere savage may not even have a name for religion; still when the Papua squats before his *karwar*, clasping his hands over his forehead, and asking himself whether what he is going to do is right or wrong, that is to him religion. Among several savage tribes, where there was no sign of a knowledge of divine beings, missionaries have recognized in the worship paid to the spirits of the departed the first faint beginnings of

opinio and *necopinus*; by the side of *rebellare*, *rebellis* and *rebellio*. Ebel (Kuhn's *Zeitschrift*, iv. p. 144) points out that by the side of *ligare* we have *lictor*, originally a binder, and that, therefore, *religio* from *religare* could be defended, at all events, grammatically. I believe that is so. Still there is no trace of *religare* having been used by the Romans themselves in the sense of restraining, still less of revering or fearing, and these after all are the original meanings in which *religio* first appears in Latin. Ebel thinks that *lex*, *leg-is*, is likewise derived from *ligare*, like *jus*, from Sanskrit *yu*, to join. The Oscan *lig-ud*, *lêge*, might seem to confirm this. But Lottner's comparison of *lex* with the Old N. *lög*, Eng. *law*, what is laid down, and is settled (*Gesetz* in German) deserves consideration (see Curtius: *Griech. Etymologie*, i. p. 367), though it must be borne in mind that the transition of h and χ into g is irregular.

religion; nor should we hesitate to recognize the last glimmerings of religion when we see a recent philosopher, after declaring both God and gods obsolete, falling down before a beloved memory, and dedicating all his powers to the service of humanity. When the publican, standing afar off, would not lift up so much as his eyes unto heaven, but smote upon his breast, saying, "God be merciful to me a sinner," that was to him religion. When Thales declared that all things were full of the gods, and when Budha denied that there were any *devas* or gods at all, both were stating their religious convictions. When the young Brahman lights the fire on his simple altar at the rising of the sun, and prays, in the oldest prayer of the world, "May the Sun quicken our minds;" or when, later in life, he discards all prayer and sacrifice as useless, nay, as hurtful, and silently buries his own self in the Eternal Self — all this is religion. Schiller declared that he professed no religion; and why? From religion. How, then, shall we find a definition of religion sufficiently wide to comprehend all these phases of thought?

DEFINITIONS OF RELIGION BY KANT AND FICHTE.

It may be useful, however, to examine at least a few of the more recent definitions of religion, if only to see that almost every one is met by another, which takes the very opposite view of what religion is or ought to be. According to Kant, religion is morality. When we look upon all our moral duties as divine commands, that, he thinks, constitutes religion.[1] And

[1] "Religion ist (subjectiv betrachtet) das Erkenntniss aller unserer Pflichten als göttlicher Gebote." — "Religion innerhalb der Grenzen der blossen Vernunft," iv. 1.

we must not forget that Kant does not consider that duties are moral duties because they rest on a divine command (that would be, according to Kant, merely revealed religion); on the contrary, he tells us that because we are directly conscious of them as duties, therefore we look upon them as divine commands. Any outward divine authority is, in the eyes of a Kantian philosopher, something purely phenomenal, or, as we should say, a mere concession to human weakness. An established religion [1] or the faith of a church, though it cannot at first dispense with statutory laws which go beyond pure morality, must, he thinks, contain in itself a principle which in time will make the religion of good moral conduct its real goal, and enable us in the end to surrender the preliminary faith of the Church.

Fichte, Kant's immediate successor, takes the very opposite view. Religion, he says, is never practical, and was never intended to influence our life. Pure morality suffices for that, and it is only a corrupt society that has to use religion as an impulse to moral action. Religion is knowledge. It gives to a man a clear insight into himself, answers the highest questions, and thus imparts to us a complete harmony with ourselves, and a thorough sanctification to our mind.

[1] See Kant, l. c. p. 183: "Weil indess jede auf statuarischen Gesetzen errichtete Kirche nur in so ferne die wahre sein kann, als sie in sich ein Princip enthält, sich dem reinen Vernunftglauben (als demjenigen, der, wenn er practisch ist, in jedem Glauben eigentlich die Religion ausmacht) beständig zu nähern, und den Kirchenglauben (nachdem was an ihm historisch ist) mit der Zeit entbehren zu können, so werden wir in diesen Gesetzen und an den Beamten der darauf gegründeten Kirche doch einen Dienst (cultus) der Kirche so ferne setzen können, als diese ihre Lehren und Anordnung jederzeit auf jenen letzten Zweck (einen öffentlichen Religionsglauben) richten."

Now Kant may be perfectly right in saying that religion *ought* to be morality, or Fichte may be perfectly right in saying that it *ought* to be knowledge. What I protest against is, that either the one or the other should be taken as a satisfactory definition of what is or was universally meant by the word religion.

RELIGION, WITH OR WITHOUT WORSHIP.

There is another view according to which religion consists in the worship of divine beings, and it has been held by many writers to be impossible that a religion could exist without some outward forms,— without what is called a *cultus*. A religious reformer has a perfect right to say so, but the historian of religion could easily point out that religions have existed, and do exist still, without any signs of external worship.

In the last number of the "Journal of the Anthropological Society" (February, 1878), Mr. C. H. E. Carmichael draws our attention to a very interesting account of a mission established by Benedictine monks in New Nursia in Western Australia, north of the Swan River, in the diocese assigned to the Roman Catholic Bishop of Perth in 1845.[1] These Benedictine monks took great pains to ascertain the religious sentiments of the natives, and for a long time they seem to have been unable to discover even the faintest traces of anything that could be called religion. After three years of mission life, Monsignor Salvado declares that the natives do not adore any

[1] *Memorie Storiche dell' Australia, particolarmente della Missione Benedettina di Nuova Norcia, e degli usi e costumi degli Australiani*, per Mgr. D. Rudesindo Salvado, O. S. B., Vescovo di Porto Vittoria. Roma, Tip. S. Cong. de Prop. Fide, 1851.

deity, whether true or false. Yet he proceeds to tell us that they believe in an Omnipotent Being, creator of heaven and earth, whom they call *Motogon*, and whom they imagine as a very tall, powerful, and wise man of their own country and complexion. His mode of creation was by breathing. To create the earth, he said, "Earth, come forth!" and he breathed, and the earth was created. So with the sun, the trees, the kangaroo, etc. *Motogon*, the author of good, is confronted by *Cienga*, the author of evil. This latter being is the unchainer of the whirlwind and the storm, and the invisible author of the death of their children, wherefore the natives fear him exceedingly. Moreover, as *Motogon* has long since been dead and decrepit, they no longer pay him any worship. Nor is *Cienga*, although the natives believe that he afflicts them with calamities, propitiated by any service. "Never," the bishop concludes, "did I observe any act of external worship, nor did any indication suggest to me that they practiced any internal worship."

If from one savage race we turn to another, we find among the Hidatsa or Grosventre Indians of the Missouri the very opposite state. Mr. Matthews,[1] who has given us an excellent account of this tribe, says (p. 48): "If we use the term worship in its most extended sense, it may be said that, besides 'the Old Man Immortal,' or 'the Great Spirit,' 'the Great Mystery,' they worship everything in nature. Not man alone, but the sun, the moon, the stars, all the lower animals, all trees and plants, rivers and lakes, many bowlders and other separated

[1] *Ethnography and Philology of the Hidatsa Indians.* By Washington Matthews. Washington, 1877.

rocks, even some hills and buttes which stand alone, —in short, everything not made by human hands, which has an independent being, or can be individualized, possesses a spirit, or, more properly, a shade. To these shades some respect or consideration is due, but not equally to all. . . . . The sun is held in great veneration, and many valuable sacrifices are made to it."

Here then among the very lowest of human beings we see how some worship everything, while others worship nothing, and who shall say which of the two is the more truly religious?

Let us now look at the conception of religion, such as we find it among the most cultivated races of Europe, and we shall find among them the same divergence. Kant declares that to attempt to please the Deity by acts which have no moral value, by mere *cultus*, *i. e.* by external worship, is not religion, but simply superstition.[1] I need not quote authorities on the other side who declare that a silent religion of the heart, or even an active religion in common life, is nothing without an external worship, without a priesthood, without ritual.

We might examine many more definitions of re-

[1] "Alles, was, ausser dem guten Lebenswandel, der Mensch noch thun zu können vermeint, um Gott wohlgefällig zu werden, ist blosser Religionswahn und Afterdienst Gottes" (l. c. iv. 2, p. 205). "Ob der Andächtler seinen statutenmässigen Gang zur Kirche, oder ob er eine Wallfahrt nach den Heiligthümern in Loretto oder Palästina anstellt, ob er seine Gebetsformeln mit den Lippen, oder wie der Tibetaner (welcher glaubt, dass diese Wünsche, auch schriftlich anfgesetzt, wenn sie nur durch irgend Etwas, z. B. auf Flaggen geschrieben, durch den Wind, oder in einer Büchse eingeschlossen, als eine Schwungmaschine mit der Hand bewegt werden ihren Zweck ebenso gut erreichen) es durch ein Gebetrad an die himmlische Behörde bringt, oder was für ein Surrogat des moralischen Dienstes Gottes es auch immer sein mag, das ist Alles einerlei und von gleichen Werth" (p. 208).

ligion, and we should always find that they contain what certain persons thought that religion ought to be; but they are hardly ever wide enough to embrace all that has been called religion at different periods in the history of the world. That being so, the next step has generally been to declare that whatever is outside the pale of any one of these definitions does not deserve to be called religion; but should be called superstition, or idolatry, or morality, or philosophy, or any other more or less offensive name. Kant would call much of what other people call religion, hallucination; Fichte would call Kant's own religion mere legality. Many people would qualify the brilliant services, whether carried on in Chinese temples or Roman Catholic cathedrals, as mere superstition; while the faith of the silent Australians, and the half-uttered convictions of Kant, would by others be classed together as not very far removed from atheism.

DEFINITION OF SCHLEIERMACHER (DEPENDENCE), AND OF HEGEL (FREEDOM).

I shall mention one more definition of religion, which in modern times has been rendered memorable and popular by Schleiermacher. According to him religion consists in our consciousness of absolute dependence on something which, though it determines us, we cannot determine in turn.[1] But here again another class of philosophers step in, declaring that feeling of dependence the very opposite of religion. There is a famous, though not very wise saying of

[1] This is, of course, a very imperfect account of Schleiermacher's view of religion, which became more and more perfect as he advanced in life. See on this point the excellent *Life of Schleiermacher*, by W. Dilthey, 1870.

Hegel, that if the consciousness of dependence constituted religion, the dog would possess most religion. On the contrary, religion, according to Hegel, is or ought to be perfect freedom; for it is neither more nor less than the Divine Spirit becoming conscious of himself through the finite spirit.

COMTE AND FEUERBACH.

From this point it required but another step, and that step was soon taken by Feuerbach in Germany, and by Comte in France, to make man himself, not only the subject, but also the object of religion and religious worship. We are told that man cannot know anything higher than man; that man therefore is the only true object of religious knowledge and worship, only not man as an individual, but man as a class. The generic concept of man, or the genius of humanity, is to be substantiated, and then humanity becomes at once both the priest and the Deity.

Nothing can be more eloquent, and in some passages really more solemn and sublime, than the religion of humanity, as preached by Comte and his disciples. Feuerbach, however, dissipates the last mystic halo which Comte had still left. "Self-love," he says, "is a necessary, indestructible, universal law and principle, inseparable from every kind of love. Religion must and does confirm this on every page of her history. Wherever man tries to resist that human egoism, in the sense in which we explained it, whether in religion, philosophy, or politics, he sinks into pure nonsense and insanity; for the sense which forms the foundation of all human instincts, desires, and actions is the satisfaction of the human being, the satisfaction of human egoism."[1]

[1] Feuerbach, *Wesen der Religion*, p. 100.

DIFFICULTY OF DEFINING RELIGION.

Thus we see that each definition of religion, as soon as it is started, seems at once to provoke another which meets it by a flat denial. There seem to be almost as many definitions of religion as there are religions in the world, and there is almost the same hostility between those who maintain these different definitions of religion as there is between the believers in different religions. What, then, is to be done ? Is it really impossible to give a definition of religion that should be applicable to all that has ever been called religion, or by some similar name? I believe it is, and you will yourselves have perceived the reason why it is so. Religion is something which has passed, and is still passing through an historical evolution, and all we can do is to follow it up to its origin, and then to try to comprehend it in its later historical developments.

SPECIFIC CHARACTERISTIC OF RELIGION.

But though an adequate definition, or even an exhaustive description, of all that has ever been called religion is impossible, what is possible is to give some specific characteristic which distinguishes the objects of religious consciousness from all other objects, and at the same time distinguishes our consciousness, as applied to religious objects, from our consciousness when dealing with other objects supplied to it by sense and reason.

Let it not be supposed, however, that there is a separate consciousness for religion. There is but one self and one consciousness, although that consciousness varies according to the objects to which it is applied. We distinguish between sense and reason, though even these two are in the highest sense different functions only of the same conscious self. In the same manner, when we speak of faith as a religious faculty in man, all that we can mean is our ordinary consciousness, so developed and modified as to enable us to take cognizance of religious objects. This is not meant as a new sense, by the side of the other senses, or as a new reason by the side of our ordinary reason, — a new soul within the soul. It is simply the old consciousness applied to new objects, and reacted upon by them. To admit faith as a separate religious faculty, or a theistic instinct, in order to explain religion as a fact, such as we find it everywhere, would be like admitting a vital force in order to explain life; it would be a mere playing with words or trifling with truth. Such explanations may have answered formerly, but at present the battle has advanced too far for any peace to be concluded on such terms.

RELIGION, AS A SUBJECTIVE FACULTY FOR THE APPREHENSION OF THE INFINITE.

In a course of introductory lectures on the Science of Religion, delivered at the Royal Institution in 1873, I tried to define the subjective side of religion, or what is commonly called faith, in the following words:[1] —

"Religion is a mental faculty which, independent of, nay, in spite of sense and reason, enables man to apprehend the infinite under different names and under varying disguises. Without that faculty, no religion, not even the lowest worship of idols and

[1] *Introduction to the Science of Religion*, 1873, p. 17.

fetishes, would be possible; and if we will but listen attentively, we can hear in all religions a groaning of the spirit, a struggle to conceive the inconceivable, to utter the unutterable, a longing after the Infinite, a love of God."

I do not quote these words because I altogether approve of them now. I very seldom approve altogether of what I have written myself some years ago. I fully admit the force of many objections that have been raised against that definition of religion, but I still think that the kernel of it is sound. I should not call it now an exhaustive definition of religion, but I believe it supplies such characteristics as will enable us to distinguish between religious consciousness on one side, and sensuous and rational consciousness on the other.

What has been chiefly objected to in my definition of religion was, that I spoke of it as a mental faculty. "Faculty" is a word that rouses the anger of certain philosophers, and to some extent I fully share their objections. It seems to be imagined that faculty must signify something substantial, a spring as it were, setting a machine in motion; a seed or a pip that can be handled, and will spring up when planted in proper soil. How faculty could be used in such a sense, I have never been able to comprehend, though I cannot deny that it has often been thus used. Faculty signifies a mode of action, never a substantial something. Faculties are neither gods nor ghosts, neither powers nor principalities. Faculties are inherent in substances, quite as much as forces or powers are. We generally speak of the faculties of conscious, of the forces of unconscious substances. Now we know that there is no force without substance, and no substance without force. To speak of gravity, for instance, as a thing by itself, would be sheer mythology. If the law of gravity had been discovered at Rome, there would have been a temple built to the goddess of gravity. We no longer build temples, but the way in which some natural philosophers speak of gravity is hardly less mythological. The same danger exists, I fully admit, with regard to the manner in which certain philosophers speak of our faculties, and we know that one faculty at least, that of Reason, has had an altar erected to her not very long ago. If, therefore, faculty is an ambiguous and dangerous, or if it is an unpopular word, let us by all means discard it. I am perfectly willing to say "potential energy" instead, and therefore to define the subjective side of religion as the potential energy which enables man to apprehend the infinite. If the English language allowed it, I should even propose to replace "faculty" by the *Not-yet*, and to speak of the *Not-yet* of language and religion, instead of their faculties or potential energies.[1] Professor Pfleiderer,

[1] Instead of slaying the slain over again, I quote the following words of Locke, *On the Understanding*, Book ii. c. 21. 17: "For if it be reasonable to suppose and talk of faculties as distinct beings, that can act (as we do, when we say the will orders, and the will is free), it is fit that we should make a speaking faculty, and a walking faculty, and a dancing faculty, by which those actions are produced, which are but several modes of motion; as well as we make the will and understanding to be faculties by which the actions of choosing and perceiving are produced, which are but several modes of thinking; and we may as properly say that it is the singing faculty sings, and the dancing faculty dances, as that the will chooses, or that the understanding conceives; or, as is usual, that the will directs the understanding, or the understanding obeys, or obeys not, the will; it being altogether as proper and intelligible to say that the power of speaking directs the power of singing, or the power of singing obeys, or disobeys the power of speaking. This way of talking, nevertheless, has prevailed, and, as I guess, produced great confusion."

"In einen Dialog sollte einmal recht persiflirt werden, wie die Leute von einzelnen Seelenvermögen reden, z. B. Kant: die reine Vernunft schmeichelt sich." — *Schleiermacher*, von Dilthey, vol. i. p. 122.

to whom we owe some excellent contributions to the science of religion, finds fault with my definition because it admits, not only a *facultas*, but a *facultas occulta*. All depends here again on the sense which we attach to *facultas occulta*. If it means no more than that there is in men, both individually and generally (ontogenetically and phylogenetically) something that develops into perception, conception, and faith, using the last word as meaning the apprehension of the infinite, then I fully admit a *facultas occulta*. Everything that develops may from one point of view be called occult. This, however, applies not only to the faculty of faith, but likewise to the faculties of sense and reason.

THE THREE FUNCTIONS OF SENSE, REASON, AND FAITH.

Secondly, it has been objected that there is something mysterious in this view of religion. As to myself, I cannot see that in admitting, besides the sensuous and rational, a third function of the conscious self, for apprehending the infinite, we introduce a mysterious element into psychology. One of the essential elements of all religious knowledge is the admission of beings which can neither be apprehended by sense nor comprehended by reason. Sense and reason, therefore, in the ordinary acceptation of these terms, would not be sufficient to account for the facts before us. If, then, we openly admit a third function of our consciousness for the apprehension of what is infinite, that function need not be more mysterious than those of sense and reason. Nothing is in reality more mysterious than sensuous perception. It is the real mystery of all mysteries. Yet we have accustomed ourselves to regard it as the most natural of all things. Next comes reason, which, to a being restricted to sensuous perception, might certainly appear very mysterious again, and which even by certain philosophers has been represented as altogether incomprehensible. Yet we know that reason is only a development of sensuous perception, possible under certain conditions. These conditions correspond to what we call the potential energy or faculty of reason. They belong to one and the same conscious self, and though reason is active in a different manner, yet, if kept under proper control, reason works in perfect harmony with sense. The same applies to religion in its subjective sense of faith. It is, as I shall try to show, simply another development of sensuous perception, quite as much as reason is. It is possible under certain conditions, and these conditions correspond to what we call the potential energy of faith. Without this third potential energy, the facts which are before us in religion, both subjectively and objectively, seem to me inexplicable. If they can be explained by a mere appeal to sense and reason, in the ordinary meaning of these words, let it be done. We shall then have a rational religion, or an intuitional faith. None of my critics, however, has done that yet; few, I believe, would like to do it.

When I say that our apprehension of the infinite takes place independent of, nay, in spite of sense and reason, I use these two words in their ordinary acceptation. If it is true that sense supplies us with finite objects only, and if reason has nothing to work on except those finite objects, then our assumed apprehension of anything infinite must surely be independent of, nay, in spite of sense or reason. Whether the premises are right is another question, which we shall have to discuss presently.

THE MEANING OF INFINITE.

Let us now see whether we can agree on some general characteristic of all that forms the object of our religious consciousness. I chose "infinite" for that purpose, as it seemed best to comprehend all that transcends our senses and our reason, taking these terms in their ordinary meaning. All sensuous knowledge, whatever else it may be, is universally admitted to be finite, finite in space and time, finite also in quantity and quality, and as our conceptual knowledge is based entirely on our sensuous knowledge, that also can deal with finite objects only. Finite being then the most general predicate of all our so-called positive knowledge, I thought infinite the least objectionable term for all that transcends our senses and our reason, always taking these words in their ordinary meaning. I thought it preferable to indefinite, invisible, supersensuous, supernatural, absolute, or divine, as the characteristic qualification of the objects of that large class of knowledge which constitutes what we call religion. All these terms are meant for the same thing. They all express different aspects of the same object. I have no predilection for infinite, except that it seems to me the widest term, the highest generalization. But if any other term seems preferable, again I say, let us adopt it by all means.

Only let us now clearly understand what we mean by infinite, or any other of these terms that may seem preferable.

If the infinite were, as certain philosophers suppose, simply a negative abstraction (*ein negativer Abstractions-begriff*), then, no doubt, reason would suffice to explain how we came to be possessed of it. But abstraction will never give us more than that from which we abstract. From a given number of perceptions we can abstract the concept of a given multitude. Infinite, however, is not contained in finite, therefore we may do what we like, we shall never be able to abstract the infinite from the finite. To say, as many do, that the infinite is a negative abstract concept, is a mere playing with words. We may form a negative abstract concept, when we have to deal with serial or correlative concepts, but not otherwise. Let us take a serial concept, such as blue, then not-blue means green, yellow, red, any color, in fact, except blue. Not-blue means simply the whole concept of color, *minus* blue. We might of course comprehend sweet, or heavy, or crooked by the negative concept of not-blue, — but our logic does not admit of such proceedings.

If we take correlative concepts, such as crooked and straight, then not-straight may by logicians be called a negative concept, but it is in reality quite as positive as crooked, not-straight being crooked, not-crooked being straight.

Now let us apply this to finite. Finite, we are told, comprehends everything that can be perceived by the senses, or counted by reason. Therefore, if we do not only form a word at random, by adding the ordinary negative particle to finite, but try to form a really negative concept, then that concept of infinite would be outside the concept of finite, and as, according to a premiss generally granted, there is nothing known to us outside the concept of the finite, the concept of the infinite would simply comprise nothing. Infinite, therefore, cannot be treated simply as a negative concept; if it were no more than that, it would be a word formed by false analogy, and signify nothing.

CAN THE FINITE APPREHEND THE INFINITE?

All the objections which we have hitherto examined proceed from friendly writers. They are amendments of my own definition of religion; they do not amount to a moving of the previous question. But it is well known that that previous question also has been moved. There is a large class, not only of philosophers by profession, but of independent thinkers in all classes of society, who look upon any attempt at defining religion as perfectly useless; who would not listen even to a discussion whether one religion was false or another true, but who simply deny the possibility of any religion whatsoever, on the ground that men cannot apprehend what is infinite, while all religions, however they may differ on other points, agree in this, that their objects transcend, either partially or entirely, the apprehensive and comprehensive powers of our senses and our reason. This is the ground on which what is now called positive philosophy takes its stand, denying the possibility of religion, and challenging all who admit any source of knowledge except sense and reason to produce their credentials.

This is not a new challenge, nor is the ground on which the battle has to be fought new ground. It is the old battle-field measured out long ago by Kant, only that the one opening which was still left in his time, viz, the absolute certainty of moral truth, and through it the certainty of the existence of a God, is now closed up. There is no escape in that direction.[1] The battle between those who believe in something which transcends our senses and our reason, who claim for man the possession of a faculty or potential energy for apprehending the infinite, and those who deny it on purely psychological grounds, must end in the victory of one, and the surrender of the other party.

CONDITIONS ACCEPTED ON BOTH SIDES.

Before we commit ourselves to this struggle for life or death, let us inspect once more the battle-field, as it is measured out for us, and survey what is the common ground on which both parties have agreed to stand or to fall. What is granted to us is that all consciousness begins with sensuous perception, with what we feel, and hear, and see. This gives us sensuous knowledge. What is likewise granted is that out of this we construct what may be called conceptual knowledge, consisting of collective and abstract

[1] One of the first who pointed out the uncertainty of the foundation on which Kant attempted to reconstruct religion, in the widest sense of the word, was Wyttenbach, *Opusc.* ii. p. 190 : "Non consentaneus sibi est (Kantius) in eo, quod, quum categorias à priori intelligibiles et antiquiores esse experientia statuit, ab his nullum progressum ad nova intelligibilia concedit. . . . . Tum quod illa tria placita, 'dei, immortalitatis, libertatis,' ex metaphysica ad ethicam, ex theoretica ratione ad practicam relegat, non modo hæc ipsa placita labefactat, ex lucido firmoque intelligentiæ fastigio in lubricam et confusam interni sensus latebram rejiciens, sed ἀφιγοσόφως agit et ipsum primum philosophiæ officium negligit. . . . . Theoretica dogmata ex practico ducuntur contra naturum philosophiæ, cujus est practica ex theoretico ducere. . . . . Illa tria theoretica dogmata longe dilucidiora et minus incerta sunt, quam ille sensus moralis dubius et controversus . . . . novo habitu imperatorio, inaudito nomine imperativi categorici in scenam revocatus et productus. Nonne hoc est Deum ex machina inducere ?" See Prantl, *Sitzungsberichte der philos. philolog. und historischen Classe der K. B. Akademie der Wissenschaften.* 1877, p. 284.

concepts. What we call thinking consists simply in addition and subtraction of percepts and concepts. Conceptual knowledge differs from sensuous knowledge, not in substance, but in form only. As far as the material is concerned, nothing exists in the intellect except what existed before in the senses. The organ of knowledge is throughout the same, only that it is more highly developed in animals that have five senses than in animals that have but one sense, and again more highly developed in man who counts and forms concepts than in all other animals who do not.

On this ground and with these weapons we are to fight. With them, we are told, all knowledge has been gained, the whole world has been conquered. If with them we can force our way to a world beyond, well and good; if not, we are asked to confess that all that goes by the name of religion, from the lowest fetishism to the most spiritual and exalted faith, is a delusion, and that to have recognized this delusion is the greatest triumph of our age.

I accept these terms, and I maintain that religion, so far from being impossible, is inevitable, if only we are left in possession of our senses, such as we really find them, not such as they have been defined for us. Thus the issue is plain. We claim no special faculty, no special revelation. The only faculty we claim is perception, the only revelation we claim is history, or, as it is now called, historical evolution.

For let it not be supposed that we find the idea of the infinite ready-made in the human mind from the very beginning of our history. There are even now millions of human beings to whom the very word would be unintelligible. All we maintain is that the germ or the possibility, the Not-yet of that idea, lies hidden in the earliest sensuous perceptions, and that as reason is evolved from what is finite, so faith is evolved from what, from the very beginning, is infinite in the perceptions of our senses.

Positive philosophy imagines that all that is supplied to us through the senses is by its very nature finite, that whatever transcends the finite is a mere delusion, that the very word infinite is a mere jingle, produced by an outward joining of the negative particle with the adjective finite, a particle which has a perfect right with serial or correlative concepts, but which is utterly out of place with an absolute or exclusive concept, such as finite. If the senses tell us that *all* is finite, and if reason draws all her capital from the senses, who has a right, they say, to speak of the infinite? It may be true that an essential element of all religious knowledge is the admission of beings which can neither be apprehended by sense nor comprehended by reason, which are in fact infinite, and not finite. But instead of admitting a third faculty or potential energy in order to account for these facts of religion, positive philosophers would invert the argument, and prove that, for that very reason, religion has no real roots in our consciousness, that it is a mere mirage in the desert, alluring the weary traveler with bright visions, and leaving him to despair, when he has come near enough to where the springs of living water seemed to flow.

Some philosophers have thought that a mere appeal to history would be a sufficient answer to this despairing view. No doubt, it is important that, so long as we know man in possession of sense and reason, we also find him in possession of religion. But not even the eloquence of Cicero has been able to raise this fact to the dignity of an invulnerable argument. That all men have a longing for the gods is an important truth, but not even the genius of Homer could place that truth beyond the reach of doubt. Who has not wondered at those simple words of Homer (Od. iii. 48), πάντες δὲ θεῶν χατέουσ' ἄνθρωποι, "All men crave for the gods;" or, as we might render it still more literally and truthfully, "As young birds ope their mouth for food, all men crave for the gods." For χατεῖν, as connected with χαίνειν, meant originally to gape, to open the mouth, then to crave, to desire. But even that simple statement is met with an equally simple denial. Some men, we are told, in very ancient times, and some in very modern times, know of no such cravings. It is not enough, therefore, to show that man has always transcended the limits which sense and reason seem to trace for him. It is not enough to show that, even in the lowest fetish worship, the fetish is not only what we can see, or hear, or touch, but something else, which we cannot see, or hear, or touch. It is not enough to show that in the worship paid to the objects of nature, the mountains, trees, and rivers are not simply what we can see, but something else which we cannot see; and that when the sky and the heavenly bodies are invoked, it is not the sun or the moon and the stars, such as they appear to the bodily eye, but again something else which cannot be seen, that forms the object of religious belief. The rain is visible; he who sends the rain is not. The thunder is heard, the storm is felt; but he who thunders and rides on the whirlwind is never seen by human eye. Even if the gods of the Greeks are sometimes seen, the Father of gods and men is not; and he who in the oldest Aryan speech was called Heaven-Father (Dyaus Pitar), in Greek Ζεὺς πατήρ, in Latin Jupiter, was no more an object of sensuous perception than He whom we call our Father in heaven.

All this is true, and it will be the object of these lectures to watch this important development of religious thought from its very beginning to its very end, though in one stream only, namely, in the ancient religion of India. But before we can do this, we have to answer the preliminary and more abstract question, Whence comes that something else, which, as we are told, neither sense nor reason can supply? Where is the rock for him to stand on, who declines to rest on anything but what is called the evidence of the senses, or to trust in anything but the legitimate deductions derived from it by reason, and who nevertheless maintains his belief in something which transcends both sense and reason?

APPREHENSION OF THE INFINITE.

We have granted that all our knowledge begins with the senses, and that out of the material, supplied by the senses, reason builds up its marvelous structure. If, therefore, all the materials which the senses supply are finite, whence, we ask, comes the concept of the infinite?

1. The Infinitely Great.

The first point that has to be settled — and on that point all the rest of our argument turns — is this: "Are all the materials which the senses supply finite, and finite only?" It is true that all we can see, and feel, and hear, has a beginning and an end, and is it only by apprehending these beginnings and ends that we gain sensuous knowledge? We perceive a body by perceiving its outline; we perceive green in large intervals between blue and yellow; we hear the musical note D between where C ends and E begins; and so with all other perceptions of the senses. This is true — true at least for all practical purposes. But let us look more carefully. When our eye has apprehended the farthest distance which it can reach, with or without instruments, the limit to which it clings is always fixed on the one side by the finite, but on the other side by what to the eye is not finite, or infinite. Let us remember that we have accepted the terms of our opponents, and that therefore we look upon man as simply endowed with sense. To most philosophers it would appear much more natural, and, I doubt not, much more convincing, to derive the idea of the infinite from a necessity of our human reason. Wherever we try to fix a point, in space or time, they say, we are utterly unable to fix it so as to exclude the possibility of a point beyond. In fact, our very idea of limit implies the idea of a beyond, and thus forces the idea of the infinite upon us, whether we like it or not.

This is perfectly true, but we must think, not of our friends, but of our opponents, and it is well known that our opponents do not accept that argument. If on one side, they say, our idea of a limit implies a beyond and leads us to postulate an infinite, on the other, our idea of a whole excludes a beyond, and thus leads us to postulate a finite. These antinomies of human reason have been fully discussed by Kant, and later philosophers have naturally appealed to them to show that what we call necessities may be after all but weaknesses of human reason, and that, like all other ideas, those of finite and infinite also, if they are to be admitted at all, must be shown to be the result, not of speculation, but of experience, and as all experience is at first sensuous, the result of sensuous experience. This is the argument we have to deal with, and here neither Sir W. Hamilton nor Lucretius can help us.

We have accepted the primitive savage with nothing but his five senses. These five senses supply him with a knowledge of finite things; our problem is, how such a being ever comes to think or speak of anything not finite or infinite.

I answer, without any fear of contradiction, that it is his senses which give him the first impression of infinite things, and supply him in the end with an intimation of the infinite. Everything of which his senses cannot perceive a limit is, to a primitive savage, or to any man in an early stage of intellectual activity, unlimited or infinite. Man sees, he sees to a certain point; and there his eyesight breaks down. But exactly where his sight breaks down, there presses upon him, whether he likes it or not, the perception of the unlimited or the infinite. It may be said that this is not perception, in the ordinary sense of the word. No more it is, but still less is it mere reasoning. In perceiving the infinite, we neither count, nor measure, nor compare, nor name. We know not what it is, but we know that it is, and we know it, because we actually feel it and are brought in contact with it. If it seems too bold to say that man actually sees the invisible, let us say that he suffers from the invisible, and this invisible is only a special name for the infinite.

Therefore, as far as mere distance or extension is concerned, it would seem difficult to deny that the eye, by the very same act by which it apprehends the finite, apprehends also the infinite. The more we advance, the wider no doubt grows our horizon; but there never is or can be to our senses a horizon, unless as standing between the visible and finite on one side and the invisible and infinite on the other. The infinite, therefore, instead of being merely a late abstraction, is really implied in the earliest manifestations of our sensuous knowledge. Theology begins with anthropology. We must begin with a man living on high mountains, or in a vast plain, or on a coral island without hills and streams, surrounded on all sides by the endless expanse of the ocean, and screened above by the unfathomable blue of the sky; and we shall then understand how, from the images thrown upon him by the senses, some idea of the infinite would arise in his mind, earlier even than the concept of the finite, and would form the omnipresent background of the faintly dotted picture of his monotonous life.

2. The Infinitely Small.

But that is not all. We apprehend the infinite, not only as beyond, but also as within the finite; not only as beyond all measure great, but also as beyond all measure small. However much our senses may contract the points of their tentacles, they can never touch the smallest objects. There is always a beyond, always a something smaller still. We may, if we like, postulate an atom in its original sense, as something that cannot be cut asunder; our senses, —and we speak of them only, for we have been restricted to them by our opponents, — admit of no real atoms, nor of imponderable substances, or, as Robert Mayer called these last gods of Greece, "immaterial matter." In apprehending the smallest extension, they apprehend a smaller extension still. Between the centre and the circumference, which every object must have in order to become visible, there is always a *radius*; and that omnipresent and never entirely vanishing radius gives us again the sensuous impression of the infinite — of the infinitely small, as opposed to the infinitely great.

And what applies to space, applies equally to time. applies equally to quality and quantity.

When we speak of colors or sounds, we seem for all practical purposes to move entirely within the finite. This is red, we say, this is green, this is violet. This is C, this is D, this is E. What can apparently be more finite, more definite? But let us look more closely. Let us take the seven colors of the rainbow; and where is the edge of an eye sharp enough to fix itself on the point where blue ends and green begins, or where green ends and yellow begins? We might as well attempt to put our clumsy fingers on the point where one millimetre ends and another begins. We divide color by seven rough degrees, and speak of the seven colors of the rainbow. Even those seven rough degrees are of late date in the evolution of our sensuous knowledge. Xenophanes says that what people call Iris is a cloud, purple (πορφύρεον), red (φοινίκεον), and yellow (χλωρόν). Even Aristotle still speaks of the tricolored rainbow, red (φοινική), yellow (ξανθή), and green (πράσινη), and in the Edda the rainbow is called a three-colored bridge. Blue, which seems to us so definite a color, was worked out of the infinity of colors at a comparatively late time.

There is hardly a book now in which we do not read of the blue sky. But in the ancient hymns of the Veda,[1] so full of the dawn, the sun, and the sky, the blue sky is never mentioned; in the Zendavesta the blue sky is never mentioned; in Homer the blue sky is never mentioned; in the Old, and even in the New Testament, the blue sky is never mentioned. It has been asked whether we should recognize in this a physiological development of our senses, or a gradual increase of words capable of expressing finer distinctions of light. No one is likely to contend that the irritations of our organs of sense, which produce sensation, as distinguished from perception, were different thousands of years ago from what they are now. They are the same for all men, the same even for certain animals, for we know that there are insects which react very strongly against differences of color. No, we only learn here again, in a very clear manner, that conscious perception is impossible without language. Who would contend that savages, unable, as we are told, to count beyond three — that is to say, not in possession of definite numerals beyond three — do not receive the sensuous impression of four legs of a cow as different from three or two? No, in this evolution of consciousness of color we see once more how perception, as different from sensation, goes hand in hand with the evolution of language, and how slowly every definite concept is gained out of an infinitude of indistinct perceptions. Demokritos knew of four colors, viz, black and white, which he treated as colors, red and yellow. Are we to say that he

[1] See a very remarkable paper, 'Über den Farbensinn der Urzeit und seine Entwickelung,' by L. Geiger in his *Vorträge zur Entwickelungsgeschichte der Menschheit*, 1871, p. 45. The same subject is treated again in his *Ursprung und Entwickelung der menschlichen Sprache und Vernunft*, Zweiter Band, p. 304 *seq.*

did not see the blue of the sky because he never called it blue, but either dark or bright? In China the number of colors was originally five. That number was increased with the increase of their power of distinguishing and of expressing their distinctions in words. In common Arabic, as Palgrave tells us, the names for green, black, and brown are constantly confounded to the present day. It is well known that among savage nations we seldom find distinct words for blue and black,[1] but we shall find the same indefiniteness of expression when we inquire into the antecedents of our own language. Though *blue* now does no longer mean black, we see in such expressions as "to beat black and blue" the closeness of the two colors. In Old Norse, too, *blár*, *blá*, *blátt* now means blue, as distinct from *blakkr*, black. But in O. N. *bláman*, the livid color of a bruise, we see the indefiniteness of meaning between black and blue, and in *blá-maðr*, a black man, a negro, *blá* means distinctly black. The etymology of these words is very obscure. Grimm derives blue, O. H. G. *plâo*, *plawes*, Med. Lat. *blavus* and *blavius*, It. *biavo*, Fr. *bleu*, from Goth. *bliggvan*, to strike, so that it would originally have conveyed the black and blue color of a bruise. He appeals in support of his derivation to Latin *lividus*, which he derives from **fligvidus* and *fligere;* nay even to *flavus*, which he proposes to derive from **flagvus* and **flagere*. *Caesius* also is quoted as an analogy, supposing it is derived from *caedere*. All this is extremely doubtful, and the whole subject of the names of color requires to be treated in the most comprehensive way before any certain results can be expected in the place of in-

[1] See Meyer, *Über die Mafoor'sche und einige andern Papúa-Sprachen*, p. 52: "Blau, prisim, wird nicht von schwarz unterschieden."

genious guesses. Most likely the root *bhrag* and *bhrag*, with r changed to l, will be found as a fertile source of names of color. To that root *bleak*, A. S. *blâc*, *blæc*, O. N. *bleikr*, O. H. G. *pleik*, has been referred, meaning originally bright, then pale; and to the same family *black* also will probably have to be traced back, A. S. *blac*, O. N. *blakkr*, O. H. G. *plack*.

As languages advance, more and more distinctions are introduced, but the variety of colors always stands before us as a real infinite, to be measured, it may be, by millions of ethereal vibrations in one second, but immeasurable and indivisible even to the keenest eye.

What applies to color applies to sounds. Our ear begins to apprehend tone when there are thirty vibrations in one second; it ceases to apprehend tone when there are four thousand vibrations in one second. It is the weakness of our ears which determines these limits; but as there is beyond the violet, which we can perceive, an ultra-violet which to our eye is utter darkness, while it is revealed in hundreds of lines through the spectroscope, so there may be to people with more perfect powers of hearing, music where to us there is but noise. Though we can distinguish tones and semitones, there are many smaller divisions which baffle our perception, and make us feel, as many other things, the limited power of our senses before the unlimited wealth of the universe, which we try slowly to divide, to fix, and to comprehend.

GROWTH OF THE IDEA OF THE INFINITE.

I hope I shall not be misunderstood, or, I ought rather to say, I fear I shall be, — as if I held the opinion that the religion of the lowest savages begins with the barren idea of the infinite, and with nothing else. As no concept is possible without a name, I shall probably be asked to produce from the dictionaries of Veddas and Papuas any word to express the infinite ; and the absence of such a word, even among more highly civilized races, will be considered a sufficient answer to my theory.

Let me, therefore, say once more that I entirely reject such an opinion. I am acting at present on the defensive only ; I am simply dealing with the preliminary objections of those philosophers who look upon religion as outside the pale of philosophy, and who maintain that they have proved once for all that the infinite can never become a legitimate object of our consciousness, because our senses, which form the only avenue to the whole domain of our human consciousness, never come in contact with the infinite. It is in answer to that powerful school of philosophy, which on that one point has made converts even amongst the most orthodox defenders of the faith, that I felt it was necessary to point out, at the very outset, that their facts are no facts, but that the infinite was present from the very beginning in all finite perceptions, just as the blue color was though we find no name for it in the dictionaries of Veddas and Papuas. The sky was blue in the days of the Vedic poets, of the Zoroastrian worshipers, of the Hebrew prophet, of the Homeric singers, but though they saw it, they knew it not : they had no name for that which is the sky's own peculiar tint, the sky-blue. We know it, for we have a name for it. We know it, at least to a certain extent, because we can count the millions of vibrations that make up what we now call the blue of the sky. We know it quantitatively, but not qualitatively. Nay, to most of us it is, and it always will be, nothing but visible darkness, half veiling and half revealing the infinite brightness beyond.

It is the same with the infinite. It was there from the very first, but it was not yet defined or named. If the infinite had not from the very first been present in our sensuous perceptions, such a word as infinite would be a sound, and nothing else. For that reason I felt it incumbent upon me to show how the presentiment of the infinite rests on the sentiment of the finite, and has its real roots in the real though not yet fully apprehended presence of the infinite in all our sensuous perceptions of the finite. This presentiment or incipient apprehension of the infinite passes through endless phases and assumes endless names. I might have traced it in the wonderment with which the Polynesian sailor dwells on the endless expanse of the sea, in the jubilant outburst with which the Aryan shepherd greets the effulgence of the dawn, or in the breathless silence of the solitary traveler in the desert when the last ray of the sun departs, fascinating his weary eyes, and drawing his dreamy thoughts to another world. Through all these sentiments and presentiments there vibrates the same chord in a thousand tensions, and if we will but listen attentively we can still perceive its old familiar ring even in such high harmonics as Wordsworth's

> "Obstinate questionings
> Of sense and outward things,
> Fallings from us, vanishings;
> Blank misgivings of a Creature
> Moving about in words not realized."

NO FINITE WITHOUT AN INFINITE.

What I hold is that with every finite perception there is a concomitant perception, or, if that word should seem too strong, a concomitant sentiment or presentiment of the infinite; that from the very first act of touch, or hearing, or sight, we are brought in contact, not only with a visible, but also at the same time with an invisible universe. Those therefore who deny the possibility or the legitimacy of the idea of the infinite in our human consciousness, must meet us here on their own ground. All our knowledge, they say, must begin with the senses. Yes, we say, and it is the senses which give us the first intimation of the infinite. What grows afterwards out of this intimation supplies materials both to the psychologist and to the historian of religion, and to both of them this indisputable sentiment of the infinite is the first pre-historic impulse to all religion. I do not say that in the first dark pressure of the infinite upon us, we have all at once the full and lucid consciousness of that highest of all concepts: I mean the very opposite. I simply say we have in it a germ, and a living germ, we have in it that without which no religion would have been possible, we have in that perception of the infinite the root of the whole historical development of human faith.

And let it not be supposed that in insisting on an actual perception of the infinite, I indulge in poetical language only, though I am the last to deny that poetical language may sometimes convey much truth, nay often more than is to be found in the confused webs of argumentative prose. I shall quote at least one of these poetical pleadings in favor of the reality of the infinite: "Et qu'on ne dise pas que l'infini et l'éternel sont inintelligibles; c'est le fini et le passager qu'on serait souvent tenté de prendre pour un rêve; car la pensée ne peut voir de terme à rien, et l'être ne saurait concevoir le néant. On ne peut approfondir les sciences exactes elles-mêmes, sans y rencontrer l'infini et l'éternel; et les choses les plus positives appartiennent autant, sous de certains rapports, à cet infini et à cet éternel, que le sentiment et l'imagination."

I fully admit that there is much truth in these impassionate utterances, but we must look for the deepest foundation of that truth, otherwise we shall be accused of using poetical or mystic assertions, where only the most careful logical argument can do real good. In postulating, or rather in laying my finger on the point where the actual contact with the infinite takes place, I neither ignore nor do I contravene any one of the stringent rules of Kant's "Critik der reinen Vernunft." Nothing, I hold, can be more perfect than Kant's analysis of human knowledge. "Sensuous objects cannot be known except such as they appear to us, never such as they are in themselves; supersensuous objects are not to us objects of theoretic knowledge." All this I fully accept. But though there is no theoretic knowledge of the supersensuous, is there no knowledge of it at all? Is it no knowledge, if we know that a thing is, though we do not know what it is? What would Kant say, if we were to maintain that because we do not know what the *Ding an sich* is, therefore we do not know that it is. He carefully guards against such a misunderstanding, which would change his whole philosophy into pure idealism. "Nevertheless," he says, "it should be observed that we must be able, if not to know, at all events to be conscious of, the same objects, also a *Dinge an sich*. Otherwise we should arrive at the irrational conclusion that there is appearance without something that appears."[1] If I differ from Kant, it is only in going a step beyond him. With him the supersensuous or the infinite would be a mere *Nooumenon*, not a *Phainomenon*. I maintain that before it becomes a *Nooumenon* it is an *Aistheton*, though not a *Phainomenon*. I maintain that we, as sentient beings, are in constant contact with the infinite, and that this constant contact is the only legitimate basis on which the infinite can and does exist for us afterwards, as a *Nooumenon* or *Pisteuomenon*. I maintain that, here as elsewhere, no legitimate concept is possible without a previous percept, and that that previous percept is as clear as daylight to all who are not blinded by traditional terminologies.

We have been told again and again that a finite mind cannot approach the infinite, and that therefore we ought to take our Bible and our Prayer-book and rest there and be thankful. This would indeed be taking a despairing view both of ourselves and of our Bible and Prayer-book. No, let us only see and judge for ourselves, and we shall find that, from the first dawn of history, and from the first dawn of our own individual consciousness, we have always been face to face with the infinite. Whether we shall ever be able to gain more than this sentiment of the real presence of the infinite, whether we shall ever be

[1] *Critik der reinen Vernunft*, 2te Auflage, Vorr; 2. 676. What Kant says in his *Critik*, 1te Auflage, pp. 288, 289, is less distinct and liable to be misunderstood.

able, not only to apprehend, but to comprehend it, that is a question which belongs to the end, not to the beginning of our subject. At present we are concerned with history only, in order to learn from its sacred annals how the finite mind has tried to pierce farther and farther into the infinite, to gain new aspects of it, and to raise the dark perception of it into more lucid intuitions and more definite names. There may be much error in all the names that man has given to the infinite, but even the history of error is full of useful lessons. After we have seen how it is possible for man to gain a presentiment of something beyond the finite, we shall watch him looking for the infinite in mountains, trees, and rivers, in the storm and lightning, in the moon and the sun, in the sky and what is beyond the sky, trying name after name to comprehend it, calling it thunderer, bringer of light, wielder of the thunderbolt, giver of rain, bestower of food and life; and, after a time, speaking of it as maker, ruler, and preserver, king and father, lord of lords, god of gods, cause of causes, the Eternal, the Unknown, the Unknowable. All this we shall see in at least one great evolution of religious thought, preserved to us in the ancient literature of India.

There are many other historical evolutions, in other countries, each leading to its own goal. Nothing can be more different than the evolution of the consciousness of the infinite or the divine among Aryan, Semitic, and Turanian races. To some the infinite first revealed itself, as to the Vedic poets, in certain visions of nature. Others were startled by its presence in the abyss of their own hearts. There were whole tribes to whom the earliest intimation of the infinite came from the birth of a child, or from the death of a friend; and whose idea of beings more than human was derived from the memory of those whom they had loved or feared in life. The sense of duty, which in ancient times had always a religious character, seems in some cases to have sprung from that feeling of burning shame which was none the less real because it could not be accounted for; while other tribes became conscious of law by witnessing the order in nature, which even the gods could not transgress. And love, without which no true religion can live, while in some hearts it burst forth as a sudden warmth kindled by the glances of the morning light, was roused in others by that deep sympathy of nature — that suffering in common — which, whether we like it or not, makes our nerves quiver at the sight of a suffering child; or was called into life by that sense of loneliness and finiteness which makes us long for something beyond our own narrow, finite self, whether we find it in other human selves, or in that infinite Self in which alone we have our being, and in which alone we find in the end our own true self.

Each religion had its own growth, each nation followed its own path through the wilderness. If these lectures continue, as I hope they may, other and better analysts of the human mind will hereafter disentangle and lay before you the manifold fibres that enter into the web of the earliest religious thoughts of man; other and more experienced guides will hereafter lead you through the valleys and deserts which were crossed by the great nations of antiquity, the Egyptians, the Babylonians, the Jews, the Chinese, it may be, or the Greeks and Romans, the Celts, the Slavs, and Germans, nay by savage and hardly human races, in their search after the infinite, that infinite which surrounded them, as it surrounds us, on every side, and which they tried, and tried in vain, to grasp and comprehend.

I shall confine myself to one race only, the ancient Aryans of India, in many respects the most wonderful race that ever lived on earth. The growth of their religion is very different from the growth of other religions; but though each religion has its own peculiar growth, the seed from which they spring is everywhere the same. That seed is the perception of the infinite, from which no one can escape who does not willfully shut his eyes. From the first flutter of human consciousness, that perception underlies all the other perceptions of our senses, all our imaginings, all our concepts, and every argument of our reason. It may be buried for a time beneath the fragments of our finite knowledge, but it is always there, and if we dig but deep enough, we shall always find that buried seed, as supplying the living sap to the fibres and feeders of all true faith.

For many reasons I could have wished that some English student, who in so many respects would have been far better qualified than I am, should have been chosen to inaugurate these lectures. There was no dearth of them, there was rather, I should say, an *embarras de richesse*. How ably would a psychological analysis of religion have been treated by the experienced hands of Dr. Martineau or Principal Caird! If for the first course of these Hibbert Lectures you had chosen Egypt and its ancient religion, you had such men as Birch, or Le Page Renouf; for Babylon and Nineveh, you had Rawlinson or Sayce; for Palestine, Stanley or Cheyne; for China, Legge or Douglas; for Greece, Gladstone or Jowett or Mahaffy; for Rome, Munro or Seely; for the Celtic races, Rhŷs; for the Slavonic races, Ralston; for the Teutonic races, Skeat or Sweet; for savage tribes in general, Tylor or Lubbock. If after considerable hesitation I decided to accept the invitation to deliver the first course of these lectures, it was because I felt convinced that the ancient literature of India, which has been preserved to us as by a miracle, gives us opportunities for a study of the origin and growth of religion such as we find nowhere else;[1] and I may add, because I know from past experience how great indulgence is shown by an English audience to one who, however badly he may say it, says all he has to say, without fear, without favor, and, as much as may be, without offense.

[1] "Die Inder bildeten ihre Religion zu einer Art von urweltlicher Classicität aus, welche sie für alle Zeiten zum Schlüssel des Götterglaubens der ganzen Menschheit macht." Geiger, *Über Ursprung und Entwickelung der menchslichen Sprache und Vernunft*, vol. ii. p. 339.

II.

IS FETISHISM A PRIMITIVE FORM OF RELIGION?

THE FIRST IMPULSE TO THE PERCEPTION OF THE INFINITE.

In my first lecture I tried to lay free the foundations on which alone a religion can be built up. If man had not the power — I do not say, to comprehend, but to apprehend the infinite, in its most primitive and undeveloped form, then he would have no right to speak of a world beyond this finite world, of time beyond this finite time, or of a Being which, even though he shrinks from calling it Zeus, or Jupiter, or Dyaus-pitar, or Lord, Lord, he may still feel after, and revere, and even love, under the names of the Unknown, the Incomprehensible, the Infinite. If, on the contrary, an apprehension of the infinite is possible and legitimate, if I have succeeded in showing that this apprehension of the infinite underlies and pervades all our perceptions of finite things, and likewise all the reasonings that flow from them, then we have firm ground to stand on, whether we examine the various forms which that sentiment has assumed among the nations of antiquity, or whether we sound the foundations of our own faith to its lowest depth.

The arguments which I placed before you in my first lecture were, however, of a purely abstract nature. It was the possibility, not the reality of the perception of the infinite which alone I wished to establish. Nothing could be farther from my thoughts than to represent the perfect idea of the infinite as the first step in the historical evolution of religious ideas. Religion begins as little with the perfect idea of the infinite as astronomy begins with the law of gravity: nay, in its purest form, that idea is the last rather than the first step in the march of the human intellect.

MANA, A MELANESIAN NAME FOR THE INFINITE.

How the idea of the infinite, of the unseen, or as we call it afterwards, the Divine, may exist among the lowest tribes in a vague and hazy form we may see, for instance, in the *Mana* of the Melanesians. Mr. R. H. Codrington, an experienced missionary and a thoughtful theologian, says in a letter, dated July 7, 1877, from Norfolk Island: "The religion of the Melanesians consists, as far as belief goes, in the persuasion that there is a supernatural power about, belonging to the region of the unseen; and, as far as practice goes, in the use of means of getting this power turned to their own benefit. The notion of a Supreme Being is altogether foreign to them, or indeed of any Being occupying a very elevated place in their world" (p. 14).

And again: "There is a belief in a force altogether distinct from physical power, which acts in all kinds of ways for good and evil, and which it is of the greatest advantage to possess or control. This is Mana. The word is common, I believe, to the whole Pacific, and people have tried very hard to describe what it is in different regions. I think I know what our people mean by it, and that meaning seems to me to cover all that I hear about it elsewhere. It is a power or influence, not physical, and, in a way, supernatural; but it shows itself in physical force, or in any kind of power or excellence which a man possesses. This Mana is not fixed in anything, and can be conveyed in almost anything; but spirits, whether disembodied souls or supernatural beings, have it, and can impart it; and it essentially belongs to personal beings to originate it, though it may act through the medium of water, or a stone, or a bone. All Melanesian religion, in fact, consists in getting this Mana for one's self, or getting it used for one's benefit — all religion, that is, as far as religious practices go, prayers and sacrifices."

This Mana is one of the early, helpless expressions of what the apprehension of the infinite would be in its incipient stages, though even the Melanesian Mana shows ample traces both of development and corruption.

My first lecture, therefore, was meant to be no more than a preliminary answer to a preliminary assertion. In reply to that numerous and powerful class of philosophers who wish to stop us on the very threshold of our inquiries, who tell us that here on earth there is no admission to the infinite, and that if Kant has done anything he has forever closed our approaches to it, we had to make good our right by producing credentials of the infinite, which even the most positive of positivists has to recognize, viz., — the evidence of our senses.

We have now to enter upon a new path; we have to show how men in different parts of the world worked their way in different directions, step by step, from the simplest perceptions of the world around them, to the highest concepts of religion and philosophy; how, in fact, the consciousness of the infinite, which lay hidden in every fold of man's earliest impressions, was unfolded in a thousand different ways till it became freer and freer of its coarser ingredients, reaching at last that point of purity which we imagine is the highest that can be reached by human thought. The history of that development is neither more nor less than the history of religion, closely connected, as that history always has been and must be, with the history of philosophy. To that history we now turn, as containing the only trustworthy illustration of the evolution of the idea of the infinite from the lowest beginnings to a height which few can reach, but to which we may all look up from the nether part of the mount.

FETISHISM, THE ORIGINAL FORM OF ALL RELIGION.

If you consulted any of the books that have been written during the last hundred years on the history of religion, you would find in most of them a striking agreement on at least one point, viz., that the lowest form of what can be called religion is *fetishism*, that it is impossible to imagine anything lower that would still deserve that name, and that therefore fetishism may safely be considered as the very beginning of all religion. Wherever I find so flagrant an instance of agreement, the same ideas expressed in almost the same words, I confess I feel suspicious, and I always think it right to go back to the first sources, in order to see under what circumstances, and for what special purpose, a theory which commands such ready and general assent has first been started.

DE BROSSES, THE INVENTOR OF FETISHISM.

The word *fetishism* was never used before the year 1760. In that year appeared an anonymous book called "Du Culte des Dieux Fétiches, ou, Parallèle de l'ancienne Religion de l'Egypte avec la Religion actuelle de Nigritie." It is known that this little book was written by De Brosses, the well-known President De Brosses, the correspondent of Voltaire, one of the most remarkable men of the Voltairian period (born in 1709, died 1777). It was at the instigation of his friend, the great Buffon, that De Brosses seems to have devoted himself to the study of savage tribes, or to the study of man in historic and prehistoric times. He did so by collecting the best descriptions which he could find in the books of old and recent travelers, sailors, missionaries, traders, and explorers of distant countries, and he published in 1756 his "Histoire des navigations aux terres Australes," two large volumes in quarto. Though this book is now antiquated, it contains two names which, I believe, occur here for the first time, which were, it seems, coined by De Brosses himself, and which will probably survive when all his other achievements, even his theory of fetishism, have been forgotten, viz., the names *Australia* and *Polynesia*.

Another book by the same author, more often quoted than read, is his "Traité de la Formation mécanique des Langues," published in 1765. This is a work which, though its theories are likewise antiquated, well deserves a careful perusal even in these heydays of comparative philology, and which, particularly in its treatment of phonetics, was certainly far in advance of its time.

Between his book on Eastern Voyages and his treatise on the Mechanical Formation of Language, lies his work on the Worship of the Fetish Deities, which may rightly be described as an essay on the mechanical formation of religion. De Brosses was dissatisfied with the current opinions on the origin of mythology and religion, and he thought that his study of the customs of the lowest savages, particularly those on the west coast of Africa, as described by Portuguese sailors, offered him the means of a more natural explanation of that old and difficult problem.

"This confused mass of ancient mythology," he says, "has been to us an undecipherable chaos, or a purely arbitrary riddle, so long as one employed for its solution the *figurism* of the last Platonic philosophers, who ascribed to ignorant and savage nations a knowledge of the most hidden causes of nature, and perceived in a heap of trivial practices of gross and stupid people intellectual ideas of the most abstract metaphysics. Nor have they fared better who tried, mostly by means of forced and ill-grounded comparisons, to find in the ancient mythology the detailed, though disfigured, history of the Hebrew nation, a nation that was unknown almost to all others, and made a point never to communicate its doctrines to strangers. . . . . Allegory is an instrument which will do anything. The system of a figurative meaning once admitted, one soon sees everything in everything, as in the clouds. The matter is never embarrassing, all that is wanted is spirit and imagination. The field is large and fertile, whatever explications may be required.

"Some scholars," he continues, "more judicious,

better instructed also in the history of the early nations whose colonies first discovered the East, and familiar with Oriental languages, have at last, after clearing mythology of the rubbish with which the Greeks had covered it, found the true key of it in the actual history of the early nations, their opinions and their rulers, in the false translations of a number of simple expressions, the meaning of which had been forgotten by those who nevertheless continued to use them; and in the homonymies which out of one object, designated by various epithets, have made so many different beings or persons.

"But these keys which open so well the meaning of historical fables, do not always suffice to give a reason for the singularity of the dogmatic opinions, nor of the practical rites of the early nations. These two portions of heathen theology depend either on the worship of the celestial bodies, well known by the name of *Sabeism*, or on the probably not less ancient worship of certain terrestrial and material objects, called *fétiche*, by the African negroes (he meant to say by those who visited the African negroes), and which for this reason I shall call *Fétichisme.* I ask permission to use this term habitually, and though in the proper signification it refers in particular to the religion of the negroes of Africa only, I give notice beforehand that I mean to use it with reference also to any other nation paying worship to animals, or to inanimate things which are changed into gods, even when these objects are less gods, in the proper sense of the word, than things endowed with a certain divine virtue, such as oracles, amulets, or protecting talismans. For it is certain that all these forms of thought have one and the same origin, which belongs to one general religion, formerly spread over the whole earth, which must be examined by itself, constituting, as it does, a separate class among the various religions of the heathen world."

De Brosses divides his book into three parts. In the first he collects all the information which was then accessible on fetishism, as still practiced by barbarous tribes in Africa and other parts of the world. In the second he compares it with the religious practices of the principal nations of antiquity. In the third he tries to show that, as these practices are very like to one another in their outward appearance, we may conclude that their original intention among the negroes of to-day and among the Egyptians, the Greeks, and Romans, was the same.

All nations, he holds, had to begin with fetishism, to be followed afterwards by polytheism and monotheism.

One nation only forms with him an exception — the Jews, the chosen people of God. They, according to De Brosses, were never fetish-worshipers, while all other nations first received a primeval divine revelation, then forgot it, and then began again from the beginning — viz., with fetishism.

It is curious to observe the influence which the prevalent theological ideas of the time exercised even on De Brosses. If he had dared to look for traces of fetishism in the Old Testament with the same keenness which made him see fetishes in Egypt, in Greece, in Rome, and everywhere else, surely the Teraphim, the Urim and Thummim, or the ephod, to say nothing of golden calves and brazen serpents, might have supplied him with ample material (Gen. xxviii. 18; Jerem. ii. 27).

But though on this and some other points those who have more recently adopted and defended the theory of De Brosses would differ from him, on the whole his view of fetishism has been maintained intact during the last hundred years. It sounded so easy, so natural, so plausible, that it soon found its way into manuals and school-books, and I believe we all of us have been brought up on it.[1] I myself certainly held it for a long time, and never doubted it, till I became more and more startled by the fact that, while in the earliest accessible documents of religious thought we look in vain for any very clear traces of fetishism, they become more and more frequent everywhere in the latter stages of religious development, and are certainly more visible in the later corruptions of the Indian religion,[2] beginning with the Atharvana, than in the earliest hymns of the Rig-Veda.

ORIGIN OF THE NAME OF FETISH.

Why did the Portuguese navigators, who were Christians, but Christians in that metamorphic state which marks the popular Roman Catholicism of the last century — why did they recognize at once what they saw among the negroes of the Gold Coast, as *feitiços?* The answer is clear. Because they themselves were perfectly familar with a *feitiço*, an amulet or a talisman; and probably all carried with them

[1] Meiners, whose *Allgemeine Kritische Geschichte der Religionen*, 1806, was for many years the chief storehouse for all who wrote on the history of religion, says: "It cannot be denied that fetishism is not only the oldest, but also the most universal worship of gods."

[2] L'étranger qui arrive dans l'Inde, et moi-même je n'ai pas fait exception à cette règle, ne découvre d'abord que des pratiques religieuses aussi dégradantes que dégradées, un vrai polythéisme, presque du fétichisme." *De la supériorité du Brahmanisme sur le Catholicisme*, Conférence donnée par M. Goblet d'Alviella.

some beads, or crosses, or images, that had been blessed by their priests before they started for their voyage. They themselves were fetish-worshipers in a certain sense. What was more natural, therefore, for them, if they saw a native hugging some ornament, or unwilling to part with some glittering stone, or it may be prostrating himself and praying to some bones, carefully preserved in his hut, than to suppose that the negroes did not only keep these things for luck, but that they were sacred relics, something in fact like what they themselves would call *feitiço*? As they discovered no other traces of any religious worship, they concluded very naturally that this outward show of regard for these *feitiços* constituted the whole of the negro's religion.

Suppose these negroes, after watching the proceedings of their white visitors, had asked on their part what the religion of those white men might be, what would they have said? They saw the Portuguese sailors handling their rosaries, burning incense to dauby images, bowing before altars, carrying gaudy flags, prostrating themselves before a wooden cross. They did not see them while saying their prayers, they never witnessed any sacrifices offered by them to their gods, nor was their moral conduct such as to give the natives the idea that they abstained from any crimes because they feared the gods. What would have been more natural, therefore, for them than to say that their religion seemed to consist in a worship of *gru-grus*, their own name for what the Portuguese called *feitiço*, and that they had no idea of a supreme spirit or a king of heaven, or offered any worship to him?

With regard to the word, it is well known that the

Portuguese *feitiço* corresponds to Latin *factitius*. *Factitius*, from meaning what is made by hand, came to mean artificial, then unnatural, magical, enchanted and enchanting. A false key is called in Portuguese *chave feitiça*, while *feitiço* becomes the recognized name for amulets and similar half-sacred trinkets. The trade in such articles was perfectly recognized in Europe during the Middle Ages, as it is still among the negroes of Africa. A manufacturer or seller of them was called *feitiçero*, a word which, however, was likewise used in the sense of a magician or conjurer. How common the word was in Portuguese we see from its being used in its diminutive form as a term of endearment, *meu feitiçinho* meaning my little fetish, or darling.

We see a similar transition of meaning in the Sanskrit *krityâ*, the Italian *fattura*, incantation, which occurs in mediæval Latin as far back as 1311;[1] also in *charme*, which was originally no more than *carmen*; and in the Greek ἐπῳδή.

WRONG EXTENSION OF THE NAME FETISH.

It will be clear from these considerations that the Portuguese sailors — for it is to them that we are indebted for the introduction of the word *fetish* — could have applied that term to certain tangible and inanimate objects only, and that it was an unwarrantable liberty taken with the word which enabled De Brosses to extend it to animals, and to such things as mountains, trees, and rivers. De Brosses imagined that the name *feitiço* was somehow related to *fatum*, and its modern derivative *fata* (nom. plur. of the

[1] "Synodus Pergam.," ann. 1311, apud Muratorium, tom. 9, col. 561; incantationes, sacrilegia, auguria, vel maleficia, quæ facturæ sive præstigia vulgariter appellantur.

neuter, used afterwards as a nom. sing. of the feminine), a *fée*, a fairy; and this may have made it appear less incongruous to him to apply the name of fetish, not only to artificial and material objects, but also to trees, mountains, rivers, and even to animals. This was the first unfortunate step on the part of De Brosses, for he thus mixed up three totally distinct phases of religion, first, physiolatry, or the worship paid to natural objects which impress the mind of man with feelings of awe or gratitude, such as rivers, trees, or mountains; secondly, zoolatry, or the worship paid to animals, as for instance by the highly-cultivated inhabitants of ancient Egypt; and lastly, fetishism proper, or the superstitious veneration felt and testified for mere rubbish, apparently without any claim to such distinction.

But this was not all. De Brosses did not keep what he calls fetish-worship distinct even from idolatry, though there is a very important distinction between the two. A fetish, properly so called, is itself regarded as something supernatural; the idol, on the contrary, was originally meant as an image only, a similitude or a symbol of something else. No doubt an idol was apt to become a fetish; but in the beginning, fetish worship, in the proper sense of the word, springs from a source totally different from that which produces idolatry.

Let us hear how De Brosses explains his idea of a fetish. "These fetishes," he says, "are anything which people like to select for adoration, — a tree, a mountain, the sea, a piece of wood, the tail of a lion, a pebble, a shell, salt, a fish, a plant, a flower, certain animals, such as cows, goats, elephants, sheep, or anything like these. These are the gods of the negro, sacred objects, talismans. The negroes offer them worship, address their prayers to them, perform sacrifices, carry them about in procession, consult them on great occasions. They swear by them, and such oaths are never broken.

"There are fetishes belonging to a whole tribe, and others belonging to individuals. National fetishes have a kind of public sanctuary; private fetishes are kept in their own place in the houses of private individuals.

"If the negroes want rain, they place an empty jar before the fetish. When they go to battle, they deposit their weapons before it or him. If they are in want of fish or meat, bare bones are laid down before the fetish; while, if they wish for palm-wine, they indicate their desire by leaving with the fetish the scissors with which the incisions are made in the palm-trees.[1] If their prayers are heard, all is right. But if they are refused, they think that they have somehow incurred the anger of their fetish, and they try to appease him."

Such is a short abstract of what De Brosses meant by fetishism, what he believed the religion of the negroes to be, and what he thought the religion of all the great nations of antiquity must have been before they reached the higher stages of polytheism and monotheism.

USEFULNESS OF THE STUDY OF SAVAGE TRIBES.

The idea that, in order to understand what the so-called civilized people may have been before they reached their higher enlightenment, we ought to study savage tribes, such as we find them still at the

[1] Similar customs mentioned by Waitz, *Anthropologie*, vol. ii. p. 177.

present day, is perfectly just. It is the lesson which geology has taught us, applied to the stratification of the human race. But the danger of mistaking metaphoric for primary igneous rocks is much less in geology than in anthropology. Allow me to quote some excellent remarks on this point by Mr. Herbert Spencer.[1] "To determine," he writes, "what conceptions are truly primitive, would be easy if we had accounts of truly primitive men. But there are sundry reasons for suspecting that existing men of the lowest types, forming social groups of the simplest kinds, do not exemplify men as they originally were. Probably most of them, if not all, had ancestors in higher states; and among their beliefs remain some which were evolved during those higher states. While the degradation theory, as currently held, is untenable, the theory of progression, taken in its unqualified form, seems to me untenable also. If, on the one hand, the notion that savagery is caused by lapse from civilization is irreconcilable with the evidence, there is, on the other hand, inadequate warrant for the notion that the lowest savagery has always been as low as it is now. It is quite possible, and, I believe highly probable, that retrogression has been as frequent as progression."

These words contain a most useful warning for those ethnologists who imagine that they have only to spend a few years among Papuas, Fuegians, or Andaman Islanders, in order to know what the primitive ancestors of the Greeks and Romans may have been. They speak of the savage of to-day as if he had only just been sent into the world, forgetting that, as a

[1] *Sociology*, p. 106. See, also, "On some Characteristics of Malayo-Polynesians," in *Journal of the Anthropological Institute*, February, 1878.

living species, he is probably not a day younger than we ourselves.[1] He may be a more stationary being, but he may also have passed through many ups and downs before he reached his present level. Anyhow, even if it could be proved that there has been a continuous progression in everything else, no one could maintain that the same applies to religion.

FREQUENT RETROGRESSION IN RELIGION.

That religion is liable to corruption is surely seen again and again in the history of the world. In one sense the history of most religions might be called a slow corruption of their primitive purity. At all events, no one would venture to maintain that religion always keeps pace with general civilization. Even admitting, therefore, that, with regard to their tools, their dress, their manners and customs, the Greeks and Romans, the Germans and Celts may have been before the first dawn of history in the same state in which we find some of the negro races of Africa at present, nothing would justify the conclusion that their religion also must have been the same, that they must have worshiped fetishes, stocks and stones, and nothing else.

We see Abraham, a mere nomad, fully impressed with the necessity of the unity of the godhead, while Solomon, famous among the kings of the earth, built high places for Chemosh and Moloch. Ephesus, in the sixth century before Christ, was listening to one of the wisest men that Greece ever produced, Herakleitos; while a thousand years later, the same town resounded with the frivolous and futile wranglings

[1] "The savage are as old as the civilized races, and can as little be named primitive." A. M. Fairbairn, *Academy*, 20 July, 1878.

of Cyrillus, and the council of Ephesus. The Hindus who, thousands of years ago, had reached in the Upanishads the loftiest heights of philosophy, are now in many places sunk into a groveling worship of cows and monkeys.

DIFFICULTY OF STUDYING THE RELIGION OF SAVAGES.

But there is another and even greater difficulty. If we feel inclined to ascribe to the ancestors of the Greeks and Romans the religion of the negroes and of other savages of the present day, have we seriously asked ourselves what we really know of the religious opinions of these so-called savages?

A hundred years ago there might have been some excuse for people speaking in the most promiscuous manner of the religion of savages. Savages were then looked upon as mere curiosities, and almost anything related of them was readily believed. They were huddled and muddled together much in the same manner as I have heard Neander and Strauss quoted from the pulpit, as representatives of German neology; and hardly any attempt was made to distinguish between negro and negro, between savage and savage.

At present, all such general terms are carefully avoided by scientific ethnologists. In ordinary parlance we may still use the name of negro for black people in general, but when we speak scientifically, negro is mostly restricted to the races on the west coast of Africa between the Senegal and the Niger, extending inland to the Lake of Tchad and beyond, we hardly know how far. When the negro is spoken of as the lowest of the low, it generally is this negro of the west coast that is intended, he from whom Europeans first took their idea of a fetish-worship.

It is not the place here to discuss the ethnography of Africa as it has been established by the latest travelers. The classification as given by Waitz will suffice to distinguish the negro of the Senegal and Niger from his nearest neighbors: —

First, the Berber and Copt tribes, inhabiting the north of Africa. For historical purposes they may be said to belong to Europe rather than to Africa. These races were conquered by the Mohammedan armies, and rapidly coalesced with their conquerors. They are sometimes called Moors, but never negroes.

Secondly, the races which inhabit Eastern Africa, the country of the Nile to the equator. They are Abyssinian or Nubian, and in language distantly allied to the Semitic family.

Thirdly, the Fulahs, who are spread over the greater part of Central Africa, and feel themselves everywhere as distinct from the negroes.

Fourthly, from the equator downward as far as the Hottentots, the Kaffer and Congo races, speaking their own well-defined languages, possessed of religious ideas of great sublimity, and physically also very different from what is commonly meant by a negro.

Lastly, the Hottentots differing from the rest, both by their language and their physical appearance.

These are only the most general divisions of the races which now inhabit Africa. If we speak of all of them simply as negroes, we do so in the same loose manner in which the Greeks spoke of Scythians, and the Romans, before Cæsar, of Celts. For scientific purposes the term negro should either be avoided altogether, or restricted to the races scattered over about twelve degrees of latitude, from the Senegal to the Niger, and extending inland to the as yet undefined regions where they are bounded by Berber, Nubian, and Kaffer tribes.

But though the ethnologist no longer speaks of the inhabitants of Africa as negroes or niggers, it is much more difficult to convince the student of history that these races cannot be lumped together as savages, but that here, too, we must distinguish before we can compare. People who talk very freely of savages, whether in Africa, or America, or Australia, would find it extremely difficult to give any definition of that term, beyond this, that savages are different from ourselves. Savages with us are still very much what barbarians were to the Greeks. But as the Greeks had to learn that some of these so-called barbarians possessed virtues which they might have envied themselves, so we also shall have to confess that some of these savages have a religion and a philosophy of life which may well bear comparison with the religion and philosophy of what we call the civilized and civilizing nations of antiquity. Anyhow, the common idea of a savage requires considerable modification and differentiation, and there is perhaps no branch of anthropology beset with so many difficulties as the study of these so-called savage races.

LANGUAGE OF SAVAGES.

Let us examine a few of the prejudices commonly entertained with regard to these so-called savages. Their languages are supposed to be inferior to our own. Now here the science of language has done some good work. It has shown, first of all, that no human beings are without language, and we know what that implies. All the stories of tribes without language, or with languages more like the twitterings of birds than the articulate sounds of human beings, belong to the chapter of ethnological fables.

What is more important still is that many of the so-called savage languages have been shown to possess a most perfect, in many cases too perfect, that is to say, too artificial a grammar, while their dictionary possesses a wealth of names which any poet might envy.[1] True, this wealth of grammatical forms [2] and this superabundance of names for special objects are, from one point of view, signs of logical weakness and of a want of powerful generalization. Languages which have cases to express nearness to an object, movement alongside an object, approach towards an object, entrance into an object, but which have no purely objective case, no accusative, may be called rich, no doubt, but their richness is truly poverty. The same applies to their dictionary. It may contain names for every kind of animal; again for the same animal when it is young or old, male or female; it may have different words for the foot of a man, a horse, a lion, a hare; but it probably is without a name for animal in general, or even for such concepts as member or body. There is here, as elsewhere, loss and gain on both sides. But however imperfect a language may be in one point or other, every language, even that of Papuas and Veddas, is such a masterpiece of abstract thought that it would baffle the ingenuity of many philosophers to produce

[1] A. B. Meyer, *On the Mafoor and other Papua Languages of New Guinea*, p. 11.

[2] See Taplin, *The Narrinyeri, South Australian Aborigines*, p. 77.

anything like it. In several cases the grammar of so-called savage dialects bears evidence to a far higher state of mental culture possessed by these people in former times. And it must not be forgotten that every language has capacities, if they are only called out, and that no language has yet been found into which it was not possible to translate the Lord's Prayer.

NUMERALS OF SAVAGES.

For a long time it was considered as the strongest proof of the low mental capacity of certain savages that they were unable to count beyond three or four or five. Now, first of all we want a good scholar [1] to vouch for such facts when they exist; but when they have been proved to exist, then let us begin to distinguish. There may be tribes by whom everything beyond five, beyond the fingers of one hand, is lumped together as many, though I confess I have grave doubts whether, unless they are idiots, any human beings could be found unable to distinguish between five or six or seven cows.

But let us read the accounts of the absence of numerals beyond two or three more accurately. It was said, for instance, that the Abipones [2] have no numbers beyond *three*. What do we really find? That they express *four* by *three* plus *one*. Now this, so far from showing any mental infirmity, proves in reality a far greater power of analysis than if four were expressed, say, by a word for hands and feet,

[1] Speaking of the Dahomans, Mr. Burton (*Memoirs of the Anthropological Society*, i. 314) says: By perpetual cowrie-handling the people learn to be ready reckoners. Amongst the cognate Yorubas the saying, "You cannot multiply nine by nine," means, "you are a dunce."

[2] Dobrizhofer, *Historia de Abiponibus*, 1784.

or for eyes and ears. Savages who expressed *four* by *two-two*, would never be in danger of considering the proposition that two and two make four, as a synthetic judgment *a priori;* they would know at once that in saying "two and two make two-two," they were simply enunciating an analytical judgment.

We must not be too eager to assert the mental superiority of the races to which we ourselves belong. Some very great scholars have derived the Aryan word for *four* (whether rightly or wrongly I do not ask) from the Sanskrit *k*a-tur, the Latin *quatuor*, from three, *tar*, preceded by *k*a, the Latin *que*, so that *k*atur, in Sanskrit too, would have been conceived originally as *one* plus *three*. If some African tribes express *seven* either by *five* plus *two* or *six* plus *one*,[1] why should this stamp them as the lowest of the low, whereas no one blames the French, marching at the head of European civilization, for expressing ninety by *quatre-vingt-dix*, fourscore ten, or the Romans for saying *undeviginti* for nineteen ?[2]

No ; here too we must learn to mete to others that measure which we wish to be measured to us again. We must try to understand, before we presume to judge.

NO HISTORY AMONG SAVAGES.

Another serious charge brought against the savage in general is that he has no history. He hardly

[1] Winterbottom, *Account of the Native Africans in the Neighborhood of Sierra Leone*. London, 1863, p. 230.

[2] Many cases of forming the words eight and nine by ten *minus* one or two will be found in the Comparative Table of Numerals at the end of my Essay on the Turanian Languages. See, also, Moseley, *On the Inhabitants of the Admiralty Islands*, p. 13, and Matthews, *Hidatsa Grammar*, p. 118.

counts the days of a year, still less the years of a life. Some negro tribes consider it wrong to do so, as showing a want of trust in God.[1] As they have no knowledge of writing, there is of course no trace of what we call history among them. I do not deny that an utter carelessness about the past and the future would be a sign of a low stage of cultivation; but this can by no means be charged against all so-called savages. Many of them remember the names and deeds of their fathers and grandfathers, and the marvel is that, without the power of writing, they should have been able to preserve their traditions, sometimes for many generations.

The following remarks from a paper by the Rev. S. J. Whitmee throw some curious light on this subject: "The keepers of these national traditions (among the brown Polynesians) usually belonged to a few families, and it was their duty to retain intact, and transmit from generation to generation, the myths and songs intrusted to their custody. The honor of the families was involved in it. It was the hereditary duty of the elder sons of these families to acquire, retain, and transmit them with verbal accuracy. And it was not only a sacred duty, but the right of holding such myths and songs was jealously guarded as a valuable and honorable privilege. Hence the difficulty of having them secured by writing. Care was taken not to recite them too frequently or too fully at one time. Sometimes they have been purposely altered in order to lead the

[1] "Things pass away very rapidly in a country where everything in the nature of a building soon decays, and where life is short, and there are no marked changes of seasons to make the people count by anything longer than months." R. H. Codrington, Norfolk Island, July 3, 1877.

hearers astray. Missionaries and other foreign residents, who have manifested an interest in these myths, have often been deceived in this way. Only a person thoroughly familiar with the language, quite conversant with the habits of the people, and who had their confidence, could secure a trustworthy version. And this was usually secured only after a promise made to the keepers of these treasures not to make them public in the islands.

"But notwithstanding these difficulties, some missionaries and others have succeeded in making large collections of choice myths and songs, and I am not without hope that before very long we may succeed in collecting them together for the formation of a comparative mythology of Polynesia.

"Most of these legends and songs contain archaic forms, both idioms and words, unknown to most of the present generation of the people.

"The way in which verbal accuracy in the transmission of the legends and songs has been secured is worth mentioning. In some islands all the principal stories, indeed all which are of value, exist in two forms, in *prose* and in *poetry*. The prose form gives the story in simple language. The poetic gives it in rhythm, and usually in rhyme also. The poetic form is used as a check on the more simple and more easily changed prose form. As it is easy to alter and add to the prose account, that is never regarded as being genuine, unless each particular has its poetic tally. An omission or interpolation in the poetic form would, of course, be easily detected. Thus the people have recognized the fact that a poetic form is more easily remembered than a prose form, and that it is better adapted for securing the strict accuracy of historical myths."[1]

Our idea of history, however, is something totally different. To keep up the memory of the kings of Egypt and Babylon, to know by heart the dates of their battles, to be able to repeat the names of their ministers, their wives and concubines, is, no doubt, something very creditable in a Civil Service examination, but that it is a sign of true culture I cannot persuade myself to believe. Sokrates was not a savage, but I doubt whether he could have repeated the names and dates of his own archons, much less the dates of the kings of Egypt and Babylon.

And if we consider how history is made in our own time, we shall perhaps be better able to appreciate the feelings of those who did not consider that every massacre between hostile tribes, every palaver of diplomatists, every royal marriage-feast deserved to be recorded for the benefit of future generations. The more one sees of how history is made, the less one thinks that its value can be what it was once supposed to be. Suppose Lord Beaconsfield, Mr. Gladstone, and Prince Gortshakoff were to write the history of the last two years, what would future generations have to believe? What will future generations have to believe of those men themselves, when they find them represented by observers who had the best opportunity of judging them, either as high-minded patriots or as selfish partisans? Even mere facts, such as the atrocities committed in Bulgaria, cannot be described by two eye-witnesses in the same manner. Need we wonder, then, that a whole na-

[1] This throws a curious light on the Buddhist literature, where we also find the same story told twice, once in metre (Gâthâ), and once in prose.

tion, I mean the old Hindus, simply despised history, in the ordinary sense of the word, and instead of burdening their memories with names and dates of kings, queens, and battles, cared more to remember the true sovereigns in the realm of thought, and the decisive battles for the conquest of truth?

NO MORALS AMONG SAVAGES.

Lastly, all savages were supposed to be deficient in moral principles. I am not going to represent the savage as Rousseau imagined him, or deny that our social and political life is an advance on the hermit or nomadic existence of the tribes of Africa and America. But I maintain that each phase of life must be judged by itself. Savages have their own vices, but they also have their own virtues. If the negro could write a black book against the white man, we should miss in it few of the crimes which we think peculiar to the savage. The truth is that the morality of the negro and the white man cannot be compared, because their views of life are totally different. What we consider wrong, they do not consider wrong. We condemn, for instance, polygamy; Jews and Mohammedans tolerate it, savages look upon it as honorable, and I have no doubt that, in their state of society, they are right. Savages do not consider European colonists patterns of virtue, and they find it extremely difficult to enter into their views of life.

Nothing puzzles the mere savage more than our restlessness, our anxiety to acquire and to possess, rather than to rest and to enjoy. An Indian chief is reported to have said to a European: "Ah, brother, you will never know the blessings of doing nothing and thinking nothing; and yet, next to sleep, that is the most delicious. Thus we were before our birth, thus we shall be again after death." The young girls in Tahiti, who were being taught weaving, very soon left the looms, and said, "Why should we toil? Have we not as many bread-fruits and cocoa-nuts as we can eat? You who want ships and beautiful dresses must labor indeed, but we are content with what we have."

Such sentiments are certainly very un-European, but they contain a philosophy of life which may be right or wrong, and which certainly cannot be disposed of by being simply called savage.

A most essential difference between many so-called savages and ourselves is the little store they set on life. Perhaps we need not wonder at it. There are few things that bind them to this life. To a woman or to a slave, in many parts of Africa or Australia, death must seem a happy escape, if only they could feel quite certain that the next life would not be a repetition of this. They are like children, to whom life and death are like traveling from one place to another; and as to the old people, who have more friends on the other side of the grave than on this, they are mostly quite ready to go; nay, they consider it even an act of filial duty that their children should kill them, when life becomes a burden to them. However unnatural this may seem to us, it becomes far less so if we consider that among nomads those who can travel no more must fall a prey to wild animals or starvation. Unless we take all this into account, we cannot form a right judgment of the morality and religion of savage tribes.

RELIGION UNIVERSAL AMONG SAVAGES.

At the time when De Brosses wrote, the wonder was that black people should possess anything that could be called morality or religion, even a worship of stocks and stones. We have learnt to judge differently, thanks chiefly to the labors of missionaries who have spent their lives among savages, have learnt their languages and gained their confidence, and who, though they have certain prejudices of their own, have generally done full justice to the good points in their character. We may safely say that, in spite of all researches, no human beings have been found anywhere who do not possess something which to them is religion; or, to put it in the most general form, a belief in something beyond what they can see with their eyes.

As I cannot go into the whole evidence for this statement, I may be allowed to quote the conclusions which another student of the science of religion, Prof. Tiele, has arrived at on this subject, particularly as, on many points, his views differ widely from my own. "The statement," he says, "that there are nations or tribes which possess no religion rests either on inaccurate observations, or on a confusion of ideas. No tribe or nation has yet been met with destitute of belief in any higher beings, and travelers who asserted their existence have been afterwards refuted by facts. It is legitimate, therefore, to call religion, in its most general sense, an universal phenomenon of humanity." [1]

[1] *Outlines*, p. 6.

STUDY OF THE RELIGION OF LITERARY NATIONS.

When, however, these old prejudices had been removed, and when it had been perceived that the different races of Africa, America, and Australia could no longer be lumped together under the common name of savages, the real difficulties of studying these races began to be felt, more particularly with regard to their religious opinions. It is difficult enough to give an accurate and scholar-like account of the religion of the Jews, the Greeks, the Romans, the Hindus and Persians; but the difficulty of understanding and explaining the creeds and ceremonials of those illiterate races is infinitely greater. Any one who has worked at the history of religion knows how hard it is to gain a clear insight into the views of Greeks and Romans, of Hindus and Persians on any of the great problems of life. Yet we have here a whole literature before us, both sacred and profane, we can confront witnesses, and hear what may be said on the one side and the other. If we were asked, however, to say, whether the Greeks in general, or one race of Greeks in particular, and that race again at any particular time, believed in a future life, in a system of rewards and punishments after death, in the supremacy of the personal gods or of an impersonal fate, in the necessity of prayer and sacrifice, in the sacred character of priests and temples, in the inspiration of prophets and lawgivers, we should find it often extremely hard to give a definite answer. There is a whole literature on the theology of Homer, but there is anything but unanimity between the best scholars who have treated on that subject during the last two hundred years.

Still more is this the case when we have to form our opinions of the religion of the Hindus and Persians. We have their sacred books, we have their own recognized commentaries: but who does not know that the decision whether the ancient poets of the Rig-Veda believed in the immortality of the soul depends sometimes on the right interpretation of a single word, while the question whether the author of the Avesta admitted an original dualism, an equality between the principle of Good and Evil,[1] has to be settled in some cases on purely grammatical grounds?

Let me remind you of one instance only. In the hymn of the Rig-Veda, which accompanies the burning of a dead body, there occurs the following passage (x. 16, 3): —

> "May the eye go to the sun, the breath to the wind,
> Go to heaven and to the earth, as it is right;
> Or go to the waters, if that is meet for thee,
> Rest among the herbs with thy limbs.
>
> The unborn part — warm it with thy warmth,
> May thy glow warm it and thy flame!
> With what are thy kindest shapes, O Fire,
> Carry him away to the world of the Blessed."

This passage has often been discussed, and its right apprehension is certainly of great importance. A*g*a means unborn, a meaning which easily passes into that of imperishable, immortal, eternal. I translate a*g*o bhâga*h* by the unborn, the eternal part, and then admit a stop, in order to find a proper construction of the verse. But it has been pointed out that a*g*a means also goat, and others have translated, "The goat is thy portion." They also must admit the same kind of aposiopesis, which no doubt is not very

[1] *Chips from a German Workshop*, i. p. 140.

frequent in Sanskrit. It is perfectly true, as may be seen in the Kalpa-Sûtras, that sometimes an animal of the female sex was led after the corpse to the pile, and was burnt with the dead body. It was therefore called the Anustara*n*i, the covering. But, first of all, this custom is not general, as it probably would be, if it could be shown to be founded on a passage of the Veda. Secondly, there is actually a Sûtra that disapproves of this custom, because, as Kâtyâyana says, if the corpse and the animal are burnt together, one might in collecting the ashes confound the bones of the dead man and of the animal. Thirdly, it is expressly provided that this animal, whether it be a cow or a goat, must always be of the female sex. If, therefore, we translate, The goat is thy share! we place our hymn in direct contradiction with the tradition of the Sûtras. There is a still greater difficulty. If the poet really wished to say, this goat is to be thy share, would he have left out the most important word, viz., thy. He does not say, the goat is thy share, but only, "the goat share."

However, even if we retain the old translation, there is no lack of difficulties, though the whole meaning becomes more natural. The poet says, first, that the eye should go to the sun, the breath to the air, that the dead should return to heaven and earth, and his limbs rest among herbs. Everything, therefore, that was born, was to return to whence it came. How natural, then, that he should ask, what would become of the unborn, the eternal part of man. How natural that, after such a question, there should be a pause, and that then the poet should continue: Warm it with thy warmth! May thy glow warm it and thy flame! Assume thy kindest form, O Fire, and carry him away to the world of the Blessed! Whom? Not surely the goat; not even the corpse, but the unborn, the eternal part of man.

It is possible, no doubt, and more than possible, that from this passage by a very natural misunderstanding the idea arose that with the corpse a goat (a*g*a) was to be burnt. We see, in the Âtharva*n*a, how eagerly the priests laid hold of that idea. We know it was owing to a similar misunderstanding that widows were burnt in India with their dead husbands, and that Yama, the old deity of the setting sun, was changed into a king of the dead, and lastly into the first of men who died. There are indeed vast distances beyond the hymns of the Veda, and many things even in the earliest hymns become intelligible only if we look upon them, not as just arising, but as having passed already through many a metamorphosis.

This is only one instance of the many difficulties connected with a right understanding of a religion, even where that religion possesses a large literature. The fact, however, that scholars may thus differ, does not affect the really scientific character of their researches. They have to produce on either side the grounds for their opinions, and others may then form their own judgment. We are here on *terra firma*.

The mischief begins when philosophers, who are not scholars by profession, use the labors of Sanskrit, Zend, or classical scholars for their own purposes. Here there is real danger. The same writers who, without any references, nay, it may be, without having inquired into the credibility of their witnesses, tell us exactly what Kaffers, Bushmen, and Hottentots believed on the soul, on death, on God and the world, seldom advance an opinion on the religion of Greeks, Romans, Persians, or Hindus which a scholar would not at once challenge. Of this, too, I must give a few instances, not in a fault-finding spirit, but simply in order to point out a very real danger against which we ought all of us to guard most carefully in our researches into the history of religion.

There is no word more frequently used by the Brahmans than the word *Om*. It may stand for *avam*, and, like French *oui* for *hoc illud*, have meant originally Yes, but it soon assumed a solemn character, something like our *Amen*. It had to be used at the beginning, also at the end of every recitation, and there are few MSS. that do not begin with it. It is even prescribed for certain salutations;[1] in fact, there were probably few words more frequently heard in ancient and modern India than *Om*. Yet we are told by Mr. H. Spencer[2] that the Hindus avoid uttering the sacred name *Om*, and this is to prove that semi-civilized races have been interdicted from pronouncing the names of their gods. It is quite possible that in a collective work, such as Dr. Muir's most excellent "Sanskrit Texts," a passage may occur in support of such a statement. In the mystic philosophy of the Upanishads, *Om* became one of the principal names of the highest Brahman, and a knowledge of that Brahman was certainly forbidden to be divulged. But how different is that from stating that "by various semi-civilized races the calling of deities by their proper names has been interdicted or considered improper. It is so among the Hindus, who avoid uttering the sacred name

[1] *Apastamba-Sûtras*, i. 4, 13, 6. Prâtisâkhya, 832, 838.
[2] *Sociology*, i. p. 298.

Om; it was so with the Hebrews, whose pronunciation of the word Jehovah is not known for this reason; and Herodotus carefully avoids naming Osiris." The last statement again will surprise those who remember how it is Herodotus who tells us that, though Egyptians do not all worship the same gods, they all worship Isis and Osiris, whom they identify with Dionysus.[1]

Dr. Muir[2] is no doubt perfectly right in saying that in some passages of the Veda "certain gods are looked upon as confessedly mere created beings," and that they like men were made immortal by drinking *soma*. But this only shows how dangerous even such careful compilations as Dr. Muir's "Sanskrit Texts" are apt to become. The gods in the Veda are called *agara* or *mrityu-bandhu* or *amartya*, immortal, in opposition to men, who are *martya*, mortal, and it is only in order to magnify the power of *soma*, that this beverage, like the Greek ἀμβροσία, is said to have conferred immortality on the gods. Nor did the Vedic poets think of their gods as what we mean by "mere created beings," because they spoke of the dawn as the daughter of the sky, or of Indra as springing from heaven and earth. At least we might say with much greater truth that the Greeks looked upon Zeus as a mere created thing, because he was the son of Kronos.

Again, what can be more misleading than, in order to prove that all gods were originally mortals, to quote Buddha's saying: "Gods and men, the rich and poor, alike must die?" In Buddha's time, nay, even before Buddha's time, the old Devas, whom we choose to call gods, had been used up. Buddha be-

[1] Her. ii. 42; 144; 156.

[2] *Sanskrit Texts*, v. p. 12.

lieved in no Devas, perhaps in no God. He allowed the old Devas to subsist as mere fabulous beings;[1] and as fabulous beings of much greater consequence than the Devas shared in the fate of all that exists, viz., an endless migration from birth to death, and from death to birth, the Devas could not be exempted from that common lot.

In forming an opinion of the mental capacities of people, an examination of their language is no doubt extremely useful. But such an examination requires considerable care and circumspection. Mr. H. Spencer says,[2] "When we read of an existing South American tribe, that the proposition, 'I am an Abipone,' is expressible only in the vague way, 'I Abipone,' we cannot but infer that by such undeveloped grammatical structures only the simplest thoughts can be rightly conveyed." Would not some of the most perfect languages in the world fall under the same condemnation?

STUDY OF THE RELIGION OF SAVAGES.

If such misunderstandings happen where they might easily be avoided, what shall we think when we read broad statements as to religious opinions of whole nations and tribes who possess no literature, whose very language is frequently but imperfectly understood, and who have been visited, it may be, by one or two travelers only for a few days, for a few weeks, or for a few years!

Let us take an instance. We are told that we may observe a very primitive state of religion among the people of Fiji. They regard the shooting-stars

[1] See M. M., *Buddhistischer Nihilismus*.
[2] *Sociology*, i. p. 149.

as gods, and the smaller ones as the departing souls of men. Before we can make any use of such a statement, ought we not to know, first, what is the exact name and concept of god among the Fijians; and secondly, of what objects besides shooting-stars that name is predicated? Are we to suppose that the whole idea of the Divine which the Fijians had formed to themselves is concentrated in shooting-stars? Or does the statement mean only that the Fijians look upon shooting-stars as one manifestation out of many of a Divine power familiar to them from other sources? If so, then all depends clearly on what these other sources are, and how from them the name and concept of something divine could have sprung.

When we are told that the poets of the Veda represent the sun as a god, we ask at once what is their name for god, and we are told *deva*, which originally meant *bright*. The biography of that single word *deva* would fill a volume, and not until we know its biography from its birth and infancy to its very end would the statement that the Hindus consider the sun as a *deva*, convey to us any real meaning.

The same applies to the statement that the Fijians or any other races look upon shooting-stars as the departing souls of men. Are the shooting-stars the souls, or the souls the shooting-stars? Surely all depends here on the meaning conveyed by the word *soul*. How did they come by that word? What was its original intention? These are the questions which ethnological psychology has to ask and to answer, before it can turn with any advantage to the numerous anecdotes which we find collected in works on the study of man.

It is a well-known fact that many words for soul meant originally shadow. But what meaning shall we attach, for instance, to such a statement as that Benin negroes regard their shadows as their souls? If soul is here used in the English sense of the word, then the negroes could never believe their English souls to be no more than their African shadows. The question is, Do they simply say that *a* (shadow) is equal to *a* (shadow), or do they want to say that *a* (shadow) is equal to something else, viz., *b* (soul)? It is true that we also do not always see clearly what we mean by soul; but what we mean by it could never be the same as mere shadow only. Unless, therefore, we are told whether the Benin negroes mean by their word for soul the *anima*, the breath, the token of life; or the *animus*, the mind, the token of thought; or the *soul*, as the seat of desires and passions; unless we know whether their so-called soul is material or immaterial, visible or invisible, mortal or immortal, the mere information that certain savage tribes look upon the shadow, or a bird, or a shooting-star as their soul seems to me to teach us nothing.

This was written before the following passage in a letter from the Rev. R. H. Codrington (dated July 3, 1877) attracted my attention, where that thoughtful missionary expresses himself in very much the same sense. "Suppose," he writes, "there are people who call the soul a shadow, I do not in the least believe they think the shadow a soul, or the soul a shadow; but they use the word shadow figuratively for that belonging to man, which is like his shadow, definitely individual, and inseparable from him, but unsubstantial. The Mota word we use for soul is in

Maori a shadow, but no Mota man knows that it ever means that. In fact, my belief is, that in the original language this word did not definitely mean either soul or shadow, but had a meaning one can conceive but not express, which has come out in one language as meaning shadow, and in the other as meaning something like soul, *i. e.*, second self."

What we must try to understand is exactly this transition of meaning, how from the observation of the shadow which stays with us by day and seems to leave us by night, the idea of a second self arose; how that idea was united with another, namely, that of breath, which stays with us during life, and seems to leave us at the moment of death; and how out of these two ideas the concept of a something, separate from the body and yet endowed with life, was slowly elaborated. Here we can watch a real transition from the visible to the invisible, from the material to the immaterial; but instead of saying that people, in that primitive stage of thought, believe their souls to be shadows, all we should be justified in saying would be that they believed that, after death, their breath, having left the body, would reside in something like the shadow that follows them during life. The superstition that a dead body casts no shadow, follows very naturally from this.

Nothing is more difficult than to resist the temptation to take an unexpected confirmation of any of our own theories, which we may meet with in the accounts of missionaries and travelers, as a proof of their truth. The word for God throughout Eastern Polynesia is *Atua* or *Akua*. Now *ata*, in the language of those Polynesian islanders, means shadow, and what would seem to be more natural than to see in this name of God, meaning originally shadow, a confirmation of a favorite theory, that the idea of God sprang everywhere from the idea of spirit, and the idea of spirit from that of shadow? It would seem mere captiousness to object to such a theory, and to advise caution where all seems so clear. Fortunately the languages of Polynesia have in some instances been studied in a more scholarlike spirit, so that our theories must submit to being checked by facts. Thus Mr. Gill,[1] who has lived twenty years at Mangaia, shows that *atua* cannot be derived from *ata*, shadow, but is connected with *fatu* in Tahitian and Samoan, and with *aitu*, and that it meant originally the core or pith of a tree. From meaning the core and kernel, *atu* came to mean the best part, the strength of a thing, and was used in the sense of lord and master. The final *a* in *Atua* is intensive in signification, so that *Atua* expresses to a native the idea of the very core and life. This was the beginning of that conception of the Deity which they express by *Atua*.

When we have to deal with the evidence placed before us by a scholar like Mr. Gill, who has spent nearly all his life among one and the same tribe, a certain amount of confidence is excusable. Still even he cannot claim the same authority which belongs to Homer, when speaking of his own religion, or to St. Augustine, when giving us his interesting account of the beliefs of the ancient Romans. And yet, who does not know how much uncertainty is left in our minds after we have read all that such men have to say with regard to their own religion, or the religion of the community in the midst of which they grew up and passed the whole of their life!

[1] *Myths and Songs from the South Pacific*, p. 33.

The difficulties which beset travelers and missionaries in their description of the religious and intellectual life of savage tribes are far more serious than is commonly supposed, and some of them deserve to be considered before we proceed farther.

INFLUENCE OF PUBLIC OPINION ON TRAVELERS.

First of all, few men are quite proof against the fluctuations of public opinion. There was a time when many travelers were infected with Rousseau's ideas, so that in their eyes all savages became very much what the Germans were to Tacitus. Then came a reaction. Partly owing to the influence of American ethnologists, who wanted an excuse for slavery, partly owing, at a later time, to a desire of finding the missing link between men and monkeys, descriptions of savages began to abound which made us doubt whether the negro was not a lower creature than the gorilla, whether he really deserved the name of man.

When it became a question much agitated, whether religion was an inherent characteristic of man or not, some travelers were always meeting with tribes who had no idea and name for gods;[1] others discovered exalted notions of religion everywhere. My friend Mr. Tylor has made a very useful collection of contradictory accounts given by different observers of the religious capacities of one and the same tribe. Perhaps the most ancient instance on record is the account given of the religion of the Germans by Cæsar and Tacitus. Cæsar states that the Germans count those only as gods whom they can perceive, and by whose gifts they are clearly benefited, such as the

[1] M. M., *History of Ancient Sanskrit Literature*, p. 538.

Sun, the Fire, and the Moon.[1] Tacitus declares "that they call by the names of gods that hidden thing which they do not perceive, except by reverence."[2]

It may, of course, be said that in the interval between Cæsar and Tacitus the whole religion of Germany had changed, or that Tacitus came in contact with a more spiritual tribe of Germans than Cæsar. But, even if granting that, do we make allowance for such influences in utilizing the accounts of early and later travelers?

ABSENCE OF RECOGNIZED AUTHORITIES AMONG SAVAGES.

And even if we find a traveler without any scientific bias, free from any wish to please the leaders of any scientific or theological school, there remains, when he attempts to give a description of savage or half-savage tribes and their religion, the immense difficulty that not one of these religions has any recognized standards, that religion among savage tribes is almost entirely a personal matter, that it may change from one generation to another, and that even in the same generation the greatest variety of individual opinion may prevail with regard to the gravest questions of their faith. True, there are priests, there may be some sacred songs and customs, and there always is some teaching from mothers to their children. But there is no Bible, no prayer-book, no catechism. Religion floats in the air, and each man takes as much or as little of it as he likes.

We shall thus understand why accounts given by

1 *De Bello Gall.* vi. 21. "Deorum numero eos solos ducunt quos cernunt, et quorum aperte opibus juvantur, Solem, et Vulcanum, et Lunam."

2 Tac. *Germ.* 9. "Deorumque nominibus appellant secretum illud quod sola reverentia vident."

different missionaries and travelers of the religion of one and the same tribe should sometimes differ from each other like black and white. There may be in the same tribe an angel of light and a vulgar ruffian, yet both would be considered by European travelers as unimpeachable authorities with regard to their religion.

That there are differences in the religious convictions of the people is admitted by the negroes themselves.[1] At Widah, Des Marchais was distinctly told that the nobility only knew of the supreme God as omnipotent, omnipresent, rewarding the evil and the good, and that they approached him with prayers only when all other appeals had failed. There is, however, among all nations, savage as well as civilized, another nobility — the divine nobility of goodness and genius — which often places one man many centuries in advance of the common crowd.

Think only what the result would be if, in England, the criminal drunkard and the sister of mercy who comes to visit him in his miserable den were asked to give an account of their common Christianity, and you will be less surprised, I believe, at the discrepancies in the reports given by different witnesses of the creed of one and the same African tribe.

AUTHORITY OF PRIESTS.

It might be said that the priests, when consulted on the religious opinions of their people, ought to be unimpeachable authorities. But is that so? Is it so with us?

We have witnessed ourselves, not many years ago, how one of the most eminent theologians declared

[1] Waitz, *Anthropologie*, ii. 171.

that one whose bust now stands with those of Keble and Kingsley in the same chapel of Westminster Abbey, did not believe in the same God as himself! Need we wonder, then, if priests among the Ashantis differ as to the true meaning of their fetishes, and if travelers who have listened to different teachers of religion differ in the accounts which they give to us? In some parts of Africa, particularly where the influence of Mohammedanism is felt, fetishes and sellers of fetishes are despised. The people who believe in them are called *thiedos*, or infidels.[1] In other parts, fetish-worship rules supreme, and priests who manufacture fetishes and live by the sale of them shout very loudly, "Great is Diana of the Ephesians."

UNWILLINGNESS OF SAVAGES TO TALK OF RELIGION.

Lastly, let us consider that, in order to get at a real understanding of any religion, there must be a wish and a will on both sides. Many savages shrink from questions on religious topics, partly, it may be, from some superstitious fear — partly, it may be, from their helplessness in putting their own unfinished thoughts and sentiments into definite language. Some races are decidedly reticent. Speaking is an effort to them. After ten minutes conversation they complain of headache.[2] Others are extremely talkative, and have an answer to everything, little caring whether what they say is true or not.[3]

This difficulty is admirably stated by the Rev. R. H. Codrington, in a letter from Norfolk Island, July

1 Waitz, ii. 200. "On Different Classes of Priests," ii. 199.

2 Burchell, *Reisen in das Innere von Südafrika*, 1823, pp. 71, 281. Schultze, *Fetischismus*, p. 36. H. Spencer, *Socio logy*, i. p. 94.

3 Mayer, *Papua-sprachen*, p. 19.

3, 1877: "But the confusion about such matters does not ordinarily lie in the native mind, but proceeds from the want of clear communication between the native and European. A native who knows a little English, or one trying to communicate with an Englishman in his native tongue, finds it very much more easy to assent to what the white man suggests, or to use the words that he knows, without perhaps exactly knowing the meaning, than to struggle to convey exactly what he thinks is the true account. Hence visitors receive what they suppose trustworthy information from natives, and then print things which read very absurdly to those who know the truth. Much amusement was caused to-day when I told a Merlav boy that I had just read in a book (Capt. Moresby's on New Guinea) of the idols he had seen in his village, which it was hoped that boy would be able to teach the natives to reject. He had a hand in making them, and they are no more idols than the gargoyles on your chapel; yet I have no doubt some native told the naval officers that they were idols, or devils, or something, when he was asked whether they were not, and got much credit for his knowledge of English."

I mentioned in my first Lecture the account of some excellent Benedictine [1] missionaries, who, after three years spent at their station in Australia, came to the conclusion that the natives did not adore any deity, whether true or false. Yet they found out afterwards that the natives believed in an omnipotent Being, who had created the world. Suppose they

[1] A Benedictine Missionary's account of the natives of Australia and Oceania. From the Italian of Don Rudesindo Salvado (Rome, 1851), by C. H. E. Carmichael. *Journal of the Anthropological Institute*, February, 1878.

had left their station before having made this discovery, who would have dared to contradict their statements?

De Brosses, when he gave his first and fatal account of fetishism, saw none of these difficulties. Whatever he found in the voyages of sailors and traders was welcome to him. He had a theory to defend, and whatever seemed to support it was sure to be true.

I have entered thus fully into the difficulties inherent in the study of the religions of savage tribes, in order to show how cautious we ought to be before we accept one-sided descriptions of these religions; still more, before we venture to build, on such evidence as is now accessible, far-reaching theories on the nature and origin of religion in general. It will be difficult indeed to eradicate the idea of a universal primeval fetishism from the text-books of history. That very theory has become a kind of scientific fetish, though, like most fetishes, it seems to owe its existence to ignorance and superstition.

Only let me not be misunderstood. I do not mean to dispute the fact that fetish-worship is widely prevalent among the negroes of Western Africa and other savage races.

What I cannot bring myself to admit is, that any writer on the subject, beginning with De Brosses, has proved, or ever attempted to prove, that what they call fetishism is a primitive form of religion. It may be admitted to be a low form, but that, particularly in religion, is very different from a primitive form of religion.

WIDE EXTENSION OF THE MEANING OF FETISH.

One of the greatest difficulties we have to encounter in attempting to deal in a truly scientific spirit with the problem of fetishism, is the wide extension that has been given to the meaning of the word fetish.

De Brosses speaks already of fetishes, not only in Africa, but among the Red Indians, the Polynesians, the northern tribes of Asia; and after his time hardly a single corner of the world has been visited without traces of fetish-worship being discovered. I am the last man to deny to this spirit which sees similarities everywhere, its scientific value and justification. It is the comparative spirit which is at work everywhere, and which has achieved the greatest triumphs in modern times. But we must not forget that comparison, in order to be fruitful, must be joined with distinction, otherwise we fall into that dangerous habit of seeing cromlechs wherever there are some upright stones and another laid across, or a dolmen wherever we meet with a stone with a hole in it.

We have heard a great deal lately in Germany, and in England also, of tree-worship and serpent-worship. Nothing can be more useful than a wide collection of analogous facts, but their true scientific interest begins only when we can render to ourselves an account of how, beneath their apparent similarity, there often exists the greatest diversity of origin.

It is the same in Comparative Philology. No doubt there is grammar everywhere, even in the languages of the lowest races; but if we attempt to force our grammatical terminology, our nominatives and accusatives, our actives and passives, our gerunds and supines upon every language, we lose the chief lesson which a comparative study of language is to teach us, and we fail to see how the same object can be realized, and was realized, in a hundred different ways, in a hundred different languages. Here, better than anywhere else, the old Latin saying applies: *Si duo dicunt idem, non est idem*, "If two languages say the same thing, it is not the same thing."

If there is fetish-worship everywhere, the fact is curious, no doubt; but it gains a really scientific value only if we can account for the fact. How a fetish came to be a fetish, that is the problem which has to be solved, and as soon as we attack fetishism in that spirit, we shall find that, though being apparently the same everywhere, its antecedents are seldom the same anywhere. There is no fetish without its antecedents, and it is in these antecedents alone that its true and scientific interest consists.

ANTECEDENTS OF FETISHISM.

Let us consider only a few of the more common forms of what has been called fetishism; and we shall soon see from what different heights and depths its sources spring.

If the bones, or the ashes, or the hair of a departed friend are cherished as relics, if they are kept in safe or sacred places, if they are now and then looked at, or even spoken to, by true mourners in their loneliness, all this may be, and has been, called fetish-worship.

Again, if a sword once used by a valiant warrior, if a banner which had led their fathers to victory, if a stick, or let us call it a sceptre, if a calabash, or let us call it a drum, are greeted with respect or enthusiasm by soldiers when going to do battle themselves, all this may be called fetish-worship. If these banners and swords are blessed by priests, or if the spirits of those who had carried them in former years are invoked, as if they were still present, all this may be put down as fetishism. If the defeated soldier breaks his sword across his knees, or tears his colors, or throws his eagles away, he may be said to be punishing his fetish , nay, Napoleon himself may be called a fetish-worshiper when, pointing to the pyramids, he said to his soldiers, "From the summit of these monuments forty centuries look down upon you, soldiers ! "

This is a kind of comparison in which similarities are allowed to obscure all differences.

No, we cannot possibly distinguish too much, if we want not only to know, but to understand the ancient customs of savage nations. Sometimes a stock or a stone was worshiped, because it was a forsaken altar, or an ancient place of judgment;[1] sometimes because it marked the place of a great battle or a murder,[2] or the burial of a king ; sometimes because it protected the sacred boundaries of clans or families. There are stones from which weapons can be made ; there are stones on which weapons can be sharpened ; there are stones, like the jade found in Swiss lakes, that must have been brought as heir-looms from great distances ; there are meteoric stones fallen from the sky. Are all these simply to be labeled fetishes, because, for very good but very different reasons, they were treated with some kind of reverence by ancient and even by modern people ?

[1] Paus. i. 28, 5.

[2] Ibid. viii. 13, 3; x. 5, 4.

Sometimes the fact that a crude stone is worshiped as the image of a god may show a higher power of abstraction than the worship paid to the master-works of Phidias; sometimes the worship paid to a stone slightly resembling the human form may mark a very low stage of religious feeling. If we are satisfied with calling all this and much more simply fetishism, we shall soon be told that the stone on which all the kings of England have been crowned is an old fetish, and that in the coronation of Queen Victoria we ought to recognize a survival of Anglo-Saxon fetishism.

Matters have at last gone so far that people traveling in Africa actually cross-examine the natives whether they believe in *fetishes*, as if the poor negro or the Hottentot or the Papua could have any idea of what is meant by such a word! Native African words for fetish are *gri-gri*, *gru-gru*, or *ju-ju*, all of them possibly the same word.[1] I must quote at least one story, showing how far superior the examinee may sometimes be to the examiners. "A negro was worshiping a tree, supposed to be his fetish, with an offering of food, when some European asked whether he thought that the tree could eat. The negro replied: 'Oh, the tree is not the fetish, the fetish is a spirit and invisible, but he has descended into this tree. Certainly he cannot devour our bodily food, but he enjoys its spiritual part, and leaves behind the bodily part, which we see.'" The story is almost too good to be true, but it rests on the authority of Halleur,[2] and it may serve at least as a warning

[1] Waitz, ii. p. 175. F. Schultze states that the negroes adopted that word from the Portuguese. Bastian gives *enquizi* as a name for fetish on the West Coast of Africa; also *mokisso* (Bastian, *St. Salvador*, pp. 254, 81).

[2] *Das Leben der Neger West-Africa's*, p. 40. Cf. Waitz, ii. p. 188. Tylor, *Primitive Culture*, ii. 197.

against our interpreting the sacrificial acts of so-called savage people by one and the same rule, and against our using technical terms so ill-chosen and so badly defined as fetishism.

Confusion becomes still worse confounded when travelers, who have accustomed themselves to the most modern acceptation of the word fetish, who use it, in fact, in the place of God, write their accounts of the savages races, among whom they have lived, in this modern jargon. Thus one traveler tells us that "the natives say that the great fetish of Bamba lives in the bush, where no man sees him or can see him. When he dies, the fetish-priests carefully collect his bones, in order to revive them and nourish them, till they again acquire flesh and blood." Now here "the great fetish" is used in the Comtian sense of the word; it means no longer *fetish*, but deity. A fetish that lives in the bush and cannot be seen is the very opposite of the *feitiço*, or the *gru-gru*, or whatever name we may choose to employ for those lifeless and visible subjects which are worshiped by men, not only in Africa, but in the whole world, during a certain phase of their religious consciousness.

UBIQUITY OF FETISHISM.

If we once go so far, we need not wonder that fetishes are found everywhere, among ancient and modern, among uncivilized and civilized people. The Palladium at Troy, which was supposed to have fallen from the sky, and was believed to make the town impregnable, may be called a fetish, and like a fetish it had to be stolen by Odysseus and Diomedes, before Troy could be taken. Pausanias[1] states that in

[1] Paus. vii. 22. 4.

ancient times the images of the gods in Greece were rude stones, and he mentions such stones as still existing in his time, in the second century of our era. At Pharae he tells us of thirty square stones (hermæ?), near the statute of Hermes, which the people worshiped, giving to each the name of a god. The Thespians, who worshiped Eros as the first among gods, had an image of him which was a mere stone.[1] The statue of Herakles, at Hyettos, was of the same character,[2] according to the old fashion, as Pausanias himself remarks. In Sicyon he mentions an image of Zeus Meilichios, and another of Artemis Patroa, both made without any art, the former a mere pyramid, the latter a column.[3] At Orchomenos again, he describes a temple of the Graces, in which they were worshiped as rude stones, which were believed to have fallen from the sky at the time of Eteokles. Statues of the Graces were placed in the temple during the life-time of Pausanias.[4]

The same at Rome. Stones which were believed to have fallen from the sky were invoked to grant success in military enterprises.[5] Mars himself was represented by a spear. Augustus, after losing two naval battles, punished Neptune like a fetish, by excluding his image from the procession of the gods.[6] Nero was, according to Suetonius, a great despiser of all religion, though for a time he professed great faith in the Dea Syria. This, however, came to an end, and he then treated her image with the greatest indignity. The fact was that some unknown person had given him a small image of a girl, as a protection

[1] Paus. ix. 27. 1.
[2] Ibid. ix. 24. 3.
[3] Ibid. ii. 9. 6.
[4] Ibid. ix. 38. 1.
[5] Plin. *N. H.* 37, 9.
[6] Suet., Aug.

against plots, and as he discovered a plot against his life immediately afterwards, he began to worship that image as the highest deity, offering sacrifices to it three times every day, and declaring that it enabled him to foresee the future.[1]

If all this had happened at Timbuktu, instead of Rome, should we not call it fetishism?

Lastly, to turn to Christianity, is it not notorious what treatment the images of saints receive at the hands of the lower classes in Roman Catholic countries? Della Valle[2] relates that Portuguese sailors fastened the image of St. Anthony to the bowsprit, and then addressed him kneeling, with the following words, "O St. Anthony, be pleased to stay there till thou hast given us a fair wind for our voyage." Frezier[3] writes of a Spanish captain who tied a small image of the Virgin Mary to the mast, declaring that it should hang there till it had granted him a favorable wind. Kotzebue[4] declares that the Neapolitans whip their saints, if they do not grant their requests. Russian peasants, we are told, cover the face of an image, when they are doing anything unseemly, nay, they even borrow their neighbors' saints, if they have proved themselves particularly successful.[5] All this, if seen by a stranger, would be set down as fetishism, and yet what a view is opened before our eye, if we ask ourselves how such worship paid to an image of the Virgin Mary or of a saint became possible in Europe? Why should it be so different among the

1 Ibid., Nero, c. 56.

2 *Voyage*, vii. 409; Meiners, i. p. 181; F. Schultze, *Fetishismus*, p. 175.

3 *Relation du Voyage de la Mer du Sud*, p. 248. F. Schultze, l. c.

4 *Reise nach Rom*, i. p. 327.

5 Rig-Veda, IV. 24, 10.

negroes of Africa? Why should all their fetishes be, as it were, of yesterday?

To sum up. If we see how all that can be called fetish in religions the history of which is known to us, is secondary, why should fetishes in Africa, where we do not know the earlier development of religion, be considered as primary? If everywhere else there are antecedents of a fetish, if everywhere else fetishism is accompanied by more or less developed religious idea, why should we insist on fetishism being the very beginning of all religion in Africa? Instead of trying to account for fetishism in all other religions by a reference to the fetishism which we find in Africa, would it not be better to try to account for the fetishism in Africa by analogous facts in religions the history of which is known to us?

NO RELIGION CONSISTS OF FETISHISM ONLY.

But if it has never been proved, and perhaps, according to the nature of the case, can never be proved that fetishism in Africa, or elsewhere, was ever in any sense of the word a primary form of religion, neither has it been shown that fetishism constituted anywhere, whether in Africa or elsewhere, the whole of a people's religion. Though our knowledge of the religion of the negroes is still very imperfect, yet I believe I may say that, wherever there has been an opportunity of ascertaining by long and patient intercourse the religious sentiments even of the lowest savage tribes, no tribe has ever been found without something beyond mere worship of so-called fetishes. A worship of visible material objects is widely spread among African tribes, far more widely than anywhere else. The intellectual and sentimental tendencies of the negro may preëminently predispose him to that kind of degraded worship. All this I gladly admit. But I maintain that fetishism was a corruption of religion, in Africa as elsewhere, that the negro is capable of higher religious ideas than the worship of stocks and stones, and that many tribes who believe in fetishes, cherish at the same time very pure, very exalted, very true sentiments of the Deity. Only we must have eyes to see, eyes that can see what is perfect without dwelling too much on what is imperfect. The more I study heathen religions, the more I feel convinced that, if we want to form a true judgment of their purpose, we must measure them as we measure the Alps, by the highest point which they have reached. Religion is everywhere an aspiration rather than a fulfillment, and I claim no more for the religion of the negro than for our own, when I say that it should be judged, not by what it appears to be, but by what it is — nay, not only by what it is, but by what it can be, and by what it has been in its most gifted votaries.

HIGHER ELEMENTS IN AFRICAN RELIGION. WAITZ.

Whatever can be done under present circumstances to gain an approximate idea of the real religion of the African negroes, has been done by Waitz in his classical work on Anthropology.[1] Waitz, the editor of Aristotle's "Organon," approached his subject in a truly scholarlike spirit. He was not only impartial himself, but he carefully examined the impartiality of his authorities before he quoted their opinions. His work is well known in England, where many of his facts and opinions have found so charm-

1 *Anthropologie*, ii. p. 167.

ing an interpreter in Mr. Tylor. The conclusions at which Waitz arrived with regard to the true character of the religion of the negroes may be stated in his own words: —

"The religion of the negro is generally considered as a peculiar crude form of polytheism and marked with the special name of fetishism. A closer inspection of it, however, shows clearly that, apart from certain extravagant and fantastic features which spring from the character of the negro and influence all his doings, his religion, as compared with those of other uncivilized people, is neither very peculiar nor exceptionally crude. Such a view could only be taken, if we regarded the outward side only of the negro's religion or tried to explain it from gratuitous antecedents. A more profound investigation, such as has lately been successfully carried out by several eminent scholars, leads to the surprising result that several negro tribes, who cannot be shown to have experienced the influence of any more highly civilized nations, have progressed much farther in the elaboration of their religious ideas than almost all other uncivilized races; so far indeed that, if we do not like to call them monotheists, we may at least say of them, that they have come very near to the boundaries of true monotheism, although their religion is mixed up with a large quantity of coarse superstitions, which with some other people seem almost to choke all pure religious ideas."

Waitz himself considers Wilson's book on West Africa, its History, Condition, and Prospects (1856), as one of the best, but he has collected his materials likewise from many other sources, and particularly from the accounts of missionaries. Wilson was the first to point out that what we have chosen to call fetishism is something very distinct from the real religion of the negro. There is ample evidence to show that the same tribes, who are represented as fetish-worshipers, believe either in gods or in a supreme good God, the creator of the world, and that they possess in their dialects particular names for him.

Sometimes it is said that no visible worship is paid to that Supreme Being, but to fetishes only. This, however, may arise from different causes. It may arise from an excess of reverence, quite as much as from negligence. Thus the Odjis [1] or Ashantis call the Supreme Being by the same name as the sky, but they mean by it a personal God, who, as they say, created all things, and is the giver of all good things. But though he is omnipresent and omniscient, knowing even the thoughts of men, and pitying them in their distress, the government of the world is, as they believe, deputed by him to inferior spirits, and among these again it is the malevolent spirits only who require worship and sacrifice from man.[2]

Cruickshank [3] calls attention to the same feature in the character of the negroes on the Gold Coast. He thinks that their belief in a supreme God, who has made the world and governs it, is very old, but he adds that they invoke him very rarely, calling him "their great friend," or "He who has made us." Only when in great distress they call out, "We are in the hands of God; he will do what seemeth right to

1 Waitz, ii. p. 171.
2 Riis, *Baseler Missions-Magazin*, 1847, iv. 244, 248.
3 Cruickshank, p. 217, quoted by Waitz, ii. p. 172.

him." This view is confirmed by the Basle missionaries,[1] who cannot certainly be suspected of partiality. They also affirm that their belief in a supreme God is by no means without influence on the negroes. Often, when in deep distress, they say to themselves, "God is the old one, he is the greatest; he sees me, I am in his hand." The same missionary adds, "If, besides this faith, they also believe in thousands of fetishes, this, unfortunately, they share in common with many Christians."

The Odjis or Ashantis,[2] while retaining a clear conception of God as the high or the highest, the creator, the giver of sunshine, rain, and all good gifts, the omniscient, hold that he does not condescend to govern the world, but that he has placed created spirits as lords over hills and vales, forests and fields, rivers and the sea. These are conceived as like unto men, and are occasionally seen, particularly by the priests. Most of them are good, but some are evil spirits, and it seems that in one respect at least these negroes rival the Europeans, admitting the existence of a supreme evil spirit, the enemy of men, who dwells apart in a world beyond.[3]

Some of the African names given to the Supreme Being meant originally sun, sky, giver of rain; others mean Lord of Heaven, Lord and King of Heaven, the invisible creator. As such he is invoked by the Yebus,[4] who in praying to him turn their faces to the ground. One of their prayers was — "God in Heaven, guard us from sickness and death; God, grant us happiness and wisdom."

[1] *Baseler Missions-Magazin*, 1855, i. p. 88; Waitz, ii. p. 173.
[2] Waitz, ii. p. 171.
[3] Waitz, ii. pp. 173, 174.
[4] Ibid. ii. p. 168; D'Avezac, p. 84, note 3.

The Edîyahs of Fernando Po[1] call the Supreme Being *Rupi*, but admit many lesser gods as mediators between him and man. The Duallahs,[2] on the Camеrunѕ, have the same name for the Great Spirit and the sun.

The Yorubas believe in a Lord of Heaven, whom they call *Olorun*.[3] They believe in other gods also, and they speak of a place called Ife, in the district of Kakanda (5° E. long. Gr. 8° N. lat.) as the seat of the gods, a kind of Olympus, from whence sun and moon always return after having been buried in the earth, and from whence men also are believed to have sprung.[4]

Among the people of Akra, we are told by Römer[5] that a kind of worship was paid to the rising sun. Zimmerman[6] denies that any kind of worship is paid there to casual objects (commonly called fetishes), and we know from the reports of missionaries that their name for the highest god is Jongmaa,[7] which signifies both rain and god. This Jongmaa is probably the same as Nyongmo, the name for God on the Gold Coast. There too it means the sky, which is everywhere, and has been from everlasting. A negro, who was himself a fetish priest, said, "Do we not see daily how the grass, the corn, and the trees grow by the rain and the sunshine which he sends!

1 Waitz, ii. p. 168.

2 Allen and Thomson, *Narrative of the Expedition to the River Niger in* 1841, ii. pp. 199, 395, note.

3 Tucker, p. 192, note.

4 Tucker, *Abbeokuta, or an Outline of the Origin and Progress of the Yoruba Mission*, 1856, p. 248.

5 Römer, *Nachrichten von der Küste Guinea*, 1769, p. 84.

6 Zimmerman, *Grammatical Sketch of the Akra or Ga Language, Vocabulary*, p. 337.

7 *Baseler Missions-Magazin*, 1837, p. 559.

How should he not be the creator?" The clouds are said to be his veil; the stars, the jewels on his face. His children are the *Wong*, the spirits which fill the air and execute his commands on earth.

These Wongs, which have likewise been mistaken for fetishes, constitute a very important element in many ancient religions, not only in Africa; they step in everywhere where the distance between the human and the divine has become too wide, and where something intermediate, or certain mediators, are wanted to fill the gap which man has created himself. A similar idea is expressed by Celsus when defending the worship of the genii. Addressing himself to the Christians, who declined to worship the old genii, he says, "God can suffer no wrong. God can lose nothing. The inferior spirits are not his rivals, that He can resent the respect which we pay to them. In them we worship only some attributes of Him from whom they hold authority, and in saying that One only is Lord, you disobey and rebel against Him." [1]

On the Gold Coast [2] it is believed that these Wongs dwell between heaven and earth, that they have children, die, and rise again. There is a Wong for the sea and all that is therein; there are other Wongs for rivers, lakes, and springs; there are others for pieces of land which have been inclosed, others for the small heaps of earth thrown up to cover a sacrifice; others, again, for certain trees, for certain animals, such as crocodiles, apes, and serpents, while other animals are only considered as sacred to the Wongs. There are Wongs for the sacred images carved by the fetishman, lastly for anything made

[1] Froude, in *Fraser's Magazine*, 1878, p. 160.
[2] Waitz, ii. p. 183.

of hair, bones, and thread, and offered for sale as talismans.[1] Here we see clearly the difference between Wongs and fetishes, the fetish being the outward sign, the Wong the indwelling spirit, though, no doubt, here too the spiritual might soon have dwindled down into a real presence.[2]

In Akwapim the word which means both God and weather is Jankkupong. In Bonny, also, and in Eastern Africa among the Makuas, one and the same word is used to signify God, heaven, and cloud.[3] In Dahomey the sun is said to be supreme, but receives no kind of worship.[4] The Ibos believe in a maker of the world whom they call Tshuku. He has two eyes and two ears, one in the sky and one on the earth. He is invisible, and he never sleeps. He hears all that is said, but he can reach those only who draw near unto him.[5]

Can anything be more simple and more true ? He can reach those only who draw near unto him ! Could we say more ?

Good people, it is believed, will see him after death, bad people go into fire. Do not some of us say the same ?

That some of the negroes are aware of the degrading character of fetish-worship is shown by the people of Akra declaring the monkeys only to be fetish-worshipers.[6]

I cannot vouch for the accuracy of every one of

1 *Baseler Missions-Magazin*, 1856, ii. 131.
2 Waitz, ii. pp. 174, 175.
3 Köler, *Einige Notizen über Bonny*, 1848, p. 61; Waitz, ii. p. 169.
4 Salt, *Voyage to Abyssinia*, 1814, p. 41.
5 Schön and Crowther, *Journal of an Expedition up the Niger, in* 1842, pp. 51, 72. Waitz, ii p. 169.
6 Waitz, ii. pp. 174-178.

these statements for reasons which I have fully explained. I accept them on the authority of a scholar who was accustomed to the collation of various readings in ancient MSS., Professor Waitz. Taken together, they certainly give a very different impression of the negroes from that which is commonly received. They show at all events that, so far from being a uniform fetishism, the religion of the negro is many-sided in the extreme. There is fetish-worship in it, perhaps more than among other nations, but what becomes of the assertion that the religion of the negro consists in fetishism and in fetishism only, and that the negro never advanced beyond this, the lowest stage of religion? We have seen that there are in the religion of the Africans very clear traces of a worship of spirits residing in different parts of nature, and of a feeling after a supreme spirit, hidden and revealed by the sun or the sky. It is generally, if not always, the sun or the sky which forms the bridge from the visible to the invisible, from nature to nature's God. But besides the sun, the moon[1] also was worshiped by the negroes, as the ruler of months and seasons, and the ordainer of time and life. Sacrifices were offered under trees, soon also to trees, particularly to old trees which for generations had witnessed the joys and troubles of a family or a tribe.

ZOOLATRY.

Besides all this which may be comprehended under the general name of physiolatry, there are clear indications also of zoolatry.[2] It is one of the most difficult problems to discover the motive which led the

[1] Waitz, ii. p. 175. [2] Ibid. ii. p. 177.

negro to worship certain animals. The mistake which is made by most writers on early religions is, that they imagine there can be but one motive for each custom that has to be explained. Generally, however, there are many. Sometimes the souls of the departed are believed to dwell in certain animals. In some places animals, particularly wolves, are made to devour the dead bodies, and they may in consequence be considered sacred.[1] Monkeys are looked upon as men, slightly damaged at the creation, sometimes also as men thus punished for their sins. They are in some places believed to be able to speak, but to sham dumbness in order to escape labor. Hence, it may be, a reluctance arose to kill them, like other animals, and from this there would be but a small step to ascribing to them a certain sacro-sanctity. Elephants, we know, inspire similar feelings by the extraordinary development of their understanding. People do not like to kill them, or if they have to do it, they ask pardon from the animal which they have killed. In Dahomey, where the elephant is a natural fetish, many purificatory ceremonies have to be performed when an elephant has been slain.[2]

In some places it is considered lucky to be killed by certain animals, as for instance by leopards in Dahomey.

There are many reasons why snakes might be looked upon with a certain kind of awe, and even kept and worshiped. Poisonous snakes are dreaded, and may therefore be worshiped, particularly after they had been (perhaps secretly) deprived of their

[1] Waitz, ii. p. 177. *Hostmann, Zur Geschichte des Nordischen Systems der drei Culturperioden.* Braunschweig, 1875, p. 13, note.

[2] Waitz, ii. p. 178.

fangs. Other snakes are useful as domestic animals, as weather prophets, and may therefore have been fed, valued, and, after a time, worshiped, taking that word in that low sense which it often has, and must have among uncivilized people. The idea that the ghosts of the departed dwell for a time in certain animals is very widely prevalent; and considering the habits of certain snakes, hiding in deserted and even in inhabited houses, and suddenly appearing, peering at the inhabitants with their wondering eyes, we may well understand the superstitious awe with which they were treated. Again, we know that many tribes assumed in modern and ancient times the name of Snakes (Nâgas), whether in order to assert their autochthonic right to the country in which they lived, or because, as Diodorus supposes, the snake had been used as their banner, their rallying sign, or, as we should say, their totem or crest. As the same Diodorus points out, people may have chosen the snake for their banner, either because it was their deity, or it may have become their deity because it was their banner. At all events, nothing would be more natural than that people who, for some reason or other, called themselves Snakes, should in time adopt a snake for their ancestor, and finally for their god. In India the snakes assume, at an early time, a very prominent part in epic and popular traditions. They soon became what fairies or bogies are in our nursery tales, and they thus appear in company with Gandharvas, Apsaras, Kinnaras, etc., in some of the most ancient architectural ornamentations of India.

Totally different from these Indian snakes is the snake of the Zendavesta, and the snake of Genesis, and the dragons of Greek and Teutonic mythology.

There is, lastly, the snake as a symbol of eternity, either on account of its leaving its skin, or because it rolls itself up into a complete circle. Every one of these creatures of fancy has a biography of his own, and to mix them all up together would be like writing *one* biography of all the people who were called Alexander.

Africa is full of animal fables, in the style of Æsop's fables, though they are not found among all tribes; and it is often related that, in former times, men and animals could converse together. In Bornu it is said that one man betrayed the secret of the language of animals to his wife, and that thenceforth the intercourse ceased.[1] Man alone is never, we are told, worshiped in Africa as a divine being; and if in some places powerful chiefs receive honors that make us shudder, we must not forget that during the most brilliant days of Rome divine honors were paid to Augustus and his successors. Men who are deformed, dwarfs, albinos, and others, are frequently looked upon as something strange and uncanny, rather than what we should call sacred.

PSYCHOLATRY.

Lastly, great reverence is paid to the spirits of the departed.[2] The bones of dead people also are frequently preserved and treated with religious respect. The Ashantis have a word *kla*,[3] which means the life of man. If used as a masculine, it stands for the voice that tempts man to evil. If used in the feminine, it is the voice that persuades us to keep aloof from evil. Lastly, *kla* is the tutelary genius of a

1 Kölle, *African Literature*, 145.

2 Waitz, ii. p. 181.

3 *Baseler Missions-Magazin*, 1856, ii. 134, 139; Waitz, ii. p. 182.

person who can be brought near by witchcraft, and expects sacrifices for the protection which he grants. When a man dies, his *kla* becomes *sisa*, and a *sisa* may be born again.

MANY-SIDEDNESS OF AFRICAN RELIGION.

Now I ask, Is so many-sided a religion to be classed simply as African fetish-worship? Do we not find almost every ingredient of other religions in the little which we know at present of the faith and worship of the negro? Is there the slightest evidence to show that there ever was a time when these negroes were fetish-worshipers only, and nothing else? Does not all our evidence point rather in the opposite direction, viz., that fetishism was a parasitical development, intelligible with certain antecedents, but never as an original impulse of the human heart?

What is, from a psychological point of view, the really difficult problem is, how to reconcile the rational and even exalted religious opinions, traces of which we discovered among many of the negro tribes, with the coarse forms of fetish-worship. We must remember, however, that every religion is a compromise between the wise and the foolish, the old and the young, and that the higher the human mind soars in its search after divine ideals, the more inevitable the symbolical representations, which are required for children and for the majority of people, incapable of realizing sublime and subtle abstractions.

Much, no doubt, may be said in explanation, even in excuse of fetishism, under all its forms and disguises. It often assists our weakness, it often reminds us of our duties, it often may lead our thoughts from material objects to spiritual visions, it often comforts us when nothing else will give us peace. It is often said to be so harmless, that it is difficult to see why it should have been so fiercely reprobated by some of the wisest teachers of mankind. It may have seemed strange to many of us, that among the ten Commandments which were to set forth, in the shortest possible form, the highest, the most essential duties of man, the second place should be assigned to a prohibition of any kind of images. "Thou shalt not make to thyself any graven image, nor the likeness of anything that is in heaven above, or in the earth beneath, or in the waters under the earth: thou shalt not bow down to them, nor worship them."

Let those who wish to understand the hidden wisdom of these words study the history of ancient religions. Let them read the descriptions of religious festivals in Africa, in America, and Australia; let them witness, also, the pomp and display in some of our own Christian churches and cathedrals. No arguments can prove that there is anything very wrong in all these outward signs and symbols. To many people, we know, they are even a help and comfort. But history is sometimes a stronger and sterner teacher than argument, and one of the lessons which the history of religions certainly teaches is this, that the curse pronounced against those who would change the invisible into the visible, the spiritual into the material, the divine into the human, the infinite into the finite, has come true in every nation on earth. We may consider ourselves safe against the fetish-worship of the poor negro; but there are few of us, if any, who have not their own fetishes, or their own idols, whether in their churches, or in their hearts.

The results at which we have arrived, after examining the numerous works on fetishism from the days of De Brosses to our own time, may be summed up under four heads: —

1. The meaning of the word fetish (*feitiço*) has remained undefined from its first introduction, and has by most writers been so much extended that it may include almost every symbolical or imitative representation of religious objects.

2. Among people who have a history, we find that everything which falls under the category of fetish points to historical and psychological antecedents. We are, therefore, not justified in supposing that it has been otherwise among people whose religious development happens to be unknown and inaccessible to us.

3. There is no religion which has kept itself entirely free from fetishism.

4. There is no religion which consists entirely of fetishism.

SUPPOSED PSYCHOLOGICAL NECESSITY OF FETISHISM.

Thus I thought I had sufficiently determined the position which I hold with regard to the theory of a universal primeval fetishism, or, at all events, to have made it clear that the facts of fetish-worship, as hitherto known to us, can in no wise solve the question of the natural origin of religion.

The objection has, however, been raised by those who cling to fetishism, or at least to the Comtian theory of fetishism, that these are after all facts only, and that a complete and far more formidable theory has to be encountered before it could be admitted that the first impulse to religion proceeded from an incipient perception of the infinite pressing upon us through the great phenomena of nature, and not from sentiments of surprise or fear called forth by such finite things as shells, stones, or bones, — that is to say, by fetishes.

We are told that whatever the *facts* may be which, after all, by mere accident, are still within our reach, as bearing witness to the earliest phases of religious thought, there *must* have been a time, whether in historic or prehistoric periods, whether during the formation of quaternary or tertiary strata, when man worshiped stocks and stones, and nothing else.

I am far from saying that under certain circumstances mere argumentative reasoning may not be as powerful as historical evidence; still I thought I had done enough by showing how the very tribes who were represented to us as living instances of fetish-worship possessed religious ideas of a simplicity and, sometimes, of a sublimity such as we look for in vain even in Homer and Hesiod. Facts had been collected to support a theory, nay had confessedly given the first impulse to a theory, and that theory is to remain, although the facts have vanished, or have at all events assumed a very different aspect. However, as it is dangerous to leave any fortress in our rear, it may be expedient to reply to this view of fetishism also, though in as few words as possible.

It may be taken for granted that those who hold the theory that religion must everywhere have taken its origin from fetishism, take fetish in the sense of casual objects which, for some reason or other, or it may be for no reason at all, were considered as endowed with exceptional powers, and gradually raised to the dignity of spirits or gods. They could not hold the other view, that a fetish was, from the beginning, an emblem or symbol only, an outward sign or token of some power previously known, which power, originally distinct from the fetish, was afterwards believed to reside in it, and in course of time came to be identified with it. For in that case the real problem for those who study the growth of the human mind would be the origin and growth of that power, previously known, and afterwards supposed to reside in a fetish. The real beginning of religious life would be there; the fetish would represent a secondary stage only. Nor is it enough to say (with Professor Zeller[1]) that "fancy or imagination personifies things without life and without reason as gods." The real question is, Whence that imagination? and whence, before all things, that unprovoked and unjustifiable predicate of God?

The theory, therefore, of fetishism with which alone we have still to deal is this, that a worship of casual objects is and must be the first inevitable step in the development of religious ideas. Religion not only does begin, but must begin, we are told, with a contemplation of stones, shells, bones, and such like things, and from that stage only can it rise to the conception of something else — of powers, spirits, gods, or whatever else we like to call it.

WHENCE THE SUPERNATURAL PREDICATE OF A FETISH?

Let us look this theory in the face. When travelers, ethnologists, and philosophers tell us that savage tribes look upon stones and bones and trees as their

[1] *Vorträge und Abhandlungen*, Zweite Sammlung, 1877, p. 32.

gods, what is it that startles us? Not surely the stones, bones, or trees; not the subjects, but that which is predicated of these subjects, viz., God. Stones, bones, and trees are ready at hand everywhere; but what the student of the growth of the human mind wishes to know is, Whence their higher predicates; or, let us say at once, whence their predicate God? Here lies the whole problem. If a little child were to bring us his cat and say it was a vertebrate animal, the first thing that would strike us would surely be, How did the child ever hear of such a name as a vertebrate animal? If the fetish-worshiper brings us a stone and says it is a god, our question is the same. Where did you ever hear of God, and what do you mean by such a name? It is curious to observe how little that difficulty seems to have been felt by writers on ancient religion.

Let us apply this to the ordinary theory of fetishism, and we shall see that the problem is really this: Can spirits or gods spring from stones? Or, to put it more clearly, Can we understand how there should be a transition from the percept of a stone to the concept of a spirit or a god?

ACCIDENTAL ORIGIN OF FETISHISM.

We are told that nothing is easier than this transition. But how? We are asked[1] to imagine a state of mind when man, as yet without any ideas beyond those supplied to him by his five senses, suddenly sees a glittering stone or a bright shell, picks it up as strange, keeps it as dear to himself, and then persuades himself that this stone is not a stone like other stones, that this shell is not a shell like other shells,

[1] Waitz, ii. p. 187.

but that it is endowed with extraordinary powers, which no other stone or shell ever possessed before. We are asked to suppose that possibly the stone was picked up in the morning, that the man who picked it up was engaged in a serious fight during the day, that he came out of it victorious, and that he very naturally ascribed to the stone the secret of his success. He would afterwards, so we are told, have kept that stone for luck; it might very likely have proved lucky more than once; in fact, those stones only which proved lucky more than once would have had a chance of surviving as fetishes. It would then have been believed to possess some supernatural power, to be not a mere stone but something else, a powerful spirit, entitled to every honor and worship which the lucky possessor could bestow on it or on him.

This whole process, we are assured, is perfectly rational in its very irrationality. Nor do I deny it; I only doubt whether it exhibits the irrationality of an uncultured mind. Is not the whole process of reasoning, as here described, far more in accordance with modern than with ancient and primitive thoughts? Nay, I ask, can we conceive it as possible except when men were already far advanced in their search after the infinite, and in full possession of those very concepts, the origin of which we want to have explained to us?

ARE SAVAGES LIKE CHILDREN?

It was formerly supposed that the psychological problem involved in fetishism could be explained by a mere reference to children playing with their dolls, or hitting the chair against which they had hit themselves. This explanation, however, has long been surrendered, for, even supposing that fetishism consisted only in ascribing to material objects life, activity, or personality, call it figurism, animism, personification, anthropomorphism or anthropopathism, the mere fact that children do the same as grown-up savages cannot possibly help us to solve the psychological problem. The fact, suppose it is a fact, would be as mysterious with children as with savages. Besides, though there is some truth in calling savages children, or children savages, we must here, too, learn to distinguish. Savages are children in some respects, but not in all. There is no savage who, on growing up, does not learn to distinguish between animate and inanimate objects, between a rope, for instance, and a serpent. To say that they remain childish on such a point is only to cheat ourselves with our own metaphors. On the other side, children, such as they now are, can help us but rarely to gain an idea of what primitive savages may have been. Our children, from the first awakening of their mental life, are surrounded by an atmosphere saturated with the thoughts of an advanced civilization. A child, not taken in by a well-dressed doll, or so perfectly able to control himself as not to kick against a chair against which he had hit his head, would be a little philosopher rather than a savage not yet emerging from fetishism. The circumstances or the surroundings are so totally different in the case of the savage and the child, that comparisons between the two must be carried out with the greatest care before they can claim any real scientific value.

I agree so far with the believers in primitive fetishism that if we are to explain religion as a universal property of mankind, we must explain it out of conditions which are universally present. Nor do I blame them if they decline to discuss the problem of the origin of religion with those who assume a primitive revelation, or a religious faculty which distinguishes man from the animal. Let us start, by all means, from common ground and from safe ground. Let us take man such as he is, possessing his five senses, and as yet without any knowledge except what is supplied to him by his five senses. No doubt that man can pick up a stone, or a bone, or a shell. But then we must ask the upholders of the primitive fetish theory, How do these people, when they have picked up their stone or their shell, pick up at the same time the concepts of a supernatural power, of spirit, of god, and of worship paid to some unseen being?

THE FOUR STEPS.

We are told that there are four steps — the famous four steps — by which all this is achieved, and the origin of fetishism rendered perfectly intelligible. First, there is a sense of surprise; secondly, an anthropopathic conception of the object which causes surprise; thirdly, the admission of a causal connection between that object and certain effects, such as victory, rain, health; fourthly, a recognition of the object as a power deserving of respect and worship. But is not this rather to hide the difficulties beneath a golden shower of words than to explain them?

Granted that a man may be surprised at a stone or a shell, though they would seem to be the very last things to be surprised at; but what is the meaning of taking an anthropopathic view of a stone or a shell? If we translate it into plain English it means neither more nor less than that, instead of taking a stone to be a stone like all other stones, we suppose that a particular stone is not an ordinary stone, but endowed with the feelings of a man. Natural as this may sound, when clothed in technical language, when we use long names, such as anthropopathism, anthropomorphism, personification, figurism, nothing would really seem to do greater violence to common sense, or to our five senses, than to say that a stone is a stone, yet not quite a stone; and again, that the stone is a man, yet not quite a man. I am fully aware that, after a long series of intermediate steps, such contradictions arise in the human mind, but they cannot spring up suddenly; they are not there from the beginning, unless we admit disturbing influences much more extraordinary than a primeval revelation. It is the object of the science of religion to find out by what small and timid steps the human mind advanced from what is intelligible to what at first sight is almost beyond our comprehension. If we take for granted the very thing that has to be explained; if we once admit that it was perfectly natural for the primitive savage to look upon a stone as something human; if we are satisfied with such words as anthropopathism, or animism, or figurism, — then all the rest no doubt is easy enough. The human stone has every right to be called superhuman, and that is not very far from divine; nor need we wonder that the worship paid to such an object should be more than what is paid to either a stone or to a man — that it too should be superhuman, which is not very far from divine.

FETISHISM NOT A PRIMARY FORM OF RELIGION.

My position then is simply this: It seems to me that those who believe in a primordial fetishism have taken that for granted which has to be proved. They have taken for granted that every human being was miraculously endowed with the concept of what forms the predicate of every fetish, call it power, spirit, or god. They have taken for granted that casual objects, such as stones, shells, the tail of a lion, a tangle of hair, or any such rubbish, possess in themselves a theogonic or god-producing character, while the fact that all people, when they have once risen to the suspicion of something supersensuous, infinite, or divine, have perceived its presence afterwards in merely casual and insignificant objects, has been entirely overlooked. They have taken for granted that there exists at present, or that there existed at any time, a religion entirely made up of fetishism; or that, on the other hand, there is any religion which has kept itself entirely free from fetishism. My last and most serious objection, however, is that those who believe in fetishism as a primitive and universal form of religion, have often depended on evidence which no scholar, no historian, would feel justified to accept. We are justified, therefore, I think, in surrendering the theory[1] that fetishism either has or must have been the beginning of all religion, and we are bound to look elsewhere, if we wish to discover what were the sensuous impressions that first filled the human mind with a suspicion of the supersensuous, the infinite, and the divine.

[1] I am glad to find that both Dr. Happel, in his work *Die Anlage des Menschen zur Religion*, 1878, and Professor Pfleiderer in his *Religionsphilosophie*, just published, take nearly the same view of the Fetish-theory.

III.

THE ANCIENT LITERATURE OF INDIA SO FAR AS IT SUPPLIES MATERIALS FOR THE STUDY OF THE ORIGIN OF RELIGION.

USEFULNESS OF THE STUDY OF LITERARY RELIGIONS.

INSTEAD of trying to study the origin of religion in the tertiary or quarternary strata of Africa, America, and Australia, it seems far wiser to look first to countries where we find, not only the latest formations, the mere surface and detritus of religious growth, but where we can see and study some at least of the lower strata on which the superficial soil of religion reposes.

I know very well that this study also has its difficulties, quite as much as the study of the religion of savage races, but the soil on which we have here to labor is deeper, and promises a richer harvest.

It is quite true that the historical documents of a religion never carry us very far. They fail us often just where they would be most instructive, near the first springs of the old stream. This is inevitable. No religion is of importance to the surrounding world in its first beginnings. It is hardly noticed, so long as it is confined to the heart of one man and his twelve disciples. This applies to national religions still more than to what I call personal religions, the latter founded by known individuals, the former elaborated by the united efforts of a whole people. For many generations a national religion has no tangible form as a body of doctrine or ceremonies: it has hardly a name. We only know a religion, after it has assumed consistency and importance, and when it has become the interest of certain individuals or of a whole class, to collect and to preserve for posterity whatever is known of its origin and first spreading. It is not by accident, therefore, but by a law of human nature, that the accounts which we possess of the origin of religions, are almost always fabulous, never historical in the strict sense of the word.

GROWTH OF RELIGIOUS IDEAS IN JUDAISM, ZOROASTRIANISM, ETC.

But though we can nowhere watch the first vital movements of a nascent religion, we can in some countries observe the successive growth of religious ideas. Among the savages of Africa, America, and Australia this is impossible. It is difficult enough to know what their religion is at present; what it was in its origin, what it was even a thousand years ago, is entirely beyond our reach.

Many of the so-called book-religions also offer the same, or at least similar, difficulties. There are traces of growth and decay in the religion of the Jews, but they have to be discovered by patient study. The object, however, of most of the writers on the O. T. seems to be to hide these traces rather than to display them. They wish to place the religion of the Jews before us as ready-made from the beginning, as perfect in all its parts, because revealed by God, and, if liable to corruption, at all events incapable of improvement. But that the Jewish monotheism was preceded by a polytheism "on the other side of the flood and in Egypt," is now admitted by most scholars, nor would it be easy to find in the same sacred code two more opposite sentiments than the rules and regulations for burnt-offerings in Leviticus, and the words of the Psalmist (li. 16): "For thou delightest not in sacrifice, else would I give it thee: thou delightest not in burnt-offerings. The sacrifices of God are a broken spirit: a broken and a contrite heart, O God, thou wilt not despise."

There is growth here, as evident as can be, however difficult it may seem to some students of religion to reconcile the idea of growth with the character of a revealed religion.

What applies to the religion of Moses, applies to that of Zoroaster. It is placed before us as a complete system from the first, revealed by Ahuramazda, proclaimed by Zarathustra. Minute scholarship only has been able to discover some older elements in the Gâthâs, but, with that exception, we find in the Avesta, too, but few acknowledged traces of real growth.

With regard, again, to the religion and mythology of Greece and Italy, it would be extremely difficult to distinguish their infancy, their youth, and their manhood. We know that certain ideas, which we find in later writers, do not occur in Homer; but it does not follow at all that therefore such ideas are all of later growth, or possess a secondary character. One myth may have belonged to one tribe, one god may have had his chief worship in one locality, and our becoming acquainted with these through a later poet does not in the least prove their later origin. Besides, there is this great disadvantage in the study of the religion of the Greeks and Romans, that we do not possess anything really deserving the name of a sacred book.

GROWTH OF RELIGION IN INDIA.

No country can be compared to India as offering opportunities for a real study of the genesis and growth of religion. I say intentionally for the growth, not for the history of religion : for history, in the ordinary sense of the word, is almost unknown in Indian literature. But what we can watch and study in India better than anywhere else is, how religious thoughts and religious language arise, how they gain force, how they spread, changing their forms as they pass from mouth to mouth, from mind to mind, yet always retaining some faint contiguity with the spring from which they rose at first.

I do not think, therefore, that I am exaggerating when I say that the sacred books of India offer for a study of religion in general, and particularly for the study of the origin and growth of religion, the same peculiar and unexpected advantages which the language of India, Sanskrit, has offered for the study of the origin and growth of human speech. It is for that reason that I have selected the ancient religion of India to supply the historical illustrations of my own theory of the origin and growth of religion. That theory was suggested to me during a life-long study of the sacred books of India ; it rests, therefore, on facts, though I am responsible for their interpretation.

THE RIGHT POSITION OF THE VEDA IN THE SCIENCE OF RELIGION.

Far be it from me to say that the origin and growth of religion must everywhere have been exactly the same as in India. Let us here, too, take a warning from the science of language. It is no longer denied that for throwing light on some of the darkest problems that have to be solved by the student of language, nothing is so useful as a critical study of Sanskrit. I go farther, even, and maintain that, in order to comprehend fully the ways and means adopted by other languages, nothing is more advantageous than to be able to contrast them with the proceedings of Sanskrit. But to look for Sanskrit, as Bopp has done, in Malay, Polynesian, and Caucasian dialects, or to imagine that the grammatical expedients adopted by the Aryan languages are the only possible expedients for realizing the objects of human speech, would be a fatal mistake; and we must guard, from the very first, against a similar danger in a scientific study of the religions of mankind. When we have learnt how the ancient inhabitants of India gained their religious ideas, how they elaborated them, changed them, corrupted them, we may be allowed to say that possibly other people also may have started from the same beginnings, and may have passed through the same vicissitudes. But we shall never go beyond, or repeat the mistake of those who, because they found, or imagined they found fetish-worship among the least cultivated races of Africa, America, and Australia, concluded that every uncultivated race must have started from fetishism in its religious career.

What, then, are the documents in which we can

study the origin and growth of religion among the early Aryan settlers of India?

DISCOVERY OF SANSKRIT LITERATURE.

The discovery of the ancient literature of India must sound to most people like a fairy-tale rather than like a chapter of history, nor do I wonder that there is, or that there has been at least for a long time, a certain incredulity, with regard to the genuineness of that literature. The number of separate works in Sanskrit, of which manuscripts are still in existence, is now estimated to amount to about 10,000.[1] What would Plato and Aristotle have said, if they had been told that at their time there existed in India, in that India which Alexander had just discovered, if not conquered, an ancient literature far richer than anything they possessed at that time in Greece?

BUDDHISM THE FRONTIER BETWEEN ANCIENT AND MODERN LITERATURE IN INDIA.

At that time the whole drama of the really ancient literature of the Brahmans had been acted. The old language had changed, the old religion, after passing through many phases, had been superseded by a new faith: for however skeptical or conscientious we may be before admitting or rejecting the claims of the Brahmans in favor of an enormous antiquity of their

[1] Rajendralal Mitra, *Catalogue of Sanskrit MSS. in the Library of the Asiatic Library of Bengal*, 1877, Preface, p. 1. The India Office Library is said to contain 4,093 separate codices; the Bodleian 854; the Berlin library about the same number. The library of the Mahárája of Tanjore is estimated at upwards of 18,000, in eleven distinct alphabets; the library of the Sanskrit College at Benares, at 2,000; the library of the Asiatic Society of Bengal at Calcutta at 3,700; that of the Sanskrit College at Calcutta at 2,000.

9

sacred literature, so much is certain and beyond the reach of reasonable doubt,[1] that *Sandrocottus*, who

[1] In my *History of Ancient Sanskrit Literature*, published in 1859 (p. 274), I had tried to lay down some general principles on which I thought the dates of Greek history might to a certain extent be reconciled with some of the traditional dates of the Northern and Southern Buddhists. The conclusions at which I then arrived were that Sandrocottus or *K*andragupta became king in 315 B. C., that he reigned 24 years, and was succeeded by Bindusâra in 291 B. C.; that Bindusâra reigned (25 or) 28 years, and was succeeded by Asoka in (266 or) 263 B. C.; and that Asoka was formally inaugurated in (262 or) 259 B. C., reigned 37 years, and died in (215 or) 212 B. C. The great Council took place in the 17th year of his reign, therefore either (245 or) 242 B. C.

In my attempt at arriving at some kind of rough chronology for the Buddhistic age, I was chiefly guided by a number of native traditions bearing on the distance between certain events and Buddha's death. Thus we find: (1.) That 162 years were supposed to have passed between Buddha's death and *K*andragupta's accession, 315 + 162 = 477, this giving us 477 B. C. as the probable date of that event. (2.) We found that 218 years were supposed to have passed between Buddha's death and Asoka's inauguration, 259 + 218 = 477, this giving us 477 B. C. as the probable date of that event.

I therefore proposed that 477 B. C. should provisionally be accepted as the probable date of Buddha's death, instead of 543 B. C., and I tried to strengthen that position by some other evidence available at the time.

An important confirmation of that hypothesis has lately been added by two inscriptions discovered by General Cunningham, and published by Dr. Bühler in the *Indian Antiquary*. Dr. Bühler seems to me to have shown conclusively in his two articles that the writer of these inscriptions could have been no other but Asoka. Asoka in these two edicts states that he has been for a long time, or for more than 33½ years, an *upâsaka* or worshiper of Buddha, and that during one year or more he has been a member of the Sa*m*gha. Now if Asoka was consecrated in 259, and became an *upâsaka* three or four years later, 255 B. C., these inscriptions would have been put up in 255 — 33½ = 221 B. C. According to the same inscriptions, 256 years had passed since the departure of Buddha (here, too, I accept Dr. Bühler's interpretation, not because all its difficulties are removed, but because, in spite of all difficulties, the inscription cannot well be interpreted differently) 221 + 256 = 477, this giving us 477 B. C. as the probable date of Buddha's death.

This confirmation was entirely unexpected, and becomes therefore all the more important.

I may add one other confirmation. Mahinda, the son of Asoka, became an ascetic in the sixth year of his father's reign, *i. e.*, in 253 B. C. At that time he was 20 years of age, and must therefore have been born in 273 B. C. Between his birth and Buddha's death 204 years are supposed to by Greek writers is mentioned as a child when Alexander invaded India, who after Alexander's retreat was king at Palibothra, who was the contemporary of Seleucus Nicator, and several times visited by Megasthenes, was the same as the *K*andragupta of Indian literature, who reigned at Pa*t*aliputra, the founder of a new dynasty, and the grandfather of Asoka. This Asoka was the famous king who made himself the patron of Buddhism, under whom the great Buddhist Council was held in 245 or 242 B. C., and of whose time we have the first inscriptions, still extant on rocks in different parts of India. These inscriptions are not in Sanskrit, but in a language which stands to Sanskrit in the same relation as Italian to Latin. The days, therefore, when Sanskrit was the spoken language of the people, were over in the third century B. C.

Buddhism, again, the religion of Asoka, stands in the same relation to the ancient Brahmanism of the Veda as Italian to Latin, or as Protestantism to Roman Catholicism. Buddhism, in fact, is only intelligible as a development of, and a reaction against, Brahmanism. As against those, therefore, who consider the whole of Indian literature a modern forgery, or against ourselves, when unwilling to trust our own eyes, we have at least these two facts, on which we can rely: that, in the third century B. C., the ancient Sanskrit language had dwindled down to a mere *volgare* or Prakrit, and that the ancient religion of the

have passed, 273 + 204 = 477, this giving us once more 477 B. C. as the probable date of Buddha's death.

I learn that so high an authority as General Cunningham has arrived at the same conclusion with regard to the date of Buddha's death, and had published it before the appearance of my *History of Sanskrit Literature*, in 1859; but I do not know whether his arguments were the same as those on which I chiefly relied.

Veda had developed into Buddhism, and had been superseded by its own offspring, the state religion in the kingdom of Asoka, the grandson of *K*andragupta.

THE VEDA PROCLAIMED AS REVEALED.

One of the principal points on which Buddhism differed from Brahmanism was the sacred and revealed character ascribed to the Veda. This is a point of so much historical importance in the growth of the early theology of India that we must examine it more carefully. The Buddhists, though on many points merely Brahmanists in disguise, denied the authority of the Veda as a divine revelation; this being so, we may advance another step, and ascribe to the theory of a divine inspiration of the Veda a pre-Buddhistic origin and prevalence.

At what time the claim of being divinely revealed, and therefore infallible, was first set up by the Brahmans in favor of the Veda, is difficult to determine. This claim, like other claims of the same kind, seems to have grown up gradually, till at last it was formulated into a theory of inspirations as artificial as any known to us from other religions.

The poets of the Veda speak in very different ways of their compositions. Sometimes they declare that they have made the hymns, and they compare their work as poets with that of the carpenter, the weaver, the maker of butter (gh*ri*ta), the rower of a ship (X. 116, 9).[1]

In other places, however, more exalted sentiments appear. The hymns are spoken of as shaped by the heart (I. 171, 2; II. 35, 2), and uttered by the

[1] A most useful collection of passages bearing on this point may be found in Dr. J. Muir's *Sanskrit Texts*, vol. iii.

mouth (VI. 32, 1). The poet says that he found the hymn (X. 67, 1); he declares himself powerfully inspired after having drunk the Soma juice (VI. 47, 3), and he compares his poem to a shower of rain bursting from a cloud (VII. 94, 1), or to a cloud impelled by the wind (I. 116, 1).

After a time the thoughts that rose in the heart and were uttered in hymns, were called God-given (I. 37, 4), or divine (III. 18, 3). The gods were supposed to have roused and sharpened the mind of the poets (VI. 47, 10); they were called the friends and helpers of the poets (VII. 88, 4; VIII. 52, 4), and at last the gods themselves were called seers or poets (I. 31, 1). If the petitions addressed to the gods in the hymns of the poets were fulfilled, these hymns were naturally believed to be endowed with miraculous powers, the thought arose of a real intercourse between gods and men (I. 179, 2; VII. 76, 4), and the ideas of inspiration and revelation thus grew up naturally, nay inevitably, in the minds of the ancient Brahmans.

By the side of it, however, there also grew up, from the very first, the idea of doubt. If the prayers were not heard, if, as in the contest between Vasish*th*a and Visvâmitra, the enemy who had called on other gods, prevailed, then a feeling of uncertainty arose which, in some passages of the hymns, goes so far as to amount to a denial of the most popular of all gods, Indra.[1]

If, however, the claims to a divine origin of the Veda had amounted to no more than these poetic thoughts, they would hardly have roused any violent opposition. It is only when the divine and infallible

[1] See this subject treated in Lecture VI.

character of the whole Veda had been asserted by the Brahmans, and when the Brâhma*n*as also, in which these claims were formulated, had been represented as divinely inspired and infallible, that a protest, like that of the Buddhists, becomes historically intelligible. This step was taken chiefly during the Sûtra period. Although in the Brâhma*n*as the divine authority of the Vedas is asserted as a fact, it is not yet, so far as I know, used as an instrument to silence all opposition; and between these two positions the difference is very great. Though *s*ruti, the later technical name for revelation, as opposed to sm*r*iti, tradition, occurs in the Brâhma*n*as (Ait. Br. VII. 9), it is not yet employed there to crush all doubt or opposition. In the old Upanishads in which the hymns and sacrifices of the Veda are looked upon as useless, and as superseded by the higher knowledge taught by the forest-sages, they are not yet attacked as mere impositions.

That opposition, however, sets in very decidedly in the Sûtra period. In the Nirukta (I. 15) Yâska quotes the opinions of Kautsa, that the hymns of the Veda have no meaning at all. Even if Kautsa be not the name of a real person, but a nickname only, the unquestioning reverence for the Veda must have been on the wane before the days of Yâska and Pâ*n*ini.[1] Nor is it at all likely that Buddha was the first and only denier of the sacred authority of the Veda, and of all the claims which the Brahmans had founded on that authority. The history of heresy is difficult to trace in India, as elsewhere. The writings of

[1] Pâ*n*ini was acquainted with infidels and nihilists, as may be seen from IV. 4, 60. Lokâyata, another name applied to unbelievers, from which Laukâyatika, is found in the Ga*n*a ukthâdi, and IV. 2, 60. Bârhaspatya occurs in the commentary only, V. 1, 121.

B*ri*haspati, one of the oldest heretics, constantly quoted in later controversial treatises, have not yet been recovered in India. Without committing myself to any opinion as to his age, I shall state here some of the opinions ascribed to B*ri*haspati, to show that even the mild Hindu can hit hard blows, and still more in order to make it clear that the stronghold of Brahmanism, namely, the revealed character of the Vedas, was not a mere theory, but a very important historical reality.

In the "Sarva-darsana-sa*m*graha" (translated by Professor Cowell, Pandit, 1874, p. 162), the first philosophical system of which an account is given is that of the *K*ârvâka, who follows the tenets of B*ri*haspati. The school to which they belonged is called the Lokâyata, *i. e.*, prevalent in the world. They hold that nothing exists but the four elements, a kind of protoplasm, from which, when changed by evolution into organic body, intelligence is produced, just as the inebriating power is developed from the mixing of certain ingredients. The self is only the body qualified by intelligence, there being no evidence for a self without a body. The only means of knowledge is perception, the only object of man, enjoyment.

But if that were so, it is objected, why should men of proved wisdom offer the Agnihotra and other Vedic sacrifices? To this the following answer is returned: —

"Your objection cannot be accepted as any proof to the contrary, since the Agnihotra, etc., are only useful as means of livelihood, for the Veda is tainted by the three faults of untruth, self-contradiction, and tautology. Then again the impostors, who call themselves Vedic pandits, are mutually destructive, as the authority of the *G*nânakâ*n*da (Upanishads) is overthrown by those who maintain that of the Karmakâ*n*da (Hymns and Brâhma*n*as), while those who maintain the authority of the *G*nânakâ*n*da reject that of the Karmakâ*n*da. Lastly, the three Vedas themselves are only the incoherent rhapsodies of knaves, and to this effect runs the popular saying : —

"The Agnihotra, the three Vedas, the ascetic's three staves, and smearing one's self with ashes,

"B*ri*haspati says, these are but means of livelihood for those who have no manliness or sense."

And again it has been said by B*ri*haspati : —

"If a beast slain in the *G*yotish*t*oma rite will itself go to heaven,

"Why then does not the sacrificer forthwith offer his own father?

"If the *S*râddha produces gratification to beings who are dead,

"Then there too, in the case of travelers when they start, it is needless to give provisions for the journey.

"If beings in heaven are gratified by our offering the *S*râddha here,

"Then why not give the food down below to those who are standing on the house-top?

"While life remains, let a man live happily, let him feed on ghee, even though he runs into debt,

"When once the body becomes ashes, how can it ever return again ?

"He who departs from the body goes to another world,

"How is it that he comes not back again, restless for love of his kindred?

"Hence it is only as a means of livelihood that Brahmans have established here

"All these ceremonies for the dead, — there is no other fruit anywhere.

"The three authors of the Vedas were buffoons, knaves, and demons,

"All the well-known formulas of the pandits, *g*arpharî turpharî, etc.

"And all the horrid rites for the queen commanded in the A*s*vamedha,

"These were invented by buffoons, and so all the various kinds of presents to the priests,

"While the eating of flesh was similarly commanded by night-prowling demons."

Some of these objections may be of later date, but most of them are clearly Buddhistic. The retort, Why if a victim slain at a sacrifice goes to heaven, does not a man sacrifice his own father, is, as Professor Burnouf has shown, the very argument used by Buddhist controversialists.[1] Though Buddhism became recognized as a state religion through Asoka in the third century only, there can be little doubt that it had been growing in the minds of the people for several generations, and though there is some doubt as to the exact date of Buddha's death, his traditional era begins 543 B. C., and we may safely assign the origin of Buddhism to about 500 B. C.

It is the Sanskrit literature before that date which is the really important, I mean historically important literature of India. Far be it from me to deny the charms of Kalidâsa's play, "*S*akuntala," which are very real, in spite of the exaggerated praises bestowed upon it. The same poet's "Meghadûta" or Cloud-Messenger, is an elegy which deserves even higher praise, as a purer and more perfect work of art. "Nala," if we could only remove some portions, would be a most charming idyll; and some of the fables of the "Pa*nk*atantra" or "Hitopade*s*a," are excellent specimens of what story-telling ought to be. But all this literature is modern, secondary, — as it were, Alexandrian.

[1] Burnouf, *Introduction à l'Histoire de Buddhisme*, p. 209.

These works are literary curiosities, but no more; and though we may well understand that they formed a pleasant occupation for such men as Sir W. Jones and Colebrooke, during their leisure hours, they could never become the object of a life-study.

HISTORICAL CHARACTER OF THE VEDIC LANGUAGE.

It is very different with the literature of the Veda. First of all, we feel in it on historical ground. The language of Vedic literature differs from the ordinary Sanskrit. It contains many forms which afterwards have become extinct, and those the very forms which exist in Greek or other Aryan dialects. Ordinary Sanskrit, for instance, has no subjunctive mood. Comparative Philology expected, nay postulated, such a mood in Sanskrit, and the Veda, when once discovered and deciphered, supplied it in abundance.

Ordinary Sanskrit does not mark its accents. The Vedic literature is accentuated, and its system of accentuation displays the same fundamental principles as the Greek system.

I like to quote one instance, to show the intimate relationship between Vedic Sanskrit and Greek. We know that the Greek Ζεύς is the same word as the Sanskrit Dyaus, the sky. Dyaus, however, occurs in the later Sanskrit as a feminine only. It is in the Veda that it was discovered, not only as a masculine, but in that very combination in which it became the name of the supreme deity in Greek and Latin. Corresponding to Jupiter, and Ζεὺς πατήρ, we find in the Veda Dyaush pitar. But more than that, Ζεύς in Greek has in the nominative the acute, in the vocative the circumflex. Dyaus in the Veda has in the nominative the acute, in the vocative the circumflex. And while Greek grammarians can give us no explanation of that change, it is a change which in Sanskrit has been shown to rest on the general principles of accentuation.[1]

Now I confess that such a vocative as Dyaus, having the circumflex instead of the acute, is to my mind a perfect gem, of the most precious material and the most exquisite workmanship. Who has not wondered lately at those curious relics of pre-Hellenic art, brought to light at Hissarlik and Mykenae by the indefatigable labors of Dr. Schliemann? I am the last man to depreciate their real value, as opening to us a new world on the classical soil of Greece. But what is a polished or perforated stone, what is a drinking-vessel, or a shield, or a helmet, or even a gold diadem, compared with this vocative of Dyaus. In the one case we have mute metal, rude art, and little thought: in the other, a work of art of the most perfect finish and harmony, and wrought of a material more precious than gold, —human thought. If it took thousands, or hundreds of thousands of men to build a pyramid, or to carve an obelisk, it took millions of men to finish that single word *Dyaus*, or Ζεύς, or *Jupiter*, originally meaning the illuminator, but gradually elaborated into a name of God! And remember, the Veda is full of such pyramids, the ground is strewn with such gems. All we want is laborers to dig, to collect, to classify, and to decipher

[1] The general rule is that in the vocative the high accent is on the first syllable of the word. Remnants only of this rule exist in Greek and Latin, while in Sanskrit it admits of no exception. Dyaus having the svarita or the combined accent in the vocative is only an apparent exception. The word was treated as dissyllabic, *di* had the high, *aus* the low accent, and the high and low accents together gave the svarita or combined accent, commonly called circumflex.

them, in order to lay free once more the lowest chambers of that most ancient of all labyrinths, the human mind.

These are not isolated facts or mere curiosities, that can be disposed of with a patronizing Indeed! That accent in the vocative of Dyaus and Ζεύς is like the nerve of a living organism, still trembling and beating, and manifesting its vitality under the microscope of the comparative philologist. There is life in it — truly historic life. As modern history would be incomplete without mediæval history, or mediæval history without Roman history, or Roman history without Greek history, so we learn that the whole history of the world would henceforth be incomplete without that first chapter in the life of Aryan humanity which has been preserved to us in Vedic literature.

It was a real misfortune to Sanskrit scholarship that our first acquaintance with Indian literature should have begun with the prettinesses of Kalidâsa and Bhavabhûti, and the hideousnesses of the religion of *S*iva and Vish*n*u. The only original, the only important period of Sanskrit literature, which deserves to become the subject of earnest study, far more than it is at present, is that period which preceded the rise of Buddhism, when Sanskrit was still the spoken language of India, and the worship of *S*iva was still unknown.

THE FOUR STRATA OF VEDIC LITERATURE.

I. Sûtra Period, 500 B. C.

We can distinguish three or four successive strata of literature in that pre-Buddhistic period. First comes the *Sûtra period*, which extends far into Buddhistic times, and is clearly marked by its own peculiar style. It is composed in the most concise and enigmatical form, unintelligible almost without a commentary. I cannot describe it to you, for there is nothing like it in any other literature that I am acquainted with. But I may quote a well-known saying of the Brahmans themselves, that the author of a Sûtra rejoices more in having saved one single letter than in the birth of a son: and remember that without a son to perform the funeral rites, a Brahman believed that he could not enter into heaven. The object of these Sûtras was to gather up the knowledge, then floating about in the old Brahmanic settlements or Parishads. They contain the rules of sacrifices, treatises on phonetics, etymology, exegesis, grammar, metre, customs and laws, geometry, astronomy, and philosophy. In every one of these subjects they contain original observations, and original thought, such as can no longer be ignored by any students of these subjects.

Ritual is not a subject that seems to possess any scientific interest at present, still the origin and growth of sacrifice is an important page in the history of the human mind, and nowhere can it be studied to greater advantage than in India.

The science of phonetics arose in India at a time when writing was unknown, and when it was of the highest importance to the Brahmans to preserve the accurate pronunciation of their favorite hymns. I believe I shall not be contradicted by Helmholtz, or Ellis, or other representatives of phonetic science, if I say that, to the present day, the phoneticians of India of the 5th century B. C. are unsurpassed in their analysis of the elements of language.

In grammar, I challenge any scholar to produce

from any language a more comprehensive collection and classification of all the facts of a language than what we find in Pâ*n*ini's Sûtras.

With regard to metre, we possess in the observations and the technical terms of the ancient Indian authors a clear confirmation of the latest theories of modern metricians, viz., that metres were originally connected with dancing and music. The very names for metre in general confirm this. *Kh*andas, metre, is connected with *scandere*, in the sense of stepping; v*r*itta, metre, from v*r*it, *verto*, to turn, meant originally the last three or four steps of a dancing movement, the turn, the *versus*, which determined the whole character of dance and of a metre. Trish*t*ubh, the name of a common metre, in the Veda,[1] meant three-step, because its turn, its v*r*itta or *versus*, consisted of three steps, ⏑ – –.

I do not feel competent to speak with equal certainty of the astronomical and geometrical observations, which we find in some of the ancient Sûtra works. It is well known that at a later time the Hindus became the pupils of the Greeks in these subjects. But I have seen no reason as yet to modify my opinion, that there was an ancient indigenous Hindu astronomy, founded on the twenty-seven Nakshatras or Lunar Mansions, and an ancient indigenous Hindu geometry, founded on the construction of altars and their inclosures. The problem, for instance, treated in the *S*ulva Sûtras,[2] how to construct a square altar that should be of exactly the same magnitude as a round altar, suggested probably

[1] M. M., *Translation of the Rig-Veda*, I., p. ci.

[2] These Sûtras have for the first time been edited and translated by Professor G. Thibaut, in the *Pandit*.

the first attempt at solving the problem of the squaring of the circle.[1] Anyhow, the terminology used in those early Sûtras seems to me home-grown, and it deserves, I believe, in the highest degree the attention of those who wish to discover the first beginnings of mathematical science.

The rules on domestic ceremonies, connected with marriage, birth, baptism, burial, the principles of education, the customs of civil society, the laws of inheritance, of property, of taxation and government, can nowhere be studied to greater advantage than in the G*ri*hya and Dharma-sûtras. These are the principal sources of those later metrical law-books, the laws of Manu, Yâ*g*navalkya, Parâsara, and the rest, which, though they contain old materials, are in their present form decidedly of a much later date.

In the same Sûtras[2] we find also certain chapters devoted to philosophy, the first germs of which exist in the Upanishads, and receive at a later time a most perfect systematic treatment in the six collections of philosophical Sûtras. These Sûtras may be of a much later date,[3] but to whatever period they belong, they contain not only, as Cousin used to say, the whole development of philosophic thought in a nut-

[1] In Greece, too, we are told that the Delians received an oracle that the misfortunes which had befallen them and all the Greeks would cease, if they built an altar double the present one. In this they did not succeed, because they were ignorant of geometry. Plato, whom they consulted, told them how to set about it, and explained to them that the real object of the oracle was to encourage them to cultivate science, instead of war, if they wished for more prosperous days. See Plutarch, *De Daemonio Socratis*, cap. VII.

[2] See Âpastamba-Sûtras, translated by G. Bühler, in *Sacred Books of the East*.

[3] The Sânkhya-kârikâ was translated into Chinese about 560 A. D. See S. Beal, *The Buddhist Tripitaka*, p. 84. I owe the date, and the fact that the translation, *The Golden Seventy Shaster*, agrees with Colebrooke's text, to a private communication from Mr. S. Beal.

shell, but they show us in many cases a treatment of philosophic problems, which, even in these days of philosophic apathy, will rouse surprise and admiration.

II. Brâhmana Period, 600–800 B. C.

This period of literature, the Sûtra period, presupposes another, *the period of the Brâhmanas*, works written in prose, but in a totally different style, in a slightly different language, and with a different object. These Brâhma*n*as, most of which are accentuated, while the Sûtras are so no longer, contain elaborate discussions on the sacrifices, handed down in different families, and supported by the names of various authorities. Their chief object is the description and elucidation of the sacrifice, but they incidentally touch on many other topics of interest. The Sûtras, whenever they can, refer to the Brâhma*n*as as their authority; in fact, the Sûtras would be unintelligible except as following after the Brâhma*n*as.

A very important portion of the Brâhma*n*as are the *Âranyakas*, the forest-books, giving an account of the purely mental sacrifices that have to be performed by the Vânaprasthas, or the dwellers in the forest, and ending with the *Upanishads*, the oldest treatises on Hindu philosophy.

If the Sûtra period began about 600 B. C., the Brâhma*n*a period would require at least 200 years to account for its origin and development, and for the large number of ancient teachers quoted as authorities. But I care little about these chronological dates. They are mere helps to our memory. What is really important is the recognition of a large stratum of literature, lying below the Sûtras, but placed itself above another stratum, which I call the *Mantra period.*

III. Mantra Period, 800–1000 B. C.

To this period I ascribe the collection and the systematic arrangment of the Vedic hymns and formulas, which we find in four books or the Sa*m*hitâs for the Rig-Veda, the Ya*g*ur-Veda, the Sâma-Veda, and the Atharva-Veda. These four collections were made with a distinct theological or sacrificial purpose. Each contains the hymns which had to be used by certain classes of priests at certain sacrifices. The Sâma-veda-sa*m*hitâ[1] contains the verses to be used by the singing priests (Udgâtri); the Ya*g*ur-veda-sa*m*hitâ the verses and formulas to be muttered by the officiating priests (Adhvaryu). These two collections followed in their arrangement the order of certain sacrifices. The Rig-veda-sa*m*hitâ contained the hymns to be recited by the Hot*ri* priests, but mixed up with a large mass of sacred and popular poetry, and *not* arranged in the order of any sacrifice. The Atharva-veda-sa*m*hitâ is a later collection, containing, besides a large number of Rig-veda verses, some curious relics of popular poetry connected with charms, imprecations, and other superstitious usages.

We move here already, not only among Epigonoi, but among priests by profession, who had elaborated a most complicated system of sacrifices, and had assigned to each minister and assistant his exact share in the performance of each sacrifice, and his portion of the ancient sacred poetry, to be recited, sung, or muttered by him, as the case might be.

[1] With the exception of about seventy-five verses, all the rest of the Sâma-veda-sa*m*hitâ is found in the Rig-Veda.

10

Fortunately for us, there was one class of priests for whom no special prayer-book was made, containing such extracts only as were required to accompany certain ceremonies, but who had to know by heart the whole treasure of their sacred and national poetry. In this manner much has been preserved to us of the ancient poetry of India, which has no special reference to sacrificial acts; we have, in fact, one great collection of ancient poetry, and that is the collection which is known by the name of the *Rig-Veda*, or the Veda of the hymns: in truth, the only real or historical Veda, though there are other books called by the same name.

This Veda consists of ten books, each book being an independent collection of hymns, though carried out under the same presiding spirit.[1] These collections were preserved as sacred heir-looms in different families, and at last united into one great body of sacred poetry. Their number amounts to 1,017 or 1,028.

The period during which the ancient hymns were collected, and arranged as prayer-books for the four classes of priests, so as to enable them to take their part in the various sacrifices, has been called the *Mantra period*, and may have extended from about 1000 to 800 B. C.

IV. Khandas *Period, 1000–X B. C.*

It is therefore before 1000 B. C. that we must place the spontaneous growth of Vedic poetry, such as we find it in the Rig-Veda and in the Rig-Veda only, the gradual development of the Vedic religion, and

[1] This is pointed out by the Paribhâshâs of the Anukrama*n*îs, which explain the order of the deities according to which the hymns in each Ma*nd*ala were arranged.

the slow formation of the principal Vedic sacrifices. How far back that period, the so-called Kh*andas period*, extended, who can tell? Some scholars extend it to two or three thousand years before our era, but it is far better to show the different layers of thought that produced the Vedic religion, and thus to gain an approximate idea of its long growth, than to attempt to measure it by years or centuries, which can never be more than guess-work.

If we want to measure the real depth of that period, we should measure it by the change of language and metre, even by the change of locality from the northwest to the southeast, clearly indicated in some of the hymns; by the old and new songs constantly spoken of by the poets; by the successive generations of kings and leaders; by the slow development of an artificial ceremonial, and lastly by the first signs of the four castes perceptible in the very latest hymns only. A comparison of the Rig-Veda with the Atharva-veda will in many cases show us how what we ourselves should expect as a later development of the more primitive ideas of the Rig-Veda is what we actually find in the hymns of the Atharva-veda, and in the later portions of the Ya*g*ur-veda; nay it is the confirmation of these expectations that gives us a real faith in the historical growth of Vedic literature.

One thing is certain: there is nothing more ancient and primitive, not only in India, but in the whole Aryan world, than the hymns of the Rig-Veda. So far as we are Aryans in language, that is in thought, so far the Rig-Veda is our own most ancient book.

And now let me tell you, what will again sound like a fairy-tale, but is nevertheless a simple fact. That Rig-Veda which, for more than three, or it may be four thousand years, has formed the foundation of the religious and moral life of untold millions of human beings, had never been published; and by a combination of the most fortunate circumstances, it fell to my lot to bring out the first complete edition of that sacred text, together with the most authoritative commentary of Hindu theologians, the commentary of Sâya*n*a Â*k*ârya.

The Rig-Veda consists of 1,017 or 1,028 hymns, each on an average of ten verses. The total number of words, if we may trust native scholars, amounts to 153,826.

THE VEDA HANDED DOWN BY ORAL TRADITION.

But how, you may ask, was that ancient literature preserved? At present, no doubt, there are MSS. of the Veda, but few Sanskrit MSS. in India are older than 1000 after Christ, nor is there any evidence that the art of writing was known in India much before the beginning of Buddhism, or the very end of the ancient Vedic literature. How, then, were these ancient hymns, and the Brâhma*n*as, and, it may be, the Sûtras too, preserved? Entirely by memory, but by memory kept under the strictest discipline. As far back as we know anything of India, we find that the years which we spend at school and at university were spent by the sons of the three higher classes in learning from the mouth of a teacher their sacred literature. This was a sacred duty, the neglect of which entailed social degradation, and the most minute rules were laid down as to the mnemonic system that had to be followed. Before the invention of writing there was no other way of preserving literature, whether sacred or profane, and in consequence every precaution was taken against accidents.

It has sometimes been asserted that the Vedic religion is extinct in India, that it never recovered from its defeat by Buddhism; that the modern Brahmanic religion, as founded on the Purâ*n*as[1] and Tantras, consists in a belief in Vish*n*u, *S*iva, and Brahma, and manifests itself in the worship of the most hideous idols. To a superficial observer it may seem to be so, but English scholars who have lived in India in intimate relations with the natives, or native scholars who now occasionally visit us in England, give a very different account. No doubt, Brahmanism was for a time defeated by Buddhism; no doubt it had, at a later time, to accommodate itself to circumstances, and tolerate many of the local forms of worship, which were established in India, before it was slowly subdued by the Brahmans. Nor did Brahmanism ever possess a state machinery to establish uniformity of religious belief, to test orthodoxy, or to punish heresy over the whole of India. But how was it that, during the late famine, many people would rather die than accept food from unclean hands?[2] Are there any

[1] We must carefully distinguish between the Purâ*n*as, such as they now exist, and the original Purâ*n*a, a recognized name for ancient tradition, mentioned already in the Atharva-Veda, XI. 7, 24, *rik*a*h* sâmâni *kh*andâ*m*si purâ*n*a*m* ya*g*ushâ saha; XV. 6, 4, itihâsa*h* purâ*n*a*m* *k*a gâthâs *k*a nârâ*s*a*m*sîs *k*a. The original Purâ*n*a formed part, from the earliest times, of the traditional learning of the Brahmans (see Â*s*v.-G*ri*hya-Sûtras, III. 3, 1), as distinct from the Itihâsas, the legends; and we hear of Purâ*n*a and Itihâ*s*as being repeated for entertainment, for instance at funerals, Â*s*v.-G*ri*hya-Sûtras, IV. 6, 6. The law-books frequently refer to the Purâ*n*a as authoritative, as distinct from Veda, Dharmâ*s*âstras and Vedâṅgas; Gautama, XI. 19. Extracts from the Purâ*n*a are given in Âpastamba's Dharmasûtras, I. 19, 13; II. 23, 3. These are metrical and repeated, the former in Manu, IV. 248, 249, the latter in Yâ*g*navalkya, III. 186. Prose quotations occur, Âpast. Dh. S., I. 29, 7. Totally distinct from this are the Purâ*n*as. So late as the time of *G*aimini no importance was attached to the Purâ*n*as, for he does not even refer to them in his system of Mîmâ*m*sâ. Cf. Sha*dd*ar*s*ana-*k*intanikâ, I. p. 164.

[2] It is curious that the popular idea that, even during a famine, food

priests in Europe or elsewhere, whose authority would be proof against starvation? The influence of the priests is still enormous in India, and all the greater, because it is embodied in the influence of custom, tradition, and superstition. Now those men who are, even at the present moment, recognized as the spiritual guides of the people, those whose influence for good or evil is even now immense, are believers in the supreme authority of the Veda. Everything, whether founded on individual opinion, on local custom, on Tantras or Purâ*n*as, nay, even on the law-books of Manu, must give way, as soon as it can be proved to be in direct conflict with a single sentence of the Veda. On that point there can be no controversy. But those Brahmans, who even in this Kali age, and during the ascendency of the Mle*kkh*as uphold the sacred traditions of the past, are not to be met with in the drawing-rooms of Calcutta. They depend on the alms of the people, and live in villages, either by themselves, or in colleges. They would lose their prestige, if they were to shake hands or converse with an infidel, and it is only in rare cases that they drop their reserve, when brought in contact with Europeans whose knowledge of their own sacred language and literature excites their wonderment, and with a little pressure, opens their heart and their mouth, like a treasure-house of ancient knowledge. Of course, they would not speak English or even Bengali. They speak Sanskrit and write Sanskrit, and I frequently receive letters from some of them, couched in the most faultless language.

And my fairy-tale is not all over yet. These men,

must not be accepted from unclean hands, rests on no sacred authority, nay is flatly contradicted by both *S*ruti and Sm*r*iti.

and I know it as a fact, know the whole Rig-Veda by heart, just as their ancestors did, three or four thousand years ago; and though they have MSS., and though they now have a printed text, they do not learn their sacred lore from them. They learn it, as their ancestors learnt it, thousands of years ago, from the mouth of a teacher, so that the Vedic succession should never be broken.[1] That oral teaching and learning became in the eyes of the Brahmans one of the great sacrifices, and though the number of those who still keep it up is smaller than it used to be, their influence, their position, their sacred authority, are as great as ever. These men do not come to England, they would not cross the sea. But some of their pupils, who have been brought up half on the native, and half on the English system, are less strict. I have had visits from natives who knew large portions of the Veda by heart. I have been in correspondence with others who, when they were twelve or fifteen years old, could repeat the whole of it.[2] They learn a few lines every day, repeat them for hours, so that the whole house resounds with the noise, and they thus strengthen their memory to that degree, that when their apprenticeship is finished, you can open them like a book, and find any passage you like, any word, any accent. One native scholar, Shankar

[1] This oral teaching is carefully described in the Prâtisâkhya of the Rig-Veda, *i. e.*, probably in the fifth or sixth century B. C. It is constantly alluded to in the Brâhmanas, but it must have existed even during the earlier periods, for in a hymn of the Rig-Veda (VII. 103), in which the return of the rainy season, and the delight and quacking of the frogs is described, we read: "One repeats the speech of the other, as the pupil (repeats the words) of the teacher." The pupil is called *s*ikshamâna*h*, the teacher *s*akta*h*, while *s*ikshâ, from the same root, is the recognized technical term for phonetics in later times.

[2] *Indian Antiquary*, 1878, p. 140. "There are thousands of Brâhmans, the editor remarks, who know the whole of the Rig-Veda by heart, and can repeat it, etc."

Pandurang, is at the present moment collecting various readings for my edition of the Rig-Veda, not from MSS., but from the oral tradition of Vaidik *S*rotriyas. He writes, on the 2d March, 1877, "I am collecting a few of our walking Rig-Veda MSS., taking your text as the basis. I find a good many differences which I shall soon be able to examine more closely, when I may be able to say whether they are various readings or not. I will of course communicate them all to you before making any use of them publicly, if I ever do this at all. As I write, a Vaidik scholar is going over your Rig-Veda text. He has his own MS. on one side, but does not open it, except occasionally. He knows the whole Sa*m*hitâ and Pada texts by heart. I wish I could send you his photograph, how he is squatting in my tent with his Upavîta (the sacred cord) round his shoulders, and only a Doti round his middle, not a bad specimen of our old Rishis."

Think of that half-naked Hindu, repeating under an Indian sky the sacred hymns which have been handed down for three or four thousand years by oral tradition. If writing had never been invented, if printing had never been invented, if India had never been occupied by England, that young Brahman, and hundreds and thousands of his countrymen, would probably have been engaged just the same in learning and saying by heart the simple prayers first uttered on the Sarasvatî, and the other rivers of the Penjab by Vasish*th*a, Visvâmitra, *S*yâvâsva, and others. And here are we, under the shadow of Westminster Abbey, in the very zenith of the intellectual life of Europe, nay, of the whole world, listening in our minds to the same sacred hymns, trying to understand them (and they are sometimes very difficult to understand), and hoping to learn from them some of the deepest secrets of the human heart, that human heart which is the same everywhere, however widely we ourselves may be separated from each other by space and time, by color and creed.

This is the story I wished to tell you to-day. And though it may have sounded to some of you like a fairy-tale, believe me it is truer in all its details than many a chapter of contemporary history.

POSTSCRIPT TO THE THIRD LECTURE.

As I find that some of my remarks as to the handing down of the ancient Sanskrit literature by means of oral tradition, and the permanence of that system to the present day, have been received with a certain amount of incredulity, I subjoin some extracts from the Rig-veda-prâtisâkhya, to show how the oral teaching of the Vedas was carried on at least 500 B. C., and some statements from the pens of two native scholars, to show how it is maintained to the present day.

The Prâtisâkhya of the Rig-Veda, of which I published the text and a German translation in 1856, contains the rules according to which the sacred texts are to be pronounced. I still ascribe this, which seems to me the oldest Prâtisâkhya, to the 5th or 6th century B. C., to a period between Yâska on one side, and Pâ*n*ini on the other, until more powerful arguments can be brought forward against this date than have been hitherto advanced. In the 15th chapter of that Prâtisâkhya we find a description of the method followed in the schools of ancient India. The teacher, we are told, must himself have passed through the recognized curriculum, and have fulfilled all the duties of a Brahmanical student (brahma*k*ârin), before he is allowed to become a teacher, and he must teach such students only who submit to all the rules of studentship. He should settle down in a proper place. If he has only one pupil or two, they should sit on his right side; if more, they must sit as there is room for them. At the beginning of each lecture the pupils embrace the feet of their teacher, and say: Read, Sir. The teacher answers: Om, Yes, and then pronounces two words, or, if it is a compound, one. When the teacher has pronounced one word or two, the first pupil repeats the first word, but if there is anything that requires explanation, the pupil says Sir; and after it has been explained to him (the teacher says), Om, Yes, Sir.

In this manner they go on till they have finished a prasna (question), which consists of three verses, or, if they are verses of more than forty to forty-two syllables, of two verses. If they are pankti-verses of forty to forty-two syllables each, a prasna may comprise either two or three; and if a hymn consists of one verse only, that is supposed to form a prasna. After the prasna is finished, they have all to repeat it once more, and then to go on learning it by heart, pronouncing every syllable with the high accent. After the teacher has first told a prasna to his pupil on the right, the others go round him to the right, and this goes on till the whole adhyâya or lecture is finished; a lecture consisting generally of sixty prasnas. At the end of the last half-verse the teacher says Sir, and the pupil replies, Om, Yes, Sir, repeating also the verses required at the end of a lecture.

The pupils then embrace the feet of their teacher, and are dismissed.

These are the general features of a lesson, but the Prâtisâkhya contains a number of minute rules besides. For instance, in order to prevent small words from being neglected, the teacher is to repeat twice every word which has but one high accent, or consists of one vowel only. A number of small words are to be followed by the particle *iti*, thus ; others are to be followed by *iti*, and then to be repeated again, *e. g.*, *k*a-iti *k*a.

These lectures continued during about half the year, the term beginning generally with the rainy season. There were, however, many holidays on which no lectures were given, and on these points also the most minute regulations are given both in the G*r*ihya and Dharma-sûtras.

This must suffice as a picture of what took place in India about 500 B. C. Let us now see what remains of the ancient system at present.

In a letter received from the learned editor of the "Sha*dd*ar*s*ana-*k*intanikâ," or Studies in Indian Philosophy, dated Poona, 8 June, 1878, the writer says:

"A student of a Rig-Veda-*s*âkhâ (a recension of the Rig-Veda), if sharp and assiduous, takes about eight years to learn the Da*s*agranthas, the ten books, which consist of

(1) The Sa*m*hitâ, or the hymns.

(2) The Brâhma*n*a, the prose treatise on sacrifices, etc.

(3) The Âra*n*yaka, the forest-book.

(4) The G*r*ihya-sûtras, the rules on domestic ceremonies.

(5–10) The six Angas, treatises on *S*ikshâ, pronunciation, *G*yotisha, astronomy, Kalpa, ceremonial, Vyâkara*n*a, grammar, Nigha*nt*u and Nirukta, etymology, *Kh*andas, metre.

"A pupil studies every day during the eight years, except on the holidays, the so-called anadhyâya, *i. e.*, non-reading days. There being 360 days in a lunar year, the eight years would give him 2,880 days. From this 384 holidays have to be deducted, leaving him 2,496 work-days during the eight years.

"Now the ten books consist on a rough calculation of 29,500 *s*lokas, so that a student of the Rig-Veda has to learn about twelve *s*lokas a day, a *s*loka consisting of thirty-two syllables.

"I ought to point out to you the source of my information. We have an association in Poona which is called the Veda*s*âstrotte*g*akasabhâ, which annually awards prizes in all recognized branches of Sanskrit learning, such as the six schools of Indian philosophy, the Alaṅkâra-*s*âstra or rhetoric, Vaidyaka or medicine, *G*yotisha or astronomy, recitation of the Veda in its different forms, such as Pada, Krama, Ghana, and *G*a*t*â, and all the subjects I have already mentioned under the name of Da*s*agrantha, in the case of the Rig-veda Brahmans. The prize-men are recommended by a board of examiners. In every subject a threefold test is employed,—theoretical knowledge of the subject (prakriyâ), general knowledge of the subject (upasthiti), and the construction of passages from recognized works in each branch of knowledge (granthârthaparîkshâ). About 1,000 rupees are distributed by the leading native gentlemen of Poona. At a meeting held the 8th May last there were about fifty Sanskrit Pandits and Vaidikas. In their presence I got the information from an old Vaidika much respected in Poona."

Another interesting account of the state of native learning comes from the pen of Professor R. G. Bhandarkar, M. A. ("Indian Antiquary," 1874, p. 132): —

"Every Brahmanic family," he writes, "is devoted to the study of a particular Veda, and a particular *s*âkhâ (recension) of a Veda; and the domestic rites of the family are performed according to the ritual described in the Sûtra connected with that Veda. The study consists in getting by heart the books forming the particular Veda. In Northern India, where the predominant Veda is the White Ya*g*ush, and the *s*âkhâ that of the Mâdhyandinas, this study has almost died out, except at Banâras, where Brahmanic families from all parts of India are settled. It prevails to some extent in Gujarât, but to a much greater extent in the Marâ*th*â country; and in Tailangana there is a large number of Brahmans who still devote their life to this study. Numbers of these go about to all parts of the country in search of dakshi*n*â (fee, alms), and all well-to-do natives patronize them according to their means, by getting them to repeat portions of their Veda, which is mostly the Black Ya*g*ush, with Âpastamba for their Sûtra. Hardly a week passes here in Bombay in which no Tailangana Brahman comes to me to ask for dakshi*n*â. On each occasion I get the men to repeat what they have learned, and compare it with the printed texts in my possession.

"With reference to their occupation, Brahmans of each Veda are generally divided into two classes, G*ri*hasthas and Bhikshukas. The former devote themselves to a wordly avocation, while the latter spend their time in the study of their sacred books and the practice of their religious rites.

"Both these classes have to repeat daily the Sandhyâ-vandana or twilight-prayers, the forms of which are somewhat different for the different Vedas. But the repetition of the Gâyatrî-mantra 'Tat Savitur vare*n*yam,' etc., five, ten, twenty-eight, or a hundred and eight times, which forms the principal portion of the ceremony, is common to all.

"Besides this, a great many perform daily what is called Brahmaya*g*na, which on certain occasions is incumbent on all. This for the Rig-vedis consists of the first hymn of the first ma*nd*ala, and the opening sentences of the Aitareya Brâhma*n*a, the five parts of the Aitareya Âra*n*yaka, the Ya*g*us-sa*m*hitâ, the Sâma-sa*m*hitâ, the Atharva-sa*m*hitâ, Â*s*valâyana Kalpa Sûtra, Nirukta, *Kh*andas, Nigha*nt*u, *G*yotisha, *S*ikshâ, Pâ*n*ini, Yâ*g*navalkya Sm*r*iti, Mahâbhârata, and the Sûtras of Ka*n*âda, *G*aimini, and Bâdarâya*n*a.

"Such Bhikshukas, however, as have studied the whole Veda repeat more than the first hymn; they repeat as much as they wish (sa yâvan manyeta tâvad adhitya, Â*s*valâyana).

"Some of the Bhikshukas are what are called Yâ*g*nikas. They follow a priestly occupation, and are skilled in the performance of sacred rites. . . . .

"But a more important class of Bhikshukas are the Vaidikas, some of whom are Yâ*g*nikas as well. Learning the Vedas by heart and repeating them in a manner never to make a single mistake, even in the accents, is the occupation of their life. The best Rig-vedi Vaidika knows by heart the Sa*m*hitâ, Pada, Krama, *G*a*t*â and Ghana of the hymns, the Aitareya Brâhma*n*a and Âra*n*yaka, the Kalpa and G*r*ihya Sûtra of Â*s*valâyana, the Nigha*nt*u, Nirukta, *Kh*andas, *G*yotisha, *S*ikshâ, and Pâ*n*ini's grammar. A Vaidika is thus a living Vedic library.

"The Sa*m*hitâ, Pada, Krama, *G*a*t*â and Ghana are different names for peculiar arrangements of the text of the hymns.

"In the Sa*m*hitâ text all words are joined according to the phonetic rules peculiar to Sanskrit.

"In the Pada text the words are divided and compounds also are dissolved.

"In the Krama text, suppose we have a line of eleven words, they are arranged as follows, the rules of Sandhi being observed throughout for letters and accent:—

"1, 2; 2, 3; 3, 4; 4, 5; 5, 6; 6, 7; 7, 8; etc. The last word of each verse, and half-verse, too, is repeated with iti (vesh*t*ana)."

These three, the Sa*m*hitâ, Pada, and Krama texts, are the least artificial, and are mentioned already in the Aitareya-âra*n*yaka, though under different and, as it would seem, older names. The Sa*m*hitâ text is called Nirbhu*g*a, *i. e.*, inclined, the final and initial letters being as it were inflected; the Pada text is called Pat*r*inna, *i. e.*, cut asunder; the Krama text, Ubhayam-antare*n*a, *i. e.*, between the two.[1]

"In the *G*atâ the words are arranged as follows:—

"1, 2, 2, 1, 1, 2; 2, 3, 3, 2, 2, 3; 3, 4, 4, 3, 3, 4; etc. The last word of each verse, and half-verse, is repeated with iti.

"In the Ghana the words are arranged as follows:
1, 2, 2, 1, 1, 2, 3, 3, 2, 1, 1, 2, 3; 2, 3, 3, 2, 2, 3, 4,

[1] *Rig-veda-prâtisakhya*, ed. M. M. p. iii. and *Nachträge*, p. 11. Quite a different nomenclature is that found in the *Samhito-panishad-brâhmana*, I. (ed. Burnell, p. 9, 11, *seq.*) The three Sa*m*hitâs mentioned there are called suddhâ, adu*h*sp*r*ish*t*â, and anirbhu*g*â. The first is explained as recited after bathing, etc., in a pure or holy place; the second as recited without any mistake of pronunciation; the third anirbhu*g*â, as recited while the arms do not extend beyond the knees, the accents being indicated with the tip of the thumb striking against the fingers.

4, 3, 2, 2, 3; 2, 3, 3, 2, 2, 3, 4, 4, 3, 2, 2, 3, 4; 3, 4, 4, 3, 3, 4, 5, 5, 4, 3, 3, 4, 5; etc. The last two words of each verse and half-verse are repeated with iti, as, *e. g.*, 7, 8, 8, 7, 7, 8; 8 iti 8; and again, 10, 11, 11, 10, 10, 11; 11 iti 11. Compounds are dissolved (avagraha).

"The object of these different arrangements is simply the most accurate preservation of the sacred text. Nor is the recital merely mechanical, the attention being constantly required for the phonetic changes of final and initial letters, and for the constant modification of the accents. The different accents are distinctly shown by modulations of the voice. The Rig-vedis, Kânvas, and Atharva-vedis do this in a way different from the Taittirîyas, while the Mâdhyandinas indicate the accents by certain movements of the right hand.

"Among the Rig-vedis it is not common to go so far as the Ghana; they are generally satisfied with Sa*m*hitâ, Pada, and Krama. Among the Taittirîyas, however, a great many Vaidikas go up to the Ghana of the hymns, since they have to get up only their Brâhma*n*a and Âra*n*yaka in addition. Some learn the Taittirîya Prâti*s*âkhya also, but the Vedângas are not attended to by that class, nor indeed by any except the Rig-vedis. The Mâdhyandinas get up the Sa*m*hitâ, Pada, Krama, *G*a*t*â, and Ghana of their hymns; but their studies generally stop there, and there is hardly one to be found who knows the whole *S*atapatha Brâhma*n*a by heart, though several get up portions of it. There are very few Atharva-vedis in the Bombay Presidency. The students of the Sâma-veda have their own innumerable modes of singing the Sâmas. They get up their Brâhma*n*as and Upanishads also.

"There is another class of Vedic students called *S*rotriyas, or popularly *S*rautîs. They are acquainted with the art of performing the great sacrifices. They are generally good Vaidikas, and in addition study the Kalpa-sûtras and the Prayogas, or manuals. Their number is very limited.

"Here and there one meets with Agnihotris, who maintain the three sacrificial fires, and perform the fortnightly Ish*t*is (sacrifices), and *K*âturmâsyas (particular sacrifices every four months). The grander Soma sacrifices are now and then brought forward, but they are, as a matter of course, very unfrequent."

These extracts will show what can be done by memory for the preservation of an ancient literature. The texts of the Veda have been handed down to us with such accuracy that there is hardly a various reading in the proper sense of the word, or even an uncertain accent, in the whole of the Rig-Veda. There are corruptions in the text, which can be discovered by critical investigation; but even these corruptions must have formed part of the recognized text since it was finally settled. Some of them belong to different *S*âkhâs or recensions, and are discussed in their bearing by ancient authorities.

The authority of the Veda, in respect to all religious questions, is as great in India now as it has ever been. It never was uncontested as little as the authority of any other sacred book has been. But to the vast majorities of orthodox believers the Veda forms still the highest and only infallible authority, quite as much as the Bible with us, or the Koran with the Mohammedans.

IV.

THE WORSHIP OF TANGIBLE, SEMI-TANGIBLE, AND INTANGIBLE OBJECTS.

LET us clearly see the place from which we start, the point which we wish to reach, and the road which we have to travel. We want to reach the point where religious ideas take their first origin, but we decline to avail ourselves of the beaten tracks of the fetish theory on the left, and of the theory of a primordial revelation on the right side, in order to arrive at our goal. We want to find a road which, starting from what everybody grants us, viz., the knowledge supplied by our five senses, leads us straight, though it may be slowly, to a belief in what is not, or at least not entirely, supplied to us by the senses, — the various disguises of the infinite, the supernatural, or the divine.

EVIDENCE OF RELIGION NEVER ENTIRELY SENSUOUS.

All religions, however they may differ in other respects, agree in this one point, that their evidence is not entirely supplied by sensuous perception. This applies, as we saw, even to fetish-worship, for in worshiping his fetish, the savage does not worship a common stone, but a stone which, besides being a stone that can be touched and handled, is supposed to be something else, this something else being beyond the reach of our hands, our ears, or our eyes.

How does this arise? What is the historical process which produces the conviction, that there is, or that there can be, anything beyond what is manifest to our senses, something invisible, or, as it is soon called, infinite, super-human, divine? It may, no doubt, be an entire mistake, a mere hallucination, to speak of things invisible, or infinite, or divine. But, in that case, we want to know all the more how it is that people, apparently sane on all other points, have, from the beginning of the world to the present day, been insane on this one point. We want an answer to this, or we shall have to surrender religion as altogether unfit for scientific treatment.

EXTERNAL REVELATION.

If we thought that mere words could help us, we should say that all religious ideas which transcend the limits of sensuous perception owed their origin to some kind of external revelation. This sounds well, and there is hardly any religion that does not put forward some such claim. But we have only to translate this argument as it meets us everywhere, into fetish language, in order to see how little it would help us in removing the difficulties which bar our way in an historical study of the origin and growth of religious ideas. Suppose we asked an Ashanti priest how he knew that his fetish was not a common stone, but something else, call it as you like; and suppose he were to say to us that the fetish himself had told him so, had revealed it to him, what should we say? Yet the theory of a primeval revelation, disguise it as you may, always rests on this very argument. How did man know that there are gods? Because the gods themselves told him so.

This is an idea which we find both among the lowest and amongst the most highly civilized races. It is a constant saying among African tribes, that "formerly heaven was nearer to men than it is now, that the highest god, the creator himself, gave formerly lessons of wisdom to human beings; but that afterwards he withdrew from them, and dwells now far from them in heaven."[1] The Hindus[2] say the same, and they, as well as the Greeks,[3] appeal to their ancestors, who had lived in closer community with the gods, as their authority on what they believe about the gods.

But the question is, how did that idea of gods, or of anything beyond what we can see, first rise up in the thoughts of men, even in the thoughts of their earliest ancestors. The real problem is, how man gained the predicate *God*: for he must clearly have gained that predicate before he could apply it to any object, whether visible or invisible.

INTERNAL REVELATION.

When it was found that the concept of the infinite, the invisible, or the divine, could not be forced into us from without, it was thought that the difficulty could be met by another word. Man, we were told, possessed a religious or superstitious instinct, by which he, alone of all other living creatures, was enabled to perceive the infinite, the invisible, the divine.

Let us translate this answer also into simple fetish

1 Waitz, ii. p. 171.

2 Rig-Veda, I. 179, 2; VII. 76, 4. Muir's *Sanskrit Texts*, iii. p. 245.

3 Nägelsbach, *Homerische Theologie*, p. 151.

language, and I think we shall be surprised at our own primitiveness.

If an Ashanti were to tell us that he could see that there was something else in his fetish beyond a mere stone, because he possessed an instinct of seeing it, we should probably wonder at the progress which he had made in hollow phraseology under the influence of European teaching, but we should hardly think that the study of man was likely to be much benefited by the help of unsophisticated savages. To admit a religious instinct, as something over and above our ordinary mental faculties, in order to explain the origin of religious ideas, is the same as to admit a linguistic instinct in order to explain the origin of language, or an arithmetic instinct in order to explain our power of counting. It is the old story of certain drugs producing sleep, because forsooth they possess a soporific quality.

I do not deny that there is a grain of truth in both these answers, but that grain must first be picked out from a whole bushel of untruth. For shortness' sake, and after we have carefully explained what *we* mean by a primeval revelation, what *we* mean by a religious instinct, we may perhaps be allowed to continue to employ these terms; but they have so often been used with a wrong purpose that it would seem wiser to avoid them in future altogether.

Having thus burnt the old bridges on which it was so easy to escape from the many difficulties which stare us in the face when we ask for the origin of religious ideas, all that remains to us now is to advance, and to see how far we shall succeed in accounting for the origin of religious ideas without taking refuge in the admission either of a primeval revelation or of a religious instinct. We have our five senses, and we have the world before us, such as it is, vouched for by the evidence of the senses. The question is, How do we arrive at a world beyond? or rather, How did our Aryan forefathers arrive there?

THE SENSES AND THEIR EVIDENCE.

Let us begin then from the beginning. We call real or manifest what we can perceive with our five senses. That is at least what a primitive man calls so, and we must not drag in here the question, whether our senses really convey to us real knowledge. We are not dealing at present with Berkeleys and Humes, not even with an Empedokles or Xenophanes, but with a quarternary, it may be a tertiary Troglodyte. To him a bone which he can touch, smell, taste, see, and, if necessary, hear, as he cracks it, is real, very real, as real as anything can be.

We should distinguish, however, even in that early stage, between two classes of senses, the senses of touch, scent, and taste, which have sometimes been called the *palaioteric* senses,[1] on one side, and the senses of sight and hearing, the so-called *neoteric* senses, on the other. The first three give us the greatest material certainty; the two last admit of doubt, and have frequently to be verified by the former.

Touch seems to offer the most irrefragable evidence of reality. It is the lowest, the least specialized and developed sense, and, from an evolutionary point of view, it has been classed as the oldest sense. Scent and taste are the next more specialized senses,

[1] H. Muirhead, *The Senses.*

and they are used, the former by animals, and the latter by children, for the purpose of further verification.

To many of the higher animals scent seems the most important test of objective reality, while with man, and particularly with civilized man, it has almost ceased to render any service for that purpose. A child makes but little use of scent, but in order to convince itself of the reality of an object, it first touches it, and afterwards, if it can, it puts it into its mouth. The latter process is surrendered as we grow older, but the former, that of touching things with our hands for the purpose of verification, remains. Many a man, even now, would say that nothing is real that cannot be touched, though he would not insist, with the same certainty, that everything that is real must have a smell or a taste.

THE MEANING OF MANIFEST.

We find this confirmed by language also. When we wish to affirm that the reality of any object cannot be reasonably doubted, we say that it is *manifest*. When the Romans formed this adjective, they knew very well what they meant, or what it meant. *Manifest* meant, with them, what can be touched or struck with the hands. *Fendo* was an old Latin verb, meaning to strike. It was preserved in *offendo*, or in *defendo*, to strike or to push away from a person. *Festus*, an old irregular participle, stands for *fend* and *tus*, just as *fus-tis*, a cudgel, stands for *fos-tis*,[1] *fons-tis*, *fond-tis*.

This *fustis*, cudgel, however, has nothing to do with *fist*.[2] *F* in English points to Latin and Greek

[1] Corssen, *Aussprache*, I. 149 ; II. 190.

[2] Grimm, *Dictionary*, s. v. faust.

p; hence *fist* is probably connected with the Greek πύξ, with clenched fists, Latin *pugna*, a battle originally a boxing, πυκτής and *pugil*, a boxer. The root of these words is preserved in the Latin verb *pungo*, *pŭpŭgi*, *punctum*, so that the invisible point in geometry, or the most abstruse point in metaphysics, takes its name from boxing.

The root which yielded *fendo*, *fustis*, and *festus* is quite different. It is *dhan* or *han*, to strike down, which appears in Greek θείνειν, to strike, θέναρ, the flat of the hand, in Sanskrit *han*, to kill, *nidhana*, death, etc.

Let us return now to the things which the early inhabitants of this earth would call manifest or real. A stone, or a bone, or a shell, a tree also, a mountain or a river, an animal also or a man, all these would be called real, because they could be struck with the hand. In fact, all the common objects of their sensuous knowledge would to them be real.

DIVISION OF SENSE-OBJECTS INTO TANGIBLE AND SEMI-TANGIBLE.

We can, however, divide this old stock of primeval knowledge into two classes: —

(1) Some objects, such as stones, bones, shells, flowers, berries, branches of wood, drops of water, lumps of earth, skins of animals, animals also themselves, all these can be touched, as it were, all round. We have them before us in their completeness. They cannot evade our grasp. There is nothing in them unknown or unknowable. They were the most familiar household words of primitive society.

(2) The case is different when we come to trees, mountains, rivers, or the earth.

TREES.

Even a tree, at least one of the old giants in a primeval forest, has something overwhelming and overawing. Its deepest roots are beyond our reach, its head towers high above us. We may stand beneath it, touch it, look up to it, but our senses cannot take it in at one glance. Besides, as we say ourselves, there is life in the tree,[1] while the beam is dead. The ancient people felt the same, and how should they express it, except by saying that the tree lives? By saying this, they did not go so far as to ascribe to the tree a warm breath or a beating heart, but they certainly admitted in the tree that was springing up before their eyes, that was growing, putting forth branches, leaves, blossoms, and fruit, shedding its foliage in winter, and that at last was cut down or killed, something that went beyond the limits of their sensuous knowledge, something unknown and strange, yet undeniably real; — and this unknown and unknowable, yet undeniable something, became to the more thoughtful among them a constant source of wonderment. They could lay hold of it on one side by their senses, but on the other it escaped from them — "it fell from them, it vanished."

MOUNTAINS.

A similar feeling of wonderment became mixed up with the perceptions of mountains, rivers, the sea, and the earth. If we stand at the foot of a mountain, and look up to where its head vanishes in the clouds, we feel like dwarfs before a giant. Nay, there are mountains utterly impassable, which, to

[1] Matthews, *Ethnography of Hidatsa Indians*, p. 48.

those who live in the valley, mark the end of their little world. The dawn, the sun, the moon, the stars, seem to rise from the mountains, the sky seems to rest on them, and when our eyes have climbed up to their highest visible peaks, we feel on the very threshold of a world beyond. And let us think, not of our own flat and densely peopled Europe, not even of the Alps in all their snow-clad majesty, but of that country where the Vedic hymns were first uttered, and where Dr. Hooker saw from one point twenty snow-peaks, each over 20,000 feet in height, supporting the blue dome of an horizon that stretched over one hundred and sixty degrees, — and we shall then begin to understand how the view of such a temple might make even a stout heart shiver before the real presence of the infinite.

RIVERS.

Next to the mountains come the waterfalls and rivers. When we speak of a river, there is nothing in reality corresponding to such a name. We see indeed the mass of water which daily passes our dwelling, but we never see the whole river, we never see the same river. The river, however familiar it may seem to us, escapes the ken of our five senses, both at its unknown source and at its unknown end.

Seneca, in one of his letters, says: "We contemplate with awe the heads or sources of the greater rivers. We erect altars to a rivulet, which suddenly and vigorously breaks forth from the dark. We worship the springs of hot water, and certain lakes are sacred to us on account of their darkness and unfathomable depth."

Without thinking as yet of all the benefits which

rivers confer on those who settle on their banks, by fertilizing their fields, feeding their flocks, and defending them, better than any fortress, against the assaults of their enemies, without thinking also of the fearful destruction wrought by an angry river, or of the sudden death of those who sink into its waves, the mere sight of the torrent or the stream, like a stranger coming they know not whence, and going they know not whither, would have been enough to call forth in the hearts of the early dwellers on earth a feeling that there must be something beyond the small speck of earth which they called their own or their home, that they were surrounded on all sides by powers invisible, infinite, or divine.

THE EARTH.

Nothing, again, may seem to us more real than the the earth on which we stand. But when we speak of the earth, as something complete in itself, like a stone, or an apple, our senses fail us, or at least the senses of the early framers of language failed them. They had a name, but what corresponded to that name was something, not finite, or surrounded by a visible horizon, but something that extended beyond that horizon, something to a certain extent visible and manifest, but, to a much greater extent, non-manifest and invisible.

These first steps which primitive man must have made at a very early time, may seem but small steps, but they were very decisive steps, if you consider in what direction they would lead. They were the steps that would lead man, whether he liked it or not, from the perception of finite things, which he could handle, to what we call the perception of things, not altogether finite, which he could neither span with his fingers, nor with the widest circle of his eyes. However small the steps at first, this sensuous contact with the infinite and the unknown gave the first impulse and the lasting direction in which man was meant to reach the highest point which he can ever reach, the idea of the infinite and the divine.

SEMI-TANGIBLE OBJECTS.

I call this second class of percepts *semi-tangible*, in order to distinguish them from the first class, which may for our purposes be designated as tangible percepts, or percepts of tangible objects.

This second class is very large, and there is considerable difference between the various percepts that belong to it. A flower, for instance, or a small tree, might scarcely seem to belong to it, because there is hardly anything in them that cannot become the object of sensuous perception, while there are others in which the hidden far exceeds the manifest or visible portion. If we take the earth, for instance, it is true that we perceive it, we can smell, taste, touch, see, and hear it. But we can never perceive more than a very small portion of it, and the primitive man certainly could hardly form a concept of the earth, as a whole. He sees the soil near his dwelling, the grass of a field, a forest, it may be, and a mountain on the horizon, — that is all. The infinite expanse which lies beyond his horizon he sees only, if we may say so, by not seeing it, or by what is called the mind's eye.

This is no playing with words. It is a statement which we can verify for ourselves. Whenever we look around us from some high mountain peak, our eye travels on from crest to crest, from cloud to cloud. We rest, not because there is nothing more to see, but because our eyes refuse to travel farther. It is not by *reasoning* only, as is generally supposed, that we know that there is an endless view beyond; we are actually brought in contact with it, we see and feel it. The very consciousness of the finite power of our perception gives us the certainty of a world beyond; in feeling the limit, we also feel what is beyond that limit.

We must not shrink from translating the facts before us into the only language that will do justice to them: we have before us, before our senses, the visible and the tangible infinite. For infinite is not only that which has no limits, but it is *to us*, and it certainly was to our earliest ancestors, that also of which *we* cannot perceive the limits.

INTANGIBLE OBJECTS.

But now let us go on. All these so-called semi-tangible percepts can still be verified, if need be, by some of our senses. Some portion, at least, of every one of them, can be touched by our hands.

But we now come to a third class of percepts where this too is impossible, where we see or hear objects, but cannot strike them with our hands. What is our attitude towards them?

Strange as it may seem to us that there should be things which we can see, but not touch, the world is really full of them; and more than that, the primitive savage does not seem to have been very much disturbed by them. The clouds to most people are visible only, not tangible. But even if, particularly in mountainous countries, we reckoned clouds among the semi-tangible percepts, there is the sky, there are the stars, and the moon, and the sun, none of which can ever be touched. This third class I call *non-tangible*, or if I might be allowed to coin such a technical term, *intangible* percepts.

We have thus, by a simple psychological analysis, discovered *three classes of things* which we can perceive with our senses, but which leave in us three very distinct kinds of impression of reality:

(1.) *Tangible* objects, such as stones, shells, bones, and the rest. These were supposed to have been the earliest objects of religious worship by that large school of philosophers who hold fetishism to be the first beginning of all religion, and who maintain that the first impulse to religion came from purely finite objects.

(2.) *Semi-tangible objects*, such as trees, mountains, rivers, the sea, the earth. These objects supply the material for what I should propose to call *semi-deities*.

(3.) *Intangible* objects, such as the sky, the stars, the sun, the dawn, the moon. In these we have the germs of what hereafter we shall have to call by the name of *deities*.

TESTIMONIES OF THE ANCIENTS AS TO THE CHARACTER OF THEIR GODS.

Let us first consider some of the statements of ancient writers as to what they considered the character of their gods to be. Epicharmos says,[1] the gods were the winds, water, the earth, the sun, fire, and the stars.

[1] Stobaeus, *Floril.* xci. 29. Ὁ μὲν Ἐπίχαρμος τοὺς θεοὺς εἶναι λέγει, Ἀνέμους, ὕδωρ, γῆν, ἥλιον, πῦρ, ἀστέρας.

Prodikos[1] says that the ancients considered sun and moon, rivers and springs, and in general all that is useful to us, as gods, as the Egyptians the Nile; and that therefore bread was worshiped as Demeter, wine as Dionysos, water as Poseidon, fire as Hephæstos.

Cæsar,[2] when giving his view of the religion of the Germans, says that they worshiped the sun, the moon, and the fire.

Herodotus,[3] when speaking of the Persians, says that they sacrificed to the sun, the moon, the earth, fire, water, and the winds.

Celsus,[4] when speaking of the Persians, says that they sacrificed on hill-tops to *Dis*, by whom they mean the circle of the sky; and it matters little, he adds, whether we name this being *Dis*, or "the Most High," Ζεύς, or Adonai, or Sabaoth, or Ammon, or with the Scythians, Papa."

Quintus Curtius gives the following account of the religion of the Indians: "Whatever they began to reverence they called gods, particularly the trees, which it is criminal to injure."[5]

TESTIMONY OF THE VEDA.

Let us now turn to the old hymns of the Veda themselves, in order to see what the religion of the Indians, described to us by Alexander's companions and their successors, really was. To whom are the hymns addressed which have been preserved to us as

[1] Zeller. *Philosophie der Griechen*, p. 926. Sext. *Math.* ix. 18, 51; Cic. *N. D.* 1, 42, 118; Epiph. *Exp. Fid.* 1088, C.

[2] *Bell. Gall.* vi. 21.

[3] Herod. i. 31.

[4] Froude, in *Fraser's Magazine*, 1878, p. 157.

[5] Curtius, lib. viii. c. 9, § 34. See Happelt, p. 119.

the most ancient relics of human poetry in the Aryan world? They are addressed, not to stocks or stones, but to rivers, to mountains, to clouds, to the earth, to the sky, to the dawn, to the sun — that is to say, not to tangible objects or so-called fetishes, but to those very objects which we called semi-tangible, or intangible.

This is indeed an important confirmation, and one that a hundred years ago no one could have looked forward to. For who would then have supposed that we should one day be able to check the statements of Alexander's historians about India and the Indians, by contemporary evidence, nay by a literature, at least a thousand years older than Alexander's expedition to India?

But we can go still farther; for by comparing the language of the Aryans of India with that of the Aryans of Greece, Italy, and the rest of Europe, we can reconstruct some portions of that language which was spoken before these different members of the Aryan family separated.

TESTIMONY OF THE UNDIVIDED ARYAN LANGUAGE.

What the ancient Aryans thought about the rivers and mountains, about the earth and the sky, the dawn and the sun, how they conceived what they perceived in them, we can still discover to a certain extent, because we know how they named them. They named them on perceiving in them certain modes of activity with which they were familiar themselves, such as striking, pushing, rubbing, measuring, joining, and which from the beginning were accompanied by certain involuntary sounds, gradually changed into what in the science of language we call *roots*.

This is, so far as I can see at present, the origin of all language and of all thought, and to have put this clearly before us, undismayed by the conflict of divergent theories and the authorities of the greatest names, seems to me to constitute the real merit of Noiré's philosophy.[1]

ORIGIN OF LANGUAGE.

Language breaks out first in action. Some of the simplest acts, such as striking, rubbing, pushing, throwing, cutting, joining, measuring, ploughing, weaving, etc., were accompanied then, as they frequently are even now, by certain involuntary sounds, sounds at first very vague and varying, but gradually becoming more and more definite. At first these sounds would be connected with the acts only. *Mar*,[2] for instance, would accompany the act of rubbing, polishing stones, sharpening weapons, without any intention, as yet, of reminding either the speaker or others of anything else. Soon, however, this sound *mar* would become not only an indication, say on the part of a father, that he was going to work, to rub and polish some stone weapons himself: pronounced with a certain unmistakable accent, and accompanied by certain gestures, it would serve as a clear indication that the father meant his children and servants not to be idle while he was at work. *Mar!* would become what we call an imperative. It would be perfectly intelligible because, according to our supposition, it had been used from the first, not by one

[1] I have lately treated this subject elsewhere in an article *On the Origin of Reason*, published in the *Contemporary Review* of February, 1878, to which, as well as to Professor Noiré's original works, I must refer for further detail.

[2] See *Lectures on the Science of Language*, vol. ii. p. 347.

person only, but by many, when engaged in some common occupation.

After a time, however, a new step would be made. *Mar* would be found useful, not only as an imperative, addressed in common to one's self and others (*mar*, let us work!), but, if it was found necessary to carry stones that had to be smoothed, from one place to another, from the sea-shore to a cave, from a chalk-pit to a bee-hive hut, *mar* would suffice to signify, not only the stones that were brought together to be smoothed and sharpened, but likewise the stones which were used for chipping, sharpening, and smoothing. *Mar* might thus become an imperative sign, no longer restricted to the act, but distinctly referring to the various objects of the art.

This extension of the power of such a sound as *mar* would, however, at once create confusion; and this feeling of confusion would naturally bring with it a desire for some expedient to avoid confusion.

If it was felt to be necessary to distinguish between *mar*, "let us rub our stones," and *mar*, "now, then, stones to rub?" it could be done in different ways. The most simple and primitive way was to do it by a change of accent, by a different tone of voice. This we see best in Chinese and other monosyllabic languages, where the same sound, pronounced in varying tones, assumes different meanings.

Another equally natural expedient was to use demonstrative or pointing signs, what are commonly called *pronominal roots*; and by joining them to such sounds as *mar*, to distinguish, for instance, between "rubbing here," which would be the man who rubs, and "rubbing there," which would be the stone that is being rubbed.

This may seem a very simple act, yet it was this act which first made man conscious of a difference between subject and object, nay which over and above the perceptions of a worker and the work done, left in his mind the concept of working as an act, that could be distinguished both from the subject of the act, and from its object or result. This step is the real *salto mortale* from sound expressive of percepts to sound expressive of concepts, which no one has hitherto been able to explain, but which has become perfectly intelligible through Noiré's philosophy. The sounds which naturally accompany repeated acts, are from the very beginning signs of incipient concepts, *i. e.*, signs of repeated sensations comprehended as one. As soon as these sounds become differentiated by accents or other outward signs, so as to express either the agent, or the instrument, or the place, or the time, or the object of any action, the element common to all these words is neither more nor less than what we are accustomed to call the root, the phonetic type, definite in form, and expressive of a general act, and therefore conceptual.

These considerations belong more properly to the science of language; yet we could not omit them here altogether in treating of the science of religion.

EARLY CONCEPTS.

If we want to know, for instance, what the ancients thought when they spoke of a river, the answer is, they thought of it exactly what they called it, and they called it, as we know, in different ways, either the runner (sarit), or the noisy (nadî or dhuni); or if it flowed in a straight line, the plougher or the plough (sîrâ, river, sîrâ, plough), or the arrow; or if it seemed to nourish the fields, the mother (mâtar); or if it separated and protected one country from another, the defender (sindhu, from sidh, sedhati, to keep off). In all these names you will observe that the river is conceived as acting. As man runs, so the river runs; as man shouts, so the river shouts; as man ploughs, so the river ploughs; as a man guards, so the river guards. The river is not called at first the plough, but the plougher; nay even the plough itself is for a long time conceived and called an agent, not a mere instrument. The plough is the divider, the tearer, the wolf, and thus shares often the same name with the burrowing boar, or the tearing wolf.[1]

EVERYTHING NAMED AS ACTIVE.

We thus learn to understand how the whole world which surrounded the primitive man was assimilated or digested by him, he discovering everywhere acts similar to his own acts, and transferring the sounds which originally accompanied his acts to these surrounding agents.

Here, in the lowest depths of language, lie the true germs of what we afterwards call figurism, animism, anthropopathism, anthropomorphism. Here we recognize them as necessities, necessities of language and thought, and not as what they appear to be afterwards, free poetical conceptions. At a time when even the stone which he had himself sharpened was still looked upon by man as his deputy, and called a *cutter*, not a something to cut with; when his measuring rod was a measurer, his plough a tearer, his ship a flier, or a bird, how could it be otherwise than that the river should be a shouter, the mountain

[1] Vrika is both wolf and plough in the Veda.

a defender, the moon a measurer? The moon in her, or rather in his daily progress, seemed to measure the sky, and in doing so helped man to measure the time of each lunation, of each moon or month. Man and moon were working together, measuring together; and as a man who helped to measure a field or to measure a beam might be called a measurer, say *mâ-s*, from *mâ*, to measure, to make, thus the moon also was called *mâs*, the measurer, which is its actual name in Sanskrit, closely connected with Greek *μείς*, Latin *mensis*, English *moon*.

These are the simplest, the most inevitable steps of language. They are perfectly intelligible, however much they may have been misunderstood. Only let us be careful to follow the growth of human language and thought step by step.

ACTIVE DOES NOT MEAN HUMAN.

Because the moon was called *measurer*, or even carpenter, it does not follow that the earliest framers of languages saw no difference between a moon and a man. Primitive men, no doubt, had their own ideas very different from our own; but do not let us suppose for one moment that they were idiots, and that, because they saw some similarity between their own acts and the acts of rivers, mountains, the moon, the sun, and the sky, and because they called them by names expressive of those acts, they therefore saw no difference between a man, called a measurer, and the moon, called a measurer, between a real mother and a river called the mother.

When everything that was known and named had to be conceived as active, and if active then as personal, when a stone was a cutter, a tooth, a grinder or an eater, a gimlet, a borer, there was, no doubt, considerable difficulty in dispersonifying, in distinguishing between a measurer and the moon, in neutralizing words, in producing in fact neuter nouns, in clearly distinguishing the tool from the hand, the hand from the man; in finding a way of speaking even of a stone as something simply trodden under foot. There was no difficulty in figuring, animating, or personifying.

Thus we see how, for our purposes, the problem of personification, which gave so much trouble to former students of religion and mythology, is completely inverted. Our problem is not, how language came to personify, but how it succeeded in dispersonifying.

GRAMMATICAL GENDER.

It has generally been supposed that grammatical gender was the cause of personification. It is not the cause, but the result. No doubt, in languages in which the distinction of grammatical gender is completely established, and particularly in the later periods of such languages, it is easy for poets to personify. But we are here speaking of much earlier times. No, even in sex-denoting languages, there was a period when this denotation of sex did not yet exist. In the Aryan languages, which afterwards developed the system of grammatical gender so very fully, some of the oldest words are without gender. *Pater* is not a masculine, nor *mater* a feminine; nor do the oldest words for river, mountain, tree, or sky disclose any outward signs of grammatical gender. But though without any signs of gender, all ancient nouns expressed activities.

In that stage of language it was almost impossible to speak of things not active, or not personal. Every name meant something active. If *calx*,[1] the heel, meant the kicker, so did *calx*, the stone. There was no other way of naming it. If the heel kicked the stone, the stone kicked the heel; they were both *calx*. *Vi* in the Veda is a bird, a flier, but the same word means also an arrow. *Yudh* meant a fighter, a weapon, and a fight.

A great step was made, however, when it was possible, by outward signs to distinguish between the Kick-here and the Kick-there, the Kicker and the Kicked, and at last between animate and inanimate names. Many languages never went beyond this. In the Aryan languages a farther step was made by distinguishing, among animate beings, between males and females. This distinction began, not with the introduction of masculine nouns, but with the introduction of feminines, *i. e.*, with the setting apart of certain derivative suffixes for females. By this all other words became masculine. At a still later time, certain forms were set apart for things that were neuter, *i. e.*, neither feminine nor masculine, but generally in the nominative and accusative only.

Grammatical gender, therefore, though it helps very powerfully in the later process of poetical mythology, is not the real motive power. That motive power is inherent in the very nature of language and thought. Man has vocal signs for his own acts, he discovers similar acts in the outward world, and he grasps, he lays hold, he comprehends the various objects of his outward world by the same vocal signs. He never dreams at first, because the

[1] Calc-s, from √ kal, cel-lo; heel, the Old N. hæl-l; Gr. λάξ for κλαξ, for καλξ. Calx, cal-cul-us, cal-cul-are, etc.

river is called a defender, that therefore the river has legs, and arms, and weapons of defence; or that the moon, because he divides and measures the sky, is a carpenter. Much of this misunderstanding will arise at a later time. At present, we move as yet in much lower strata of thought.

AUXILIARY VERBS.

We imagine that language is impossible without sentences, and that sentences are impossible without the copula. This view is both right and wrong. If we mean by sentence what it means, namely, an utterance that conveys a sense, then it is right; if we mean that it is an utterance consisting of several words, a subject, and a predicate, and a copula, then it is wrong. The mere imperative is a sentence; every form of the verb may be a sentence. What we now call a noun was originally a kind of sentence, consisting of the root and some so-called suffix, which pointed to something of which that root was predicated. So again, when there is a subject and a predicate, we may say that a copula is understood, but the truth is that at first it was not expressed, it was not required to be expressed; nay, in primitive languages it was simply impossible to express it. To be able to say *vir est bonus*, instead of *vir bonus*, is one of the latest achievements of human speech.

We saw that the early Aryans found it difficult to speak, that is to think, of anything except as active. They had the same difficulties to overcome, when trying to say that a thing simply is or was. They could only express that idea at first, by saying that a thing did something which they did themselves. Now the most general act of all human beings was the act of breathing, and thus, where we say that things are, they said that things breathe.

AS, TO BREATHE.

The root *as*, which still lives in our *he is*, is a very old root: it existed in its abstract sense previous to the Aryan separation. Nevertheless we know that *as*, before it could mean to be, meant to breathe.

The simplest derivation of *as*, to breathe, was *as-u*, in Sanskrit, breath; and from it probably *asu-ra*, those who breathe, who live, who are, and at last, the oldest name for the living gods, the Vedic *Asura*.[1]

BHÛ, TO GROW.

When this root *as*, to breathe, was felt to be inconvenient, as applied, for instance, to trees and other things which clearly do not breathe, a second root was taken, *bhû*, meaning originally to grow, the Greek φύ-ω, which still lives in our own *to be*. It was applicable, not to the animal world only, but also to the vegetable world, to everything growing, and the earth itself was called *Bhûs* the growing one.

VAS, TO DWELL.

Lastly, when a still wider concept was wanted, the root *vas* was taken, meaning originally to abide, to dwell. We find it in Sanskrit *vas-tu*, a house, the Greek ἄστυ, town, and it still lingers on in the Eng-

[1] This Sanskrit *asu* is the Zend *ahu*, which in the Avesta has the meanings of conscience and world (see Darmesteter, *Ormazd et Ahriman*, p. 47). If *ahu* in Zend is used also in the sense of *lord*, it does not follow that therefore *ahura* in *Ahura mazda*, meant lord, and was formed by a secondary suffix *ra*. Zend may have assigned to *ahu* two meanings, breath and lord, as it did in the case of *ratu*, order and orderer. But to assign to Sanskrit *asura* the meaning of lord, because *Ahu* in Zend is used in that sense, seems inadmissible.

lish *I was*. This could be used of all things which fall neither under the concept of breathing nor under that of growing. It was the first approach to an expression of impersonal or dead being. There is, in fact, a certain analogy between the formation of masculine, feminine, and neuter nouns and the introduction of these three auxiliary verbs.

PRIMITIVE EXPRESSION.

Let us apply these observations to the way in which it was possible for the early Aryan speakers to say anything about the sun, the moon, the sky, the earth, the mountains, and the rivers. When we should say, the moon exists, the sun is there, or it blows, it rains, they could only think and say, the sun breathes (sûryo asti), the moon grows (ma bhavati), the earth dwells (bhûr vasati), the wind or the blower blows (vâyur vâti), the rain rains (indra unatti, or v*ri*shâ varshati, or soma*h* sunoti).

We are speaking here of the earliest attempts at comprehending and expressing the play of nature, which was acted before the eyes of man. We are using Sanskrit only as an illustration of linguistic processes long anterior to Sanskrit. How the comprehension determined the expression, and how the various expressions, in becoming traditional, reacted on the comprehension, how that action and reaction produced by necessity ancient mythology, all these are problems which belong to a later phase of thought, and must not be allowed to detain us at present. One point only there is which cannot be urged too strongly. Because the early Aryans had to call the sun by names expressive of various kinds of activity, because he was called illuminator or warmer, maker or nourisher, because they called the moon the measurer, the dawn the awakener, the thunder the roarer, the rain the rainer, the fire the quick runner, do not let us suppose that they believed these objects to be human beings, with arms and legs. Even when they still said "the sun is breathing," they never meant that the sun was a man or at least an animal, having lungs and a mouth to breathe with. Our troglodyte ancestors were neither idiots nor poets. In saying "the sun or the nourisher is breathing," they meant no more than that the sun was active, was up and doing, was moving about like ourselves. The old Aryans did not yet see in the moon two eyes, a nose, and a mouth, nor did they represent to themselves the winds that blew, as so many fat-cheeked urchins, puffing streams of wind from the four corners of the sky. All that will come by and by, but not in these early days of human thought.

LIKENESS, ORIGINALLY CONCEIVED AS NEGATION.

During the stage in which we are now moving, I believe that our Aryan ancestors, so far from animating, personifying, or humanizing the objects, which we described as semi-tangible or intangible, were far more struck by the difference between them and themselves than by any imaginary similarities.

And here let me remind you of a curious confirmation of this theory preserved to us in the Veda. What we call comparison is still, in many of the Vedic hymns, negation. Instead of saying as we do, "firm like a rock," the poets of the Veda say, "firm, not a rock;" [1] that is, they lay stress on the dissimi-

[1] Rig-Veda, I. 52, 2, *sah* parvata*h* na a*k*yuta*h*; I. 64, 7, giraya*h* na svatavasa*h*. The *na* is put after the word which serves as a comparison, so

larity, in order to make the similarity to be felt. They offer a hymn of praise to the god, not sweet food,[1] that is, as if it were sweet food. The river is said to come near roaring, not a bull, *i. e.*, like a bull; and the Maruts or storm-gods are said [2] to hold their worshipers in their arms, "a father, not the son," viz., like as a father carries his son in his arms.

Thus the sun and the moon were spoken of, no doubt, as moving about, but *not* as animals; the rivers were roaring and fighting, but they were *not* men; the mountains were not to be thrown down, but they were *not* warriors; the fire was eating up the forest, yet it was *not* a lion.

In translating such passages from the Veda, we always render *na*, not, by like; but it is important to observe that the poets themselves were originally struck by the dissimilarity quite as much, if not more than by the similarity.

STANDING EPITHETS.

In speaking of these various objects of nature, which from the earliest times excited their attention, the poets would naturally use certain epithets more frequently than others. These objects of nature were different from each other, but they likewise shared a certain number of qualities in common; they therefore could be called by certain common epithets, and afterwards fall into a class, under each epithet, and thus constitute a new concept. All this was possible: let us see what really happened.

We turn to the Veda, and we find that the hymns

that the original conception was, "he, a rock, no;" *i. e.*, he not altogether, but only to a certain point, a rock.

[1] Rig-Veda, I. 61, 1.

[2] Rig-Veda, I. 38, 1.

which have been preserved to us are all addressed, according to the views of the old Indian theologians, to certain *devatâs*.[1] This word *devatâ* corresponds exactly to our word deity, but in the hymns themselves *devatâ* never occurs in that sense. The idea of deity as such had not yet been formed. Even the old Hindu commentators say that what they mean by *devatâ* is simply whatever or whoever is addressed in a hymn, the object of the hymn, while they call *rishi* or seer, whoever addresses anything or anybody, the subject of the hymn. Thus when a victim that has to be offered is addressed, or even a sacrificial vessel, or a chariot, or a battle-axe, or a shield, all these are called *devatâs*. In some dialogues which are found among the hymns, whoever speaks is called the *rishi*, whoever is spoken to is the *devatâ*. *Devatâ* has become in fact a technical term, and means no more in the language of native theologians than the object addressed by the poet. But though the abstract term *devatâ*, deity, does not yet occur in the hymns of the Rig-Veda, we find that most of the beings to whom the ancient poets of India addressed their hymns were called *deva*. If the Greeks had to translate this *deva* into Greek, they would probably use θεός, just as we translate the Greek θεοί by gods, without much thinking what we mean by that term. But when we ask ourselves what thoughts the Vedic poets connected with the word *deva*, we shall find that they were very different from the thoughts expressed by the Greek θεός or the English god; and that even in the Veda, the Brâhma*n*as, the Âra*n*yakas and Sûtras, the meaning of that word is constantly

[1] Anukrama*n*ikâ: Yasya vâkyam sa *rishih*, yâ teno*k*yate, sâ devatâ. Tena vâkyena prâtipâdyam yad vastu, sâ devatâ.

growing and changing. The true meaning of *deva* is its history, beginning from its etymology and ending with its latest definition.

Deva, from the root *div*, to shine, meant originally bright: the dictionaries give its meaning as god or divine. But if in translating the hymns of the Veda we always translate *deva* by *deus*, or by god, we should sometimes commit a mental anachronism of a thousand years. At the time of which we are now speaking, gods, in our sense of the word, did not yet exist. They were slowly struggling into existence, that is to say, the concept and name of deity was passing through the first stages of its evolution. "In contemplation of created things men were ascending step by step to God."[1] And this is the real value of the Vedic hymns. While Hesiod gives us, as it were, the past history of a theogony, we see in the Veda the theogony itself, the very birth and growth of the gods, *i. e.*, the birth and growth of the words for god; and we also see in later hymns — later in character, if not in time — the subsequent phases in the development of these divine conceptions.

Nor is *deva* the only word in the Veda which, from originally expressing one quality shared in common by many of the objects invoked by the Rishis, came to be used at last as a general term for deity. *Vasu*, a very common name for certain gods in the Veda, meant likewise originally bright.

Some of these objects struck the mind of the early poets as unchangeable and undecaying, while everything else died and crumbled away to dust. Hence they called them *amarta*, ἄμβροτος, not dying, *agara*, ἀγήρως, not growing old or decaying.

[1] Brown, *Dionysiak Myth*, i. p. 50.

When the idea had to be expressed, that such objects as the sun or the sky were not only unchangeable, undecaying, undying, while everything else, even animals and men, changed, decayed, and died, but that they had a real life of their own, the word *asura* was used, derived, as I have little doubt, from *asu*, breath. While *deva*, owing to its origin, was restricted to the bright and kindly appearances of nature, *asura* was under no such restriction, and was therefore, from a very early time, applied not only to the beneficent, but also to the malignant powers of nature. In this word *asura*, meaning originally endowed with breath, and afterwards god, we might recognize the first attempt at what has sometimes been called animism in later religions.

Another adjective, *ishira*, had originally much the same meaning as *asura*. Derived from *ish*, sap, strength, quickness, life, it was applied to several of the Vedic deities, particularly to Indra, Agni, the Asvins, Maruts, Âdityas, but likewise to such objects as the wind, a chariot, the mind. Its original sense of quick and lively crops out in Greek ἱερὸς ἰχθύς, and ἱερὸν μένος,[1] while its general meaning of divine or sacred in Greek must be accounted for like the meaning of *asura*, god, in Sanskrit.

TANGIBLE OBJECTS AMONG THE VEDIC DEITIES.

To return to our three classes of objects, we find the first hardly represented at all among the so-called deities of the Rig-Veda. Stones, bones, shells, herbs, and all the other so-called fetishes, are simply absent in the old hymns, though they appear in more mod-

[1] The identity of ἱερός with ishira was discovered by Kuhn, *Zeitschrift*, ii. 274. See also Curtius, *Zeitschrift*, iii. 154.

ern hymns, particularly those of the Atharva-Veda. When artificial objects are mentioned and celebrated in the Rig-Veda, they are only such as might be praised even by Wordsworth or Tennyson — chariots, bows, quivers, axes, drums, sacrificial vessels, and similar objects. They never assume any individual character, they are simply mentioned as useful, as precious, it may be, as sacred.[1]

SEMI-TANGIBLE OBJECTS AMONG THE VEDIC DEITIES.

But when we come to the second class, the case is very different. Almost every one of the objects which we defined as semi-tangible meets us among the so-called deities of the Veda. Thus we read Rig-Veda I. 90, 6–8: —

"The winds pour down honey upon the righteous, the rivers pour down honey; may our plants be sweet," 6.

"May the night be honey, and the dawn; may the sky above the earth be full of honey; may heaven, our father, be honey;" 7.

[1] It has been stated that utensils or instruments never become fetishes; see Kapp, *Grundlinien der Philosophie der Technik*, 1878, p. 104. He quotes Caspari, *Urgeschichte der Menschheit*, i. 309, in support of his statement. In H. Spencer's *Principles of Sociology*, i. 343, we read just the contrary: "In India the woman adores the basket which seems to bring or to hold her necessaries, and offers sacrifices to it; as well as the rice mill and other implements that assist her in her household labors. A carpenter does the like homage to his hatchet, his adz, and his other tools; and likewise offers sacrifices to them. A Brahman does so to the style with which he is going to write; a soldier to the arms he is to use in the field; a mason to his trowel." This statement of Dubois would not carry much conviction. But a much more competent authority, Mr. Lyall, in his *Religion of an Indian Province*, says the same: "Not only does the husbandman pray to his plough, the fisher to his net, the weaver to his loom; but the scribe adores his pen, and the banker his account books." The question only is, What is meant here by adoring?

"May our trees be full of honey, may the sun be full of honey; may our cows be sweet;" 8.

I have translated literally, and left the word *madhu*, which means honey, but which in Sanskrit has a much wider meaning. Honey meant food and drink, sweet food and sweet drink; and hence refreshing rain, water, milk, anything delightful was called honey. We can never translate the fullness of those ancient words; only by long and careful study can we guess how many chords they set vibrating in the minds of the ancient poets and speakers.

Again, Rig-Veda X. 64, 8, we read: —

"We call to our help the thrice-seven running rivers, the great water, the trees, the mountains, and fire."

Rig-Veda VII. 34, 23. "May the mountains, the waters, the generous plants, and heaven, may the earth with the trees, and the two worlds (rodasî), protect our wealth."

Rig-Veda VII. 35, 8. "May the far-seeing sun rise propitious, may the four quarters be propitious; may the firm mountains be propitious, the rivers, and the water."

Rig-Veda III. 54, 20. "May the strong mountains hear us."

Rig-Veda V. 46, 6. "May the highly-praised mountains and the shining rivers shield us."

Rig-Veda VI. 52, 4. "May the rising dawns protect me! May the swelling rivers protect me! May the firm mountains protect me! May the fathers protect me, when we call upon the gods!"

Rig-Veda X. 35, 2. "We choose the protection of heaven and earth; we pray to the rivers, the mothers, and to the grassy mountains, to the sun and the dawn, to keep us from guilt. May the Soma juice bring us health and wealth to-day!"

Lastly, one more elaborate invocation of the rivers, and chiefly of the rivers of the Penjâb, whose borders form the scene of the little we know of Vedic history:—

Rig-Veda X. 75. "Let the poet declare, O waters, your exceeding greatness, here in the seat of Vivasvat. By seven and seven they have come forth in three courses, but the Sindhu (Indus) exceeds all the other travelers (rivers) by her strength;" 1.

"Varu*n*a dug out a path for thee to walk on, when thou rannest for the prizes. Thou proceedest on a precipitous ridge of the earth, when thou art lord in the van of all moving streams;" 2.

"The sound rises up to heaven above the earth; she raises an endless roar with sparkling splendor. As from a cloud, the showers thunder forth, when the Sindhu comes, roaring like a bull;" 3.

"As mothers go to their young, the lowing cows (rivers) come to thee with their milk. Like a king in battle thou leadest the two wings, when thou reachest the front of these down-rushing rivers;" 4.

"Accept, O Gangâ (Ganges), Yamunâ (Jumna), Sarasvatî (Sursûti), *S*utudri (Sutlej), Parush*n*î (Ravi), my praise! With the Asiknî (Akesines), listen O Marudv*ri*dhâ, and with the Vitastâ (Hydaspes, Behat), O Ar*g*ikîyâ, listen with the Sushomâ!" 5.

"First united with the T*ri*sh*t*âmâ for thy journey, with the Susartu, the Rasâ, and the *S*vetî, thou goest, O Sindhu, with the Kubhâ (Kophen, Cabul river), to the Gomatî (Gomal), with the Mehatnu to the Krumu (Kurum), that thou mayest proceed with them on the same path;" 6.

"Sparkling, bright, with mighty splendor she carries the clouds across the plains, the unconquered Sindhu, the quickest of the quick, like a beautiful mare, a sight to see;" 7.

"Rich in horses, in chariots, in garments, in gold, in fodder, in wool, and in grass, the Sindhu, handsome and young, spreads over a land that is flowing with honey;" 8.

"The Sindhu has yoked her easy chariot with horses; may she conquer booty for us in this fight! For the glory of that irresistible, famous, and glorious chariot is celebrated as great;" 9.

I have chosen these invocations out of thousands, because they are addressed to what are still perfectly intelligible beings, to semi-tangible objects, to semi-deities.

The question which we have to answer now is this: Are these beings to be called gods? In some passages decidedly not, for we ourselves, though we are not polytheists, could honestly join in such language as that the trees, and the mountains, and the rivers, the earth, the sky, the dawn, and the sun may be sweet and pleasant to us.

An important step, however, is taken when the mountains, and the rivers, and all the rest, are invoked to protect man. Still even that might be intelligible. We know what the ancient Egyptians felt about the Nile, and even at present a Swiss patriot might well invoke the mountains and rivers to protect him and his house against foreign enemies.

But one step follows another. The mountains are asked to listen; this, too, is to a certain extent intelligible still; for why should we address them, if they were not to listen?

The sun is called far-seeing — why not? Do we not see the first rays of the rising sun, piercing through the darkness, and glancing every morning at our roof? Do not these rays enable us to see? Then, why should not the sun be called far-lighting, far-glancing, far-seeing?

The rivers are called mothers! Why not? Do they not feed the meadows, and the cattle on them? Does not our very life depend on the rivers not failing us with their water at the proper season?

And if the sky is called "not a father," or "like a father," or at last father, — does not the sky watch over us, protect us, and protect the whole world? Is there anything else so old, so high, at times so kind, at times so terrible as the sky?[1]

If all these *beings*, as we call them in our language, *devas*,[2] bright ones, as they were often called in the language of our forefathers, were implored to grant

[1] We seldom meet with writers who defend their belief in the powers of nature against the attacks of believers in one supreme God; nay, it is difficult for us to imagine how, when the idea of one God has once been realized, a faith in independent deities could still be sustained. Yet such passages exist. Celsus, whoever he was, the author of the *True Story*, which we know as quoted and refuted by Origen, distinctly defends the Greek polytheism against the Jewish or Christian monotheism: "The Jews," he writes, "profess to venerate the heavens and the inhabitants of the heavens; but the grandest, the most sublime, of the wonders of those high regions they will not venerate. They adore the phantasm of the dark, the obscure visions of their sleep; but for those bright and shining harbingers of good, those ministers by whom the winter rains and the summer warmth, the clouds and the lightnings and the thunders, the fruits of the earth and all living things are generated and preserved, those beings in whom God reveals his presence to us, those fair celestial heralds, those angels which are angels indeed, for them they care not, they heed them not." Froude, *On Origen and Celsus*, in Fraser's *Magazine*, 1878, p. 157.

[2] In the Upanishads *deva* is used in the sense of forces or faculties; the senses are frequently called devas, also the prâ*n*as, the vital spirits. Devatâ, too, sometimes must be translated by a being; cp. *Kh*ând. Up. 6, 3, 2 *seq*.

honey, that is joy, food, happiness, we are not startled; for we too know there are blessings proceeding from all of them.

The first prayer that sounds really strange to us is when they are implored to keep us from guilt. This is clearly a later thought; nor need we suppose, because it comes from the Veda, that all we find there belongs to one and the same period. Though the Vedic hymns were collected about 1000 B. C., they must have existed for a long, long time before they were collected. There was ample time for the richest growth, nor must we forget that individual genius, such as finds expression in these hymns, frequently anticipates by centuries the slow and steady advance of the main body of the great army for the conquest of truth.

We have advanced a considerable way, though the steps which we had to take were simple and easy. But now let us suppose that we could place ourselves face to face with the poets of the Veda, even with those who called the rivers mothers, and the sky father, and who implored them to listen, and to free them from guilt; what would they say, if we asked them whether the rivers, and the mountains, and the sky were their *gods?* I believe they would not even understand what we meant. It is as if we asked children whether they considered men, horses, flies, and fishes as animals, or oaks and violets as vegetables. They would certainly answer, No; because they had not yet arrived at the higher concept which, at a later time, enables them to comprehend by one grasp objects so different in appearance. The concept of *gods* was no doubt silently growing up, while men were assuming a more and more definite attitude towards these semi-tangible and intangible objects. The search after the intangible, after the unknown, which was hidden in all these semi-tangible objects, had begun as soon as one or two more of our perceptive tentacles were disappointed in their search after a corresponding object. Whatever was felt to be absent in the full reality of a perception, which full reality meant perceptibility by all five senses, was taken for granted, or looked for elsewhere. A world was thus being built up, consisting of objects perceptible by two senses, or by one sense only, till at last we approach a world of objects, perceptible by none of our senses, and yet acknowledged as real, nay as conferring benefits on mankind in the same manner as trees, rivers, and mountains.

Let us look more closely at some of the intermediate steps which lead us from semi-tangible to intangible, from natural to supernatural objects: and first the *fire*.

THE FIRE.

Now the fire may seem not only very visible, but also very tangible; and so, no doubt, it is. But we must forget the fire as we know it now, and try to imagine what it was to the early inhabitants of the earth. It may be that, for some time, man lived on earth, and began to form his language, and his thoughts, without possessing the art of kindling fire. Even before the discovery of that art, however, which must have marked a complete revolution in his life, he had seen the sparks of lightning, he had seen and felt the light and warmth of the sun, he may have watched even, in utter bewilderment, the violent destruction of forests by conflagration, caused either by lightning or friction of trees in summer. In all these appearances and disappearances there was something extremely perplexing. At one moment the fire was here, at another it had gone out. Whence did it come? Whither did it go? If there ever was a ghost, in our sense of the word, it was fire. Did it not come from the clouds? Did it not vanish in the sea? Did it not live in the sun? Did it not travel through the stars? All these are questions that may sound childish to us, but which were very natural before men had taught fire to obey their commands. And even after they had learnt to produce fire by friction, they did not understand cause and effect. They saw the sudden appearance of what we call light and heat. They felt fascinated by it, they played with it, as children are fascinated by it even now, and will play with fire, whatever we say. And when they came to speak and think of it, what could they do? They could only call it from what it did, and so they spoke of the fire as an illuminator or a burner, who seemed to be the same as the burner in a flash of lightning, or the illuminator in the sun. Men were struck most by his quick movements, his sudden appearance and disappearance, and so they called him the quick or ag-ile, in Sanskrit *Ag-nis*, in Latin *ig-nis.*

So many things could be told of him, how that he was the son of the two pieces of wood; how, as soon as he was born, he devoured his father and mother, that is, the two pieces of wood from which he sprang; how he disappeared or became extinguished, when touched by water; how he dwelt on the earth as a friend; how he mowed down a whole forest; how at a later time he carried the sacrificial offerings from earth to heaven, and became a messenger and mediator between the gods and men: that we need not wonder at his many names and epithets, and at the large number of ancient stories or myths told of Agni; nor need we wonder at the oldest of all myths, that there was in the fire something invisible and unknown, yet undeniable, — it may be, the Lord.

THE SUN.

Next to the fire, and sometimes identified with it, comes the sun. It differs from all the objects hitherto mentioned, by its being altogether beyond the reach of the senses, except the sense of sight. What position the sun must have occupied in the thoughts of the early dwellers on earth, we shall never be able to fully understand. Not even the most recent scientific discoveries described in Tyndall's genuine eloquence, which teach us how we live, and move, and have our being in the sun, how we burn it, how we breathe it, how we feed on it — give us any idea of what this source of light and life, this silent traveler, this majestic ruler, this departing friend or dying hero, in his daily or yearly course, was to the awakening consciousness of mankind. People wonder why so much of the old mythology, the daily talk, of the Aryans, was solar: what else could it have been? The names of the sun are endless, and so are his stories; but who he was, whence he came and whither he went, remained a mystery from beginning to end. Though known better than anything else, something in him always remained unknown. As man might look into the eye of man, trying to fathom the deep abyss of his soul, and hoping at last to reach his inmost self, — he never finds it, never sees or touches it, — yet he always believes in it, never doubts it, it may be he reveres it and loves it too; so man looked up to the sun, yearning for the response of a soul, and though that response never came, though his senses recoiled, dazzled and blinded by an effulgence which he could not support, yet he never doubted that the invisible was there, and that, where his senses failed him, where he could neither grasp nor comprehend, he might still shut his eyes and trust, fall down and worship.

A very low race, the Santhals in India, are supposed to worship the sun. They call the sun *Chando*, which means bright, and is at the same time a name for the moon also, probably the Sanskrit *K*andra. They declared to the missionaries who settled among them, that Chando had created the world; and when told that it would be absurd to say that the sun had created the world, they replied with. "We do not mean the visible Chando, but an invisible one."[1]

THE DAWN.

The dawn was originally the dawning sun; the twilight, the setting sun. But after a time these two manifestations became differentiated, giving rise to an abundant wealth of story and myth. By the side of dawn and evening, we soon have day and night, and their various dual representatives, the Dioskouroi, in Sanskrit the two Asvinau, the twins, also sky and earth, and their manifold progeny. We are, in fact, in the very thick of ancient mythology and religion.

[1] *What is the Correct Name for God in Santhali?* by L. O. Skrefsrud, 1876, p. 7.

AUDIBLE OBJECTS AMONG THE VEDIC DEITIES.

All the intangible objects which we have hitherto considered were brought near to us, and could all be tested by the sense of sight. We have now to consider others, which are brought near to us by the sense of hearing only, while they withdraw themselves from all other senses.[1]

THUNDER.

We hear the noise of thunder, but we cannot see the thunder, nor can we feel, smell, or taste it. An impersonal howl or thunder, which satisfies us could not be conceived by the ancient Aryans. When they heard the thunder, they spoke of the thunderer, just as when they heard a howling noise in the forest, they thought at once of a howler, of a lion or something else, whatever it might be. An impersonal howl did not exist for them. Here, therefore, we have, in the name of thunderer or howler, the first name of some one who can never be seen, but yet whose existence, whose awful power for good or evil, cannot be doubted. In the Veda that thunderer is called *Rudra*, and we may well understand how, after such a name had once been created, Rudra or the howler should be spoken of as wielding the thunderbolt, as carrying bows and arrows, as strik-

[1] Thus Xenophon says (*Mem.* iv. 3, 14); "Consider also that the sun, who seems to be visible to all, does not allow men to look at him accurately, but takes away the eyesight, if any one tries to stare at him. You will also find that the ministers of the gods are invisible. For it is clear that the lightning is sent from above and overcomes all that is in its way; but it is not seen while it comes, while it strikes, or while it goes away. Nor are the winds seen, though what they do is clear to us, and we perceive them approaching." See, also, Minucius Felix, as quoted by Feuerbach, *Wesen der Religion*, p. 145.

ing down the wicked and sparing the good, as bringing light after darkness, refreshment after heat, health after sickness. In fact, after the first leaflets have opened, the further growth of the tree, however rapid, need not surprise us.

THE WIND.

Another precept, which chiefly depends on our sense of touch, though frequently supported by the evidence of our ears, and indirectly of our eyes, is the *wind*.

Here, too, early thought and speech do not distinguish as we do, between the blower and the blast. Both are one, both are something like ourselves. Thus we find in the Veda hymns addressed to *Vâyu*, the blower, and to *Vâta*, the blast, but this too as a masculine, not as a neuter. Though the wind is not often praised, he too, when he is praised, holds a very high position. He is called the king of the whole world, the first-born, the breath of the gods, the germ of the world, whose voices we hear, though we can never see him.[1]

MARUTAS, THE STORM-GODS.

Besides the wind, there is the storm, or as they are called in the Veda, the *Maruts*, the pounders, the strikers, who come rushing on like madmen, with thunder and lightning, whirling up the dust, bending and breaking the trees, destroying dwellings, killing even men and cattle, rending the mountains and breaking in pieces the rocks. They too come and go, but no one can catch them, no one can tell whence and whither? Yet who would doubt the existence of these storm-gods? Who would not bow down

[1] Rig Veda X. 168.

before them, or even propitiate them, it may be, either by good words, or good thoughts, or good deeds? "They can pound us, we cannot pound them," this feeling, too, contained a germ of religious thought; nay, it is a lesson which even in our days would perhaps be better understood by many than Schleiermacher's consciousness of absolute dependence on something which, though it determines us, we cannot determine in turn. Need we wonder, therefore, at the growth of another old myth, that, as in the fire, so in the wind, there was something invisible, unknown, yet undeniable, — it may be, the Lord.

THE RAIN AND THE RAINER.

Lastly, we have to consider the rain. This, no doubt, seems hardly to come under the category of intangible objects; and if it were simply considered as water, and named accordingly, it would seem to be a tangible object in every sense of the word. But early thought dwells more on differences than on similarities. Rain to the primitive man is not simply water, but water of which he does not yet know whence it comes; water which, if it is absent for a long time, causes the death of plants and animals, and men; and when it returns produces a very jubilee of nature. In some countries the howler (the thunderer), or the blower (the wind), were conceived as the givers of rain. But in other countries, where the annual return of rain was almost a matter of life or death to the people, we need not wonder that, by the side of a thunderer and blower, a rainer or irrigator should have been established. In Sanskrit the drops of rain are called *ind-u*,[1]

[1] Cf. sindhu and sidhrá, mandú and mandrá, ripú and riprá, etc.

masculine themselves; he who sends them is called *Índ-ra*, the rainer, the irrigator, and in the Veda the name of the principal deity, worshiped by the Aryan settlers in India, or the land of the Seven Rivers.

VEDIC PANTHEON.

We have thus seen how the sky, originally the light-giver, the illuminator of the world, and for that reason called *Dyaus*, or Ζεύς, or *Jupiter*, might be replaced by various gods who represent some of the principal activities of the sky, such as thunder, rain, and storm. Besides these, there was, if not the activity, yet the capacity of covering and protecting the whole world, which might likewise lead to the conception of a covering, all-embracing god, in place of the sky, as a mere firmament. In that capacity the covering god might easily merge into a god of night, opposed to a god of day, and this might again give rise to a concept of correlative gods, representing night and day, morning and evening, heaven and earth. Now every one of these changes passes before our eyes in the Veda, and they give rise to such pairs of gods as Varu*n*a, the all-embracing god, the Greek οὐρανός, and Mitra, the bright sun of day; the A*s*vinau, morning and evening; Dyâvâp*ri*thivî, heaven and earth, etc.

We have thus seen, rising as it were before our eyes, almost the whole pantheon of the poets of the Veda, the oldest pantheon of the Aryan world. We have watched the germs only, but we can easily imagine how rich their growth would be, if once exposed to the rays of poetry, or to the heat of philosophic speculation. We have learnt to distinguish three classes of deities or gods: I use the word because there is no other; beings, powers, forces, spirits, being all too abstract.

(1.) *Semi-deities*, such as trees, mountains, and rivers, the earth, the sea (semi-tangible objects).

(2.) *Deities*, such as the sky, the sun, the moon, the dawn, the fire (intangible objects); also thunder, lightning, wind, and rain, though the last four, owing to their irregular appearance, might be made to constitute a separate class, assuming generally the character of preëminently active or dramatic gods.

THE DEVAS.

No word seems more incongruous for all these beings than gods and deities. To use our own word for god in the plural, is itself a logical solecism, as if we were to speak of two centres of a circle. But, apart from this, even *deities*, or the Greek θεοί, the Latin *dii*, is an anachronism. The best would be to retain the Sanskrit word, and call them *devas*. *Deva*, as we saw, meant originally bright, and it was an epithet applicable to the fire, the sky, the dawn, the sun, also to the rivers, and trees, and mountains. It thus became a general term, and even in the Veda there is no hymn so ancient that *deva* does not display in it already the first traces of the general concept of bright, heavenly beings, opposed on the other side to the dark powers of the night and of winter. Its etymological meaning becoming forgotten, *deva* became a mere name for all those bright powers, and the same word lives on in the Latin *deus*, and in our own *deity*. There is a continuity of thought, as there is of sound, between the *devas* of the Veda and "the *divinity* that shapes *our* ends."

THE VISIBLE AND THE INVISIBLE.

We have thus seen, what I wished to show you, a real transition from the visible to the invisible, from the bright beings, the Devas, that could be touched, like the rivers, that could be heard, like the thunder, that could be seen, like the sun, to the Devas or gods that could no longer be touched, or heard, or seen. We have in such words as *deva* or *deus* the actual vestiges of the steps by which our ancestors proceeded from the world of sense to the world beyond the grasp of the senses. The way was traced out by nature herself; or if nature, too, is but a Deva in disguise,[1] by something greater and higher than nature. That old road led the ancient Aryans, as it leads us still, from the known to the unknown, from nature to nature's God.

But, you may say, "that progress was unjustified. It may lead us on to polytheism and monotheism, but it will eventually land all honest thinkers in atheism. Man has no right to speak of anything but acts and facts, not of agents or factors."

My answer is: "True, that path led the Vedic Aryans to polytheism, monotheism, and to atheism; but after the denial of the old Devas or gods, they did not rest till they found what was higher than the gods, the true Self of the world, and at the same time, their own true Self. As to ourselves, we are not different from the old Aryans. We, too, must postulate an agent when we see an act, a factor when we see a fact. Take that away, and facts themselves are no longer facts, acts are no longer acts. Our

[1] Seneca, *Benef.* IV. 7, 1. "Quid enim aliud est natura quam Deus et divina ratio toti mundo et partibus ejus inserta?" Pfleiderer, *Religionsphilosophie*, p. 345.

whole language, that is our whole thought, our whole being, rests on that conviction. Take that away, and the eyes of our friends lose their responsive power, they are glass eyes, not sunny eyes. Take that away, and our own self vanishes. We, too, are no longer agents, but only acts; machines without a motive power, beings without a self.

No, that old road on which the Aryans proceeded from the visible to the invisible, from the finite to the infinite, was long and steep; but it was the right road, and though we may never here on earth reach the end of it, we may trust it, because there is no other road for us. From station to station man has advanced on it farther and farther. As we mount higher, the world grows smaller, heaven comes nearer. With each new horizon our view grows wider, our hearts grow larger, and the meaning of our words grows deeper.

Let me quote the words of one of my best friends, whose voice not long ago was heard in Westminster Abbey, and whose living likeness, as drawn by a loving hand, will be present before the minds of many of my hearers: "Those simple-hearted forefathers of ours — so says Charles Kingsley — looked round upon the earth, and said within themselves, 'Where is the All-father, if All-father there be? Not in this earth; for it will perish. Nor in the sun, moon, or stars; for they will perish too. Where is He who abideth forever?'

"Then they lifted up their eyes, and saw, as they thought, beyond sun, and moon, and stars, and all which changes and will change, the clear blue sky, the boundless firmament of heaven.

"That never changed; that was always the same.

The clouds and storms rolled far below it, and all the bustle of this noisy world; but there the sky was still, as bright and calm as ever. The All-father must be there, unchangeable in the unchanging heaven; bright, and pure, and boundless like the heavens; and, like the heavens too, silent and far off."

And how did they call that All-father?

Five thousand years ago, or it may be earlier, the Aryans, speaking as yet neither Sanskrit, Greek, nor Latin, called him *Dyu patar*, Heaven-father.

Four thousand years ago, or it may be earlier, the Aryans who had traveled southward to the rivers of the Penjâb called him *Dyaush-pitâ*, Heaven-father.

Three thousand years ago, or it may be earlier, the Aryans on the shores of the Hellespont called him Ζεὺς πατήρ, Heaven-father.

Two thousand years ago, the Aryans of Italy looked up to that bright heaven above, *hoc sublime candens*, and called it *Ju-piter*, Heaven-father.

And a thousand years ago the same Heaven-father and All-father was invoked in the dark forests of Germany by our own peculiar ancestors, the Teutonic Aryans, and his old name of *Tiu* or *Zio* was then heard, perhaps, for the last time.

But no thought, no name, is ever entirely lost. And when we here in this ancient Abbey, which was built on the ruins of a still more ancient Roman temple, if we want a name for the invisible, the infinite, that surrounds us on every side, the unknown, the true Self of the world, and the true Self of ourselves — we, too, feeling once more like children, kneeling in a small dark room, can hardly find a better name than: "Our Father, which art in Heaven."

V.

THE IDEAS OF INFINITY AND LAW.

NIHIL IN FIDE QUOD NON ANTE FUERIT IN SENSU.

EVERY day, every week, every month, every quarter, the most widely read journals seem just now to vie with each other in telling us that the time for religion is past, that faith is a hallucination or an infantine disease, that the gods have at last been found out and exploded, that there is no possible knowledge except what comes to us through our senses, that we must be satisfied with facts and finite things, and strike out such words as infinite, supernatural, or divine from the dictionary of the future.

It is not my object in these lectures either to defend or to attack any form of religion: there is no lack of hands for either the one or the other task. My own work, as I have traced it out for myself, and as it seemed to be traced out for me by the spirit of the founder of these lectures, is totally different. It is historical and psychological. Let theologians, be they Brâhma*n*as or *S*rama*n*as, Mobeds or Mollahs, Rabbis or Doctors of Divinity, try to determine whether any given religion be perfect or imperfect, true or false; what we want to know is, how religion is possible; how human beings, such as we are, came to have any religion at all; what religion is, and how it came to be what it is.

When we are engaged in the science of language, our first object is, not to find out whether one language is more perfect than another, whether one contains more anomalous nouns or miraculous verbs than another. We do not start with a conviction that in the beginning there was one language only, or that there is at present, or that there will be in the future, one only that deserves to be called a language. No: we simply collect facts, classify them, try to understand them, and thus hope to discover more and more the real antecedents of all language, the laws which govern the growth and decay of human speech, and the goal to which all language tends.

It is the same with the science of religion. Each of us may have his own feeling as to his own mother-tongue, or his own mother-religion ; but as historians we must allow the same treatment to all. We have simply to collect all the evidence that can be found on the history of religion all over the world, to sift and classify it, and thus to try to discover the necessary antecedents of all faith, the laws which govern the growth and decay of human religion, and the god to which all religion tends. Whether there ever can be one perfect universal religion, is a question as difficult to answer as whether there ever can be one perfect universal language. If we can only learn that even the most imperfect religion, like the most imperfect language, is something beyond all conception wonderful, we shall have learnt a lesson which is worth many a lesson in the various schools of theology.

It is a very old saying, that we never know a thing unless we know its beginnings. We may know a great deal about religion, we may have read many of the sacred books, the creeds, the catechisms, and liturgies of the world, and yet religion itself may be something entirely beyond our grasp, unless we are able to trace it back to the deepest sources from whence it springs.

In doing this, in trying to discover the living and natural springs of religion, we must take nothing for granted, except what is granted us by all philosophers, whether positive or negative. I explained in my first lecture how I was quite prepared to accept their terms, and I mean to keep to these terms to the very end of my course. We were told that all knowledge, in order to be knowledge, must pass through two gates and two gates only; the gate of the senses and the gate of reason. Religious knowledge also, whether true or false, must have passed through these two gates. At these two gates, therefore, we take our stand. Whatever claims to have entered in by any other gate, whether that gate be called primeval revelation or religious instinct, must be rejected as contraband of thought; and whatever claims to have entered by the gate of reason, without having first passed through the gate of the senses, must equally be rejected, as without sufficient warrant, or ordered at least to go back to the first gate, in order to produce there its full credentials.

Having accepted these conditions, I made it the chief object of my lectures to lay hold of religious ideas on their passing for the first time through the gates of our senses; or, in other words, I tried to find out what were the sensuous and material beginnings of those ideas which constitute the principal elements of religious thought.

I endeavored to show, first of all, that the idea of the infinite, which is at the root of all religious thought, is not simply evolved by reason out of nothing, but supplied, to us, in its original form, by our senses. If the idea of the infinite had no sensuous percept to rely on, we should, according to the terms of our agreement, have to reject it. It would not be enough to say with Sir W. Hamilton, that the idea of the infinite is a logical necessity; that we are so made that wherever we place the boundary of space or time, we are conscious of space and time beyond. I do not deny that there is truth in all this, but I feel bound to admit that our opponents are not obliged to accept such reasoning.

I therefore tried to show that beyond, behind, beneath and within the finite, the infinite is always present to our senses. It presses upon us, it grows upon us from every side. What we call finite in space and time, in form and word, is nothing but a veil or a net which we ourselves have thrown over the infinite. The finite by itself, without the infinite, is simply inconceivable; as inconceivable as the infinite without the finite. As reason deals with the finite materials, supplied to us by our senses, faith, or whatever else we like to call it, deals with the infinite that underlies the finite. What we call sense, reason, and faith, are three functions of one and the same perceptive self; but without sense both reason and faith are impossible, at least to human beings like ourselves.

The history of the ancient religion of India, so far as we have hitherto been able to trace it, is to us a history of the various attempts at naming the infinite that hides itself behind the veil of the finite. We saw how the ancient Aryans of India, the poets of the Veda, first faced the invisible, the unknown, or the infinite in trees, mountains, and rivers; in the dawn and the sun; in the fire, the storm-wind, and the thunder; how they ascribed to all of them a self, a substance, a divine support, or whatever else we like to call it; and how, in doing so, they always felt the presence of something which they could not see behind what they could see, of something supernatural behind the natural, of something super-finite or infinite behind or within the finite. The names which they gave, the *nomina*, may have been wrong: but the search itself after the *numina* was legitimate. At all events, we saw how that search led the ancient Aryans as far as it has led most amongst ourselves, viz., to the recognition of a Father which is in heaven.

Nay, we shall see that it led them farther still. The idea that God is *not* a father, then, *like* a father, and lastly a father, appears in the Veda at a very early time. In the very first hymn of the Rig-Veda, which is addressed to Agni, we read: "Be kind to us, as a father to his son." The same idea occurs again and again in the Vedic hymns. Thus we read, Rig-Veda I. 104, 9, "Hear us, Indra, like a father!" In III. 49, 3, the poet says that Indra gives food, bears our call, and is kind to us, like a father. In VII. 54, 2, Indra is asked to be kind, as a father to his sons. Again, Rig-Veda VIII. 21, 14, we read: "When thou thunderest and gatherest the clouds, then thou art called like a father." Rig-Veda X. 33, 3, "As mice eat their tails, sorrows eat me up, me thy worshiper, all-powerful god! For once, O mighty Indra, be gracious to us! Be to us like a father!" Rig-Veda X. 69, 10, "Thou borest him as a father bears his son in his lap." Rig-Veda III. 53, 2, "As a son lays hold of his father by his skirt, I lay hold of thee by this sweetest song." In fact, there are few nations who do not apply to their god or gods the name of Father.

But though it was a comfort to the early Aryans in the childhood of their faith, as it is to us in the faith of our childhood, to call God father, they soon perceived that this too was a human name, and that, like all human names, it said but little, compared with what it was meant to say. We may envy our ancient forefathers, as we envy a child that lives and dies full of faith that he is going from one home to another home, from one father to another father. But as every child grows up to learn that his father is but a child, the son of another father; as many a child, on becoming a man, has to surrender one idea after another that seemed to form the very essence of father, so the ancients learnt, and we all of us have to learn it, that we must take out of that word father one predicate after another, all in fact that is conceivable in it, if we wish to apply it still to God. So far as the word is applicable to man, it is inapplicable to God; so far as it is applicable to God, it is inapplicable to man. "Call no man your father upon the earth: for one is your Father, which is in heaven." Matt. xxiii. 9. Comparison, as it began, so it often ends with negation. *Father* is, no doubt, a better name than fire, or the storm-wind, or the heaven, or the Lord, or any other name which man has tried to give to the infinite, that infinite of which he felt the presence everywhere. But father too is but a weak human name, the best, it may be, which the poets of the Veda could find, but yet as far from him whom they were feeling after as the east is from the west.

Having watched the searchings of the ancient Aryans after the infinite in every part of nature, and having tried to understand the names which they gave to it, beginning with trees and rivers and mountains, and ending with their Heaven-father, we have now to consider the origin of some other ideas which, at first, might seem completely beyond the reach of our senses, but which nevertheless can be shown to have had their deepest roots and their true beginnings in that finite or natural world which, it is difficult to say why, we are so apt to despise, while it has been everywhere and is still the only royal road that leads us on from the finite to the infinite, from the natural to the supernatural, from nature to nature's God.

THEOGONY OF THE VEDA.

By imagining ourselves placed suddenly in the midst of this marvelous world, we try to find out what would be the objects most likely to have started, to have fascinated, to have awed our earliest forefathers; what would have roused and awakened them from mere staring and solid wonderment, and have set them for the first time musing, pondering, and thinking on the visions floating past their eyes. And having done that, we tried to verify our anticipations by comparing notes with the poets of the Veda, in whose songs the most ancient records of religious thought are preserved to us, at least so far as that branch of humanity is concerned to which we ourselves belong. No doubt, between the first daybreak of human thought and the first hymns of praise, composed in the most perfect metre and the most polished language, there may be, nay there must be, a gap that can only be measured by generations, by hundreds, aye by thousands of years. Yet such is the continuity of human thought, if once controlled by human language, that, on carefully examining the Vedic hymns, we found most of our anticipations realized, far beyond what we had any right to expect. The very objects which we had singled out as most likely to impress the mind with the sense that they were something more than what could be seen, or heard, or felt in them, had really served, if we might trust the Veda, as "the windows through which the ancient Aryans first looked into infinitude.

THE INFINITE IN ITS EARLIEST CONCEPTION.

When I say infinitude, do not let us take the infinite in its quantitative sense only, as the infinitely small or the infinitely great. Though this is perhaps the most general concept of the infinite, yet it is at the same time the poorest and emptiest. To the ancient Aryans the aspect of the infinite varied with the aspect of each finite object of which it, the infinite, was the ever present background or complement. The more there was of the visible or audible or tangible or finite, the less there was of the invisible, the inaudible, the intangible, or the infinite in the consciousness of man. As the reach of the senses varied, so varied the suspicion of what might be beyond their reach.

The concept, for instance, of a river or a mountain would require far less of invisible background than the concept of the dawn or the storm-wind. The dawn approaches every morning, but what it is, and whence it comes, no one can tell. "The wind bloweth where it listeth, and thou hearest the sound thereof, but canst not tell whence it cometh and whither it goeth." It was easy to understand the ravages caused by the inundation of a river or by the fall of a mountain; it was more difficult to understand what causes the trees to bend before the approach of a hurricane, and who it is that, during a dark thunder-storm, breaks asunder the mountains and overthrows the stables and huts.

The so-called semi-deities, therefore, which always remained to a great extent within the reach of the senses, seldom assumed that dramatic character which distinguishes other deities; and among those deities, again, those who were entirely invisible, and had nothing in nature to represent them, such as Indra, the rainer, Rudra, the howler, the Maruts, the pounders or storm-gods, even Varu*n*a, the all-embracer, would soon assume a far more personal and mythological aspect than the bright sky, the dawn, or the sun. Again, what constitutes the infinite or supernatural character of all these beings, would at once be clothed in a simply human form. They would not be called infinite, but rather inconquerable, imperishable, undecaying, immortal, unborn, present everywhere, knowing everything, achieving everything, and at the very last only should we expect for them names of so abstract a nature as infinite.

I say, we should expect this, but I must say at the same time that this expecting attitude is often very dangerous. In exploring new strata of thought, it is always best to expect nothing, but simply to collect facts, to accept what we find, and to try to digest it.

ADITI, THE INFINITE.

You will be surprised, for instance, as I certainly was surprised when the fact first presented itself to me, that there really is a deity in the Veda who is simply called the boundless or the infinite, in Sanskrit *A-diti.*

Aditi is derived from *diti*, and the negative particle *a.* Diti, again, is regularly derived from a root DÂ (dyati), to bind, from which *dita*, the participle, meaning bound, and *diti*, a substantive, meaning binding and bond. *Aditi*, therefore, must originally have meant without bonds, not chained or inclosed, boundless, infinite, infinitude. The same root shows itself in Greek δέω, I bind, διάδημα, a diadem, that is bound round the head. The substantive *diti* would in Greek be represented by δέσις, *a-diti* by ά-δεσις.

It is easy to say that a deity, having such a name as *Aditi*, the infinite, must be of late origin. It is much wiser to try to learn what is, than to imagine what must be. Because the purely abstract concept of the infinite seemed modern, several of our most learned Vedic students have at once put down *Aditi* as a late abstraction, as being invented simply to account for the name of her sons, the well-known Âdityas, or solar deities. From the fact that there are no hymns entirely addressed to her, they have concluded that Aditi, as a goddess, came in at the very last moments of Vedic poetry.

The same might be said of Dyaus, a name corresponding with the Greek Ζεύς. He occurs even less frequently than Aditi amongst the deities to whom long hymns are addressed in the Veda. But so far from being a modern invention, we know now that he existed before a word of Sanskrit was spoken in India, or a word of Greek in Greece; that he is in fact one of the oldest Aryan deities, who at a later time was crowded out, if I may use that expression, by Indra, Rudra, Agni and other purely Indian gods.

ADITI NOT A MODERN DEITY.

The same, I believe, is the case with Aditi. Her name occurs in invocations together with Dyaus, the sky, P*ri*thvî, the earth, Sindhu, the rivers, and other really primitive deities; and far from being a purely hypothetical mother of the Âdityas, she is represented as the mother of all the gods.

In order to understand this, we must try to find out what her own birthplace was, what could have suggested the name of Aditi, the boundless, the infinite, and what was the visible portion in nature to which that name was originally attached.

NATURAL ORIGIN OF ADITI.

I believe that there can be little doubt that Aditi, the boundless, was one of the oldest names of the dawn, or, more correctly, of that portion of the sky from whence every morning the light and life of the world flashed forth.

Look at the dawn, and forget for a moment your astronomy; and I ask you whether, when the dark veil of the night is slowly lifted, and the air becomes transparent and alive, and light streams forth, you know not whence, you would not feel that your eye, stretching as far as it can stretch, and yet stretching in vain, was looking into the very eye of the infinite? To the ancient seers the dawn seemed to open the golden gates of another world, and while these gates were open for the sun to pass in triumph, their eyes and their mind strove in their childish way to pierce beyond the limits of this finite world. The dawn came and went, but there remained always behind the dawn that heaving sea of light or fire from which she springs. Was not this the visible infinite? And what better name could be given than that which the Vedic poets gave to it, Aditi, the boundless, the yonder, the beyond all and everything?

Thus, I believe, we can understand how a deity, which at first seemed to us so abstract as to have no birthplace anywhere in nature, so modern that we could hardly believe in its occurrence in the Veda, may have been one of the earliest intuitions and creations of the Hindu mind.[1] In later times the boundless Aditi may have become identified with the sky, also with the earth, but originally she was far beyond the sky and the earth.

Thus we read in a hymn[2] addressed to Mitra and Varu*n*a, representatives of day and night, "O Mitra and Varu*n*a, you mount your chariot which, at the dawning of the dawn, is golden-colored and has iron poles at the setting of the sun:[3] from thence you see Aditi and Diti"— that is, what is yonder and what is here, what is infinite and what is finite, what is mortal and what is immortal.[4]

Another poet speaks of the dawn as the face of Aditi,[5] thus indicating that Aditi is here not the dawn itself, but something beyond the dawn.

As the sun and all the solar deities rise from the east, we can well understand how Aditi came to be

[1] I have treated fully of Aditi in the Rig-Veda, in my translation of the Rig-Veda Sanhitâ, vol. i. pp. 230–251. There is an excellent essay by Dr. Alfred Hillebrandt, *Über die Göttin Aditi*, 1876. He (p. 11) derives the word from dâ, "to bind," but prefers to explain Aditi by imperishableness, and guards against the idea that Aditi could mean omnipresent.

[2] Rig-Veda, V. 62, 8.

[3] The contrast between the light of the morning and the evening seems expressed by the color of the two metals, gold and iron.

[4] Rig-Veda, I. 35, 2.

[5] Ibid. I. 113, 19, áditer ánîkam.

called the mother of the bright gods, and more particularly of Mitra and Varu*n*a (Rig-Veda, X. 36, 3), of Aryaman and Bhaga, and at last of the seven, or even eight so-called Âdityas, that is, the solar deities, rising from the east. Sûrya, the sun, is called not only Âditya (Rig-Veda, VIII. 101, 11, ba*t* mahân asi sûrya, ba*t* âditya mahân asi, "Truly, Sûrya, thou art great; truly, Âditya, thou art great"); but also Âditeya (Rig-Veda, X. 88, 11).

It was, no doubt, the frequent mention of these her sons that gave to Aditi almost from the beginning a decidedly feminine character. She is the mother, with powerful, terrible, with royal sons. But there are passages where Aditi seems to be conceived as a male deity, or anyhow as a sexless being.

Though Aditi is more closely connected with the dawn, yet she is soon invoked, not only in the morning, but likewise at noon, and in the evening.[1] When we read in the Atharva-Veda, X. 8, 16: "That whence the sun rises, and that where he sets, that I believe is the oldest, and no one goes beyond," we might almost translate "the oldest" by Aditi. Aditi soon receives her full share of veneration and worship, and she is implored, not only to drive away darkness and the enemies that lurk in the dark, but likewise to deliver man from any sin which he may have committed.

DARKNESS AND SIN.

These two ideas — darkness and sin — which seem to us far apart, are closely connected with each other in the minds of the early Aryans. I shall read you some extracts to show how often one idea, the fear of enemies, evokes the other, the fear of sin, or what

[1] Rig-Veda, V. 69, 3.

we should call our worst enemy. "O Âdityas,[1] deliver us from the mouth of the wolves, like a bound thief, O Aditi!" "May Aditi[2] by day protect our cattle, may she, who never deceives, protect by night; may she, with steady increase, protect us from evil." (A*m*hasa*h*, literally, from anxiety, from choking produced by the consciousness of sin.) "And may she, the wise Aditi, come with help to us by day! may she kindly bring happiness, and drive away all enemies!"

Or again:[3] "Aditi, Mitra, and also Varu*n*a, forgive, if we have committed any sin against you! May I obtain the wide fearless light, O Indra! May not the long darkness come over us!" "May Aditi grant us sinlessness!"[4]

One other idea seems very naturally to have sprung up from the concept of Aditi. Wherever we go, we find that one of the earliest imaginings of a future life arose from the contemplation of the daily coming and going of the sun and other heavenly bodies.[5] As we still say, "his sun has set," they said and believed that those who departed this life would go to the west, to the setting of the sun. The sun was supposed to be born in the morning and to die in the evening; or, if a longer life was given to him, it was the short life of one year. At the end of that the sun died, as we still say, the old year dies.

IMMORTALITY.

But by the side of this conception another would spring up. As light and life come from the east, the

[1] Rig-Veda, VIII. 67, 14.
[2] Ibid. VIII. 18, 6, 7.
[3] Ibid. II. 27, 14.
[4] Ibid. I. 162, 22.
[5] H. Spencer, *Sociology*, i. p. 221.

east, among many of the nations of antiquity, was looked upon as the abode of the bright gods, the eternal home of the immortals; and when the idea had once arisen that the departed or blessed among men joined the company of the gods, then they also might be transferred to the east.

In some such sense we see that Aditi is called "the birthplace of the immortals;" and in a similar sense one of the Vedic poets sings:[1] "Who will give us back to the great Aditi; that I may see father and mother?" Is not this a beautiful intimation of immortality, simple and perfectly natural; and if you look back to the steps which led to it, suggested by the ordinary events of every-day life, interpreted by the unassisted wisdom of the human heart?

Here is the great lesson which the Veda teaches us! All our thoughts, even the apparently most abstract, have their natural beginnings in what passes daily before our senses. *Nihil in fide nisi quod ante fuerit in sensu.* Man may for a time be unheedful of these voices of nature; but they come again and again, day after day, night after night, till at last they are heeded. And if once heeded, those voices disclose their purport more and more clearly, and what seemed at first a mere sunrise, becomes in the end a visible revelation of the infinite, while the setting of the sun is transfigured into the first vision of immortality.

OTHER RELIGIOUS IDEAS IN THE VEDA.

Let us examine one more of those ideas which to us seem too abstract and too artificial to be ascribed to a very early stratum of human thought, but which,

[1] Rig-Veda, I. 24, 1.

if we may judge from the Veda, had risen in the human heart at the very first burst of its intellectual spring-tide. I do not mean to make the Veda more primitive than it is. I know full well the interminable vista of its antecedents. There is ring within ring in the old tree, till we can count no longer, and are lost in amazement at the long, slow growth of human thought. But by the side of much that sounds recent, there is much that sounds ancient and primitive. And here we ought, I think, to learn a lesson from archæology, and not try to lay down from the beginning a succession of sharply divided periods of thought. For a long time archæologists taught that there was first a period of stone, during which no weapons, no tools of bronze or iron, could possibly occur. That period was supposed to be followed by the bronze period, where the graves might yield both bronze and stone implements in abundance, but not a single trace of iron. Lastly, we were told, came the third period, clearly marked by the prevalence of iron instruments, which, when they had once been introduced, soon superseded both stone and bronze workmanship altogether.

This theory of the three periods, with their smaller subdivisions, contained no doubt some truth, but being accepted as a kind of archæological dogma, it impeded for a long time, like all dogma, the progress of independent observation; till at last it was discovered that much in the successive or contemporaneous use of the metals depended on local conditions, and that where mineral or palustric or meteoric iron existed in an easily accessible form, iron implements might be found and were found together with stone weapons, and previous to bronze workmanship.

This ought to be a warning to us against our preconceived theories as to the succession of intellectual periods. There are in the Veda thoughts as rude and crude as any paleolithic weapons, but by the side of them, we find thoughts with all the sharpness of iron and all the brilliancy of bronze. Are we to say that the bright and brilliant thoughts must be more modern than the rudely chipped flints that lie by their side? They may be, but let us remember who the workman is, and that there has been genius at all times, and that genius is not bound by years. To a man who has faith in himself and in the world around him, one glance is as good as a thousand observations; to a true philosopher, the phenomena of nature, the names given to them, the gods who represent them, all vanish by one thought like the mist of the morning, and he declares in the poetical language of the Veda, "There is but One, though the poets call it by many names," *Ekam sat viprâ bahudhâ vadanti.*

No doubt, we may say, the many names of the poets must have come first, before the philosophers could discard them. True, but the poets may have continued for ages invoking Indra, Mitra, Varuna, or Agni, while at the same time the philosophers of India protested, as Herakleitos protested and protested in vain, against the many names and the many temples and the many legends of the gods.

THE IDEA OF LAW.

It has often been said that if there is an idea which we look for in vain among savage or primitive people, it is the idea of law. It would be difficult to find, even in Greek and Latin, a true rendering of "the reign of law" once chosen as the title of an important book by the Duke of Argyll. And yet that idea, in its first half-conscious form, is as old as almost anything in the Veda. Much has been written of late of unconscious cerebration, and most exaggerated accounts have been given of it. Yet there is a great deal of mental work going on, which we may call unconscious, viz., all mental work that has not yet found expression in language. The senses go on receiving thousands of impressions, most of which pass unheeded, and seem wiped out forever from the tablets of our memory. But nothing is ever really wiped out, the very law of the conservation of force forbids it. Each impress leaves its mark, and by frequent repetition these marks accumulate until, from faint dots, they grow into sharp lines, and in the end determine the whole surface, the light, and shade, aye the general character, of our mental landscape.

Thus we can understand that while the great, and at first overpowering phenomena of nature were exciting awe, terror, admiration, and joy in the human mind, there grew up by the daily recurrence of the same sights, by the unerring return of day and night, by the weekly changes of the waning and increasing moon, by the succession of the seasons, and by the rhythmic dances of the stars, a feeling of relief, of rest, of security — a mere feeling at first, as difficult to express as it is still to express in French or Italian "our feeling at home," a kind of unconscious cerebration, if you like, but capable of being raised into a concept, as soon as the manifold perceptions which made up that feeling could be comprehended, and being comprehended could be expressed in conscious language.

This feeling has found expression in various ways among the early philosophers of Greece and Rome. What did Herakleitos[1] mean when he said, "The sun or Helios will not overstep the bounds" (τὰ μέτρα), *i. e.*, the path measured out for him; and what if he said the Erinys, the helpers of right, would find him out if he did? Nothing can show more clearly that he had recognized a law, pervading all the works of nature, a law which even Helios, be he the sun or a solar deity, must obey. This idea proved most fertile in Greek philosophy; as for religion, I believe we can trace in it the first germ of the Greek moira or fate.

Though we cannot expect to meet with any very ancient and original thoughts among the philosophers of Rome, yet I may quote here a well-known saying of Cicero's, containing a very true application of the thought indicated by Herakleitos: Cicero says[2] that men were intended, not only to contemplate the order of the heavenly bodies, but to imitate it in the order and constancy of their lives; exactly what, as we shall see, the poets of the Veda tried to express in their own simple language.

Let us ask now again, as we did when looking for the first germs of the concept of the infinite, what could have been the birthplace of the idea of order, measure, or law in nature? What was its first name, its first conscious expression?

I believe it was the Sanskrit *Ri*ta, a word which sounds like a deep key-note through all the chords of the religious poetry of India, though it has hardly

[1] *Heracliti Reliquiae*, xxix.

[2] *De Senectute*, xxi. "Sed credo deos immortales sparsisse animos in corpora humana ut essent qui terras tuerentur, quique coelestium ordinem contemplantes imitarentur cum vitae ordine et constantia."

ever been mentioned by writers on the ancient religion of the Brahmans.[1]

THE SANSKRIT *RITA*.

Nearly all the gods have epithets applied to them, which are derived from this *Ri*ta, and which are meant to convey the two ideas, first, that the gods founded the order of nature, and that nature obeys their commands; secondly, that there is a moral law which man must obey, and for the transgression of which he is punished by the gods. Such epithets are far more important, as giving us an insight into the religion of ancient India, than the mere names of the gods, and their relation to certain phenomena in nature; but their accurate understanding is beset with many difficulties.

The primary, secondary, and tertiary meanings of such words as *Ri*ta occur sometimes in one and the same hymn; the poet himself may not always have distinguished very clearly between them; and few interpreters would venture to do for him what he has not done for himself. When *we* speak of law, do we always make it quite clear to ourselves what we mean by it? And can we expect that ancient poets should have been more accurate speakers and thinkers than modern philosophers?

No doubt, in most places where *Ri*ta occurs, a vague and general rendering of it, such as law, order, sacred custom, sacrifice, may pass unchallenged; but if we look at any of the translations of the Vedic hymns, and ask ourselves what definite meaning we can connect with these high-sounding words, we shall

[1] Ludwig, *Anschauungen des Veda*, p. 15, has given the best account of *Ri*ta.

often feel tempted to shut up the book in despair. If Agni, the god of fire, or some other solar deity is called "the first-born of divine truth," what possible idea can such a translation convey? Fortunately, there is a sufficient number of passages left in which *Ri*ta occurs, and which enable us to watch the gradual growth of the word and its meanings.

Much, no doubt, in the reconstruction of such ancient buildings must of necessity be conjectured, and I offer my own ideas as to the original foundation of the word *Ri*ta and the superstructures of later periods, as no more than a guess and a first attempt.

THE ORIGINAL MEANING OF *RI*TA.

*Ri*ta, I believe, was used originally to express the settled movement of the sun, and of all the heavenly bodies. It is a participle of the verb *Ri*, which may convey the sense either of joined, fitted, fixed; or of gone, the going, the path followed in going. I myself prefer the second derivation, and I recognize the same root in another word, Nir-*ri*ti, literally going away, then decay, destruction, death, also the place of destruction, the abyss, and in later times (like An*ri*ta), the mother of Naraka, or hell.

The going, the procession, the great daily movement, or the path followed every day by the sun from his rising to his setting, followed also by the dawn, by day and night, and their various representatives, a path which the powers of night and darkness could never impede, would soon be regarded as the right movement, the good work, the straight path.[1]

It was not, however, so much the daily movement,

[1] Rig-Veda, VII. 40, 4.

or the path which it followed, as the original direction which determined it, the settled point from which it started and to which it returned, that became most prominent in the thoughts of the Vedic poets when speaking of *Ri*ta. Hence they speak of the path of *Ri*ta, which we can only translate by the right path; but which to them was the path determined by that unknown power which they had tried to grasp by the name of *Ri*ta.

If you remember how Aditi, the boundless, was at first meant for the east, which every morning seemed to reveal an endless distance beyond the sky from which the sun arose for his daily course, you will not be surprised to find that the *Ri*ta, the place or the power which determines the path of the sun, should occasionally in the Veda take the place of Aditi. As the dawn was called the face of Aditi, we find that the sun is called the bright face of *Ri*ta;[1] nay, we find invocations in which the great *Ri*ta[2] occupies a place next to Aditi, and heaven and earth. The abode of *Ri*ta is evidently the east,[3] where, according to a very ancient legend, the light-bringing gods are supposed every morning to break open the dark cave, the hiding-place of the robber, and to bring forth the cows,[4] that is to say, the days, each day being conceived as a cow, walking slowly from the dark stable across the bright pasture-ground of the earth and the sky. When that imagery is changed, and the sun is supposed to yoke his horses in the morning and to run his daily course across the world, then *Ri*ta is called the place where they unharness

[1] Rig-Veda, VI. 51, 1. [2] Ibid. X. 66, 4. [3] Ibid. X. 68, 4.

[4] Sometimes these cows seem to be meant also for the clouds carried off from the visible sky to the dark abyss beyond the horizon.

his horses.[1] Sometimes it is said that the dawns dwell in the abyss of *Ri*ta,[2] and many stories are told, how either the dawns were recovered, or how the dawn herself assisted Indra and the other gods in recovering the stolen cattle, or the stolen treasure, hidden in the dark stable of the night.

STORY OF SARAMÂ.

One of the best known stories was that of Indra, who first sent Saramâ, the peep of day, to find out where the cows were hidden. When Saramâ had heard the lowing of the cows, she returned to tell Indra, who then gave battle to the robbers, and brought forth the bright cows. This Saramâ was afterwards represented as the dog of Indra, and the metronymic name given to her sons, Sârameya, having by Professor Kuhn been identified with Hermeias, or Hermes, was one of the first indications to point out to comparative mythologists the right path (the panthâ *ri*tasya) into the dark chambers of ancient Aryan mythology. Well, this Saramâ, this old pointer of the dawn, is said to have found the cows, "by going on the path of *Ri*ta, the right path, or by going to the *Ri*ta, the right place."[3] One poet says: "When Saramâ found the cleft of the rock, she made the old great path to lead to one point. She, the quick-footed, led the way; knowing the noise of the imperishable (cows or days), she went first towards them" (Rig-Veda, III. 31, 6).

In the preceding verse, the very path which was followed by the gods and their companions, the old poets, in their attempts to recover the cows, *i. e.*, day-

[1] Rig-Veda, V. 62, 1. [2] Ibid. III. 61, 7.

[3] Ibid. V. 45, 7, ritám yatī́ sarámâ gấ avindat; V. 45, 8.

light, is called the path of the *Rita*; but in another place it is said that Indra and his friends tore Vala, the robber or his cave, to pieces, after finding out the *Rita*, the right place.[1]

That right, immovable, eternal place is likewise mentioned when a ποῦ στῶ is looked for from which the gods could have firmly established both heaven and earth. Thus Varu*n*a is introduced as saying, "I supported the sky in the seat of *Rita*;"[2] and later on, *Rita*, like Satya, the true, is conceived as the eternal foundation of all that exists.

The path of *Rita* occurs again and again as followed by the dawn, or the sun, or day and night, and the only way in which we can generally translate it is the path of right, or the right path.

Thus we read of the dawn:[3] —

"She follows the path of *Rita*, the right path; as if she knew them before, she never oversteps the regions."

"The dawn,[4] who is born in the sky, dawned forth on the right path; she came near, revealing her greatness. She drove away the evil spirits, and the unkindly darkness."

Of the sun it is said:[5] —

"The god Savit*ri* toils on the right way, the horn of the *Rita* is exalted far and wide; the *Rita* resists even those who fight well."

When the sun rises, the path of *Rita* is said to be surrounded with rays,[6] and the same thought which was uttered by Herakleitos, "Helios will not overstep the bounds," finds expression in a verse of the

[1] Rig-Veda, X. 138, 1.
[2] Ibid. IV. 42, 4.
[3] Ibid. I. 124, 3; cf. V. 80, 4.
[4] Ibid. VII. 75, 1.
[5] Ibid. VIII. 86, 5; X. 92, 4; VII. 44, 5.
[6] Ibid. I. 136, 2; I. 46, 11.

Rig-Veda: "Sûrya does not injure the appointed places."[1] This path, which is here called the path of *Ri*ta, is in other places called the broad walk,[2] gâtu; and like *Ri*ta, this gâtu also, the walk, finds sometimes a place among the ancient deities of the morning.[3] It is evidently the same path on which day and night are said to travel in turn,[4] and as that path varies from day to day, we also hear of many paths which are traveled on by the Asvinau, day and night, and similar deities.[5]

Another important feature is that this path, which is commonly called the path of *Ri*ta, is sometimes spoken of as the path which King Varu*n*a, one of the oldest Vedic gods, made for the sun to follow (I. 24, 8); for we thus begin to understand why what in some places is called the law of Varu*n*a is in others called the law of *Ri*ta;[6] how, in fact, Varu*n*a, the god of the all-embracing sky, could sometimes be supposed to have settled and determined what in other places is called the *Ri*ta, as an independent power.

When it had once been recognized that the gods overcame the powers of darkness by following the straight path or the path of right, it was but a small step for their worshipers to pray that they also might be allowed to follow that right path. Thus we read:[7] "O Indra, lead us on the path of *Ri*ta, on the right path over all evils."

Or, "May we, O Mitra and Varu*n*a, on your path

[1] Rig-Veda, III. 30, 12; cf. I. 123, 9; 124, 3. [2] Ibid. I. 136, 2.

[3] Ibid. III. 31, 15. Indra produced together the sun, the dawn, the walk, and Agni.

[4] Ibid. I. 113, 3.

[5] Ibid. VIII. 22, 7.

[6] Ibid. I. 123, 8, 9, varu*n*asya dhâma and *ri*tasya dhâma.

[7] Ibid. X. 133, 6.

of right, cross over all evils, as one crosses the waters in a ship."[1] The same gods, Mitra and Varu*n*a, are said to proclaim the praises of the great *Ri*ta.[2] Another poet says: "I follow the path of *Ri*ta well."[3] Evil-doers, on the contrary, are said never to cross the path of *Ri*ta.[4]

*RI*TA, THE SACRIFICE.

If we remember how many of the ancient sacrifices in India depended on the course of the sun, how there were daily sacrifices at the rising of the sun, at noon, and at the setting of the sun;[5] how there were offerings for the full moon and the new moon, while other sacrifices followed the three seasons, and the half-yearly or yearly progress of the sun; we may well understand how the sacrifice itself came in time to be called the path of *Ri*ta.[6]

At last *Ri*ta assumed the meaning of law in general. The rivers, which in some places are said to follow the path of *Ri*ta,[7] are spoken of in other hymns as following the *Ri*ta or law of Varu*n*a. There are many more meanings or shades of meaning conveyed by *Ri*ta, which, however, are of less importance for our purpose. I have only to add that as *Ri*ta came to express all that is right, good, and true, so An*ri*ta was used to express whatever is false, evil, and untrue.

[1] Rig-Veda, VII. 65, 3.
[2] Ibid. VIII. 25, 4; cf. I. 151, 4-6.
[3] Ibid. X. 66, 13.
[4] Ibid. IX. 73, 6.
[5] Manu, IV. 25, 26.
[6] Rig-Veda, I. 128, 2; X. 31, 2; 70, 2; 110, 2; etc.
[7] Ibid. II. 28, 4; I. 105, 12; VIII. 12, 3.

THE DEVELOPMENT OF *RITA*.

I do not know whether I have succeeded in giving you a clear idea of this *Ri*ta in the Veda, how it meant originally the firmly established movement of the world, of the sun, of morning and evening, of day and night; how the spring of that movement was localized in the far East; how its manifestation was perceived in the path of the heavenly bodies, or, as we should say, in day and night; and how that right path on which the gods brought light out of darkness became afterward the path to be followed by man, partly in his sacrifices, partly in his general moral conduct.[1] You must not expect in the development of these ancient conceptions too much accuracy and definiteness of thought. It was not there, it could not be there, and if we attempt to force those poetical imaginings into the various categories of rigorous thought, we shall only break their wings and crush out their soul: we shall have the dry bones, but no flesh, no blood, no life.

DIFFICULTY OF TRANSLATING.

The great difficulty in all discussions of this kind arises from the fact that we have to transfuse thought from ancient into modern forms. In that process some violence is inevitable. We have no word so pliant as the Vedic *Ri*ta, so full of capability, so ready to reflect new shades of thought. All we can do is to find, if possible, the original focus of thought, and then to follow the various directions taken by

[1] There is a similar development to be observed in the Hebrew yâshâr, straight, from âshar to go forward, a root which has supplied some mythical germs in Hebrew also. See Goldziher, *Mythology among the Hebrews*, p. 123.

the rays that proceeded from it. This is what I have endeavored to do, and if in so doing, I may seem to "have put a new garment upon an old," all I can say is that I see no other way, unless we all agree to speak not only Sanskrit, but Vedic Sanskrit.

A great English poet and philosopher has lately been much blamed for translating the old Hebrew belief in a personal Jehovah into a belief "in an eternal power, not ourselves, that makes for righteousness." It has been objected that it would be impossible to find in Hebrew an expression for so abstract, so modern, so purely English a thought as this. This may be true. But if the ancient poets of the Veda were to live to-day, and if they had to think modern thought and to speak modern speech, I should say that an eternal power, not ourselves, that makes for righteousness, would not be a very unlikely rendering they might feel themselves inclined to give of their ancient *Ri*ta.

WAS *RI*TA A COMMON ARYAN CONCEPT?

One more point, however, has to be settled. We have seen that in the Veda, *ri*ta belongs to one of the earliest strata of thought: the question now is, was *ri*ta a purely Vedic, or was it, like Dyaus, Zeus, Jupiter, a common Aryan concept?

It is difficult to speak confidently. There were, as we shall see, cognate ideas that found expression in Latin and German in words derived from the same root *ar*, but there is not sufficient evidence to show that, like the *Ri*ta of the Vedic poets, these words started from the conception of the daily, weekly, monthly, and annual movement of the heavenly bodies, and from nothing else.

In Sanskrit we have beside *ri*ta, the common word for seasons, *ri*tu, meaning originally the regular steps or movements of the year. In Zend *ratu* is the same word, but it means not only order, but also he who orders.[1]

It has been frequently attempted to identify the Sanskrit *ri*tu, season, and *ri*ta, settled, regular, particularly as applied to the course of the heavenly bodies and to the order of the ancient sacrifices, with the Latin *rîte*, according to religious usage, and *rîtus*, a rite, the form and manner of religious ceremonies. But *rî* in Latin never corresponds to Skt. *ri*, which is really a shortened form of *ar* or *ra*, and therefore represented in Latin by *or*, *er*, *ur*, and more rarely by *re*.

There seems, however, no difficulty in connecting the Latin *ordo* with our root *ar* or *ri*; and Benfey has shown that *ordo*, *ordinis*, would correspond to a Sanskrit form *ri*-tvan. *Ordior*, to weave, would seem to have meant originally a careful and orderly arrangement of anything, more particularly of threads.

The nearest approach to *ri*ta is to be found in the Latin *rătus*, particularly when we consider that *rătus* was originally referred in Latin also to the constant movement of the stars. Thus Cicero (Tusc. v. 24, 69) speaks of the *motus* (*stellarum*) *constantes et rati;* and again (N. D. ii. 20, 51) of the *astrorum rati immutabilesque cursus.* I incline myself to the opinion that this *rătus* in Latin is identical in origin and also in intention with Skt. *ri*ta, only that it never became developed and fixed in Latin as a religious concept, such as we saw in the Vedic *Ri*ta. But though I hold to this opinion, I do not wish to dis-

[1] Darmesteter, *Ormazd et Ahriman*, p. 12.

guise its difficulties. *Ri*ta, if it was preserved in Latin, might have been *artus*, *ertus*, *ortus*, or *urtus*, but not *ratus*, not even *rĭtus*, as it appears in *irrĭtus*, vain, *i. e.*, unsettled. I fully admit that phonetically Professor Kuhn's identification of Latin *rătus* with Sanskrit *râta* is far more regular. He derives it from *râ*, to give, and as from the root *dâ* we have in Latin *dătum* and *redditum*, so from the root *râ* we should have quite regularly *rătum* and *irritum*. The difficulty in Professor Kuhn's etymology is the meaning. *Râta* means *given*, and though it assumes the meaning of granted, assigned to, determined, and though in Zend too, dâta, law, comes from dâ (dhâ), both to give and to settle,[1] yet there is, as Corssen remarks, no trace of this having ever been the original meaning of Latin *rătum*.[2]

Nor are the phonetic difficulties in identifying Latin *ratus* with Skt. *ri*ta insurmountable. The Latin *rătis*, float, is generally connected with the Skt. root, *ar*, to row, and Latin *gracilis* with Skt. k*ri*sa. If then Latin *rătus* is the same word as the Sanskrit *ri*ta, there is every reason to suppose that it too referred originally to the regular and settled movements of the heavenly bodies, and that like *considerare*, *contemplari*, and many such words, it became afterwards despecialized. In that case it would be interesting to observe that while in Sanskrit *ri*ta, from meaning the order of the heavenly movements, became in time the name for moral order and righteousness, *rătus*, though starting from the same source,

1 Darmesteter, l. c. p. 253.

2 Kuhn ingeniously compares the superlative râtatamâ brahmâ*n*i with the beneficia ratissima et gratissima, in Festus, ed. Lindemann, p. 236.

lent itself in Latin and German to express intellectual order and reasonableness. For from the same root and closely connected with *ratus* (*pro ratâ*) we have the Latin *ratio*, settling, counting, adding and subtracting, reason, and Gothic *rathjo*, number, *rathjan*, to number; Old High German, *radja*, speech, and *redjon*, to speak.[1]

RITA IS ASHA IN ZEND.

But though we look in vain among the other Aryan languages for anything exactly corresponding to the Vedic *ri*ta, and cannot therefore claim for it, as in the case of Dyaus and Zeus, an antiquity exceeding the first separation of the Aryan races, we can show that both the word and the concept existed before the Iranians, whose religion is known to us in the Zend-avesta, became finally separated from the Indians, whose sacred hymns are preserved to us in the Veda. It has long been known that these two branches of Aryan speech, which extended in a southeasterly direction, must have remained together for a long time after they had separated from all the other branches, which took a northwesterly course. They share words and thoughts in common to which we find nothing analogous anywhere else. Particularly in their religion and ceremonial, there are terms which may be called technical, and which nevertheless are to be found both in Sanskrit and in Zend. The word which in Zend corresponds to Sanskrit *ri*ta is asha. Phonetically asha may seem far removed from *ri*ta, but *ri*ta is properly arta, and

[1] For further derivatives see Corssen, *Aussprache des Lateinischen*, i. p. 477.

the transition of Sanskrit *rt* into Zend *sh* is possible.[1] Hitherto asha in Zend has been translated by purity, and the modern Parsis always accept it in that sense. But this is a secondary development of the word, as has lately been shown by a very able French scholar, M. Darmesteter;[2] and by assigning to it the meaning which *ri*ta has in the Veda, many passages in the Avesta receive for the first time their proper character. It cannot be denied, that in the Avesta,[3] as in the Veda, asha may often be translated by purity, and that it is most frequently used in reference to the proper performance of the sacrifices. Here the Asha consists in what is called "good thoughts, good words, good deeds," good meaning ceremonially good or correct, without a false pronunciation, without a mistake in the sacrifice. But there are passages which show that Zoroaster also recognized the existence of a kosmos, or *ri*ta. He also tells how the mornings go, and the noon, and the nights; and how they follow a law that has been traced for them; he too admires the perfect friendship between the sun and the moon, and the harmonies of living nature, the miracles of every birth, and how at the right

1 The identity of arta (rita) and asha was first pointed out by de Lagarde (*Gesammelte Abhandlungen*, p. 152), and by Oppert (*Inscriptions des Achémenides*, p. 105). It was accepted by Haug (*Das* 18 *Capitel des Vendidad, Sitzungsberichte der Kgl. Bayer. Akad. der Wissenschaften*, 1868, p. 526), and supported by Hübschmann (*Ein Zoroastrisches Lied*, p. 76). Thus Skt. martya = Zend mashya; Skt. pritanâ = Zend peshanâ; Skt. bhartar = Zend bâshar; Skt. mrita = Zend mesha; Zend peretu = Zend peshu. Spiegel (*Arische Studien*, p. 33) challenges some of these identifications, and explains them differently. Still he too admits the possible interchange of Skt. *rt* and Zend *sh*. See Pischel, *Gött. gel. Anzeigen*, 1877, p. 1554.

2 *Ormazd et Ahriman, leurs origines et leur histoire*, par James Darmesteter, Paris, 1877.

3 Darmesteter, l. c. p. 14.

time there is food for the mother to give to her child. As in the Veda, so in the Avesta, the universe follows the Asha, the worlds are the creation of Asha. The faithful, while on earth, pray for the maintenance of Asha, while after death they will join Ormazd in the highest heaven, the abode of Asha. The pious worshiper protects the Asha, the world grows and prospers by Asha. The highest law of the world is Asha, and the highest ideal of the believer is to become an Ashavan, possessed of Asha, *i. e.*, righteous.

This will suffice to show that a belief in a cosmic order existed before the Indians and Iranians separated, that it formed part of their ancient, common religion, and was older therefore than the oldest Gâthâ of the Avesta, and the oldest hymn of the Veda. It was not the result of later speculation, it did not come in only after the belief in the different gods and their more or less despotic government of the world had been used up. No, it was an intuition which underlay and pervaded the most ancient religion of the Southern Aryans, and for a true appreciation of their religion it is far more important than all the stories of the dawn, of Agni, Indra, and Rudra.

Think only what it was to believe in a *Ri*ta, in an order of the world, though it be no more at first than a belief that the sun will never overstep his bounds. It was all the difference between a chaos and a kosmos, between the blind play of chance and an intelligible and therefore an intelligent providence. How many souls, even now, when everything else has failed them, when they have parted with the most cherished convictions of their childhood, when their faith in man has been poisoned, and when the apparent triumph of all that is selfish, ignoble, and hideous has made them throw up the cause of truth, of righteousness, and innocence as no longer worth fighting for, at least in this world; how many, I say, have found their last peace and comfort in a contemplation of the *Ri*ta, of the order of the world, whether manifested in the unvarying movement of the stars, or revealed in the unvarying number of the petals and stamens and pistils of the smallest forget-me-not! How many have felt that to belong to this kosmos, to this beautiful order of nature, is something at least to rest on, something to trust, something to believe, when everything else has failed! To us this perception of the *Ri*ta, of law and order in the world, may seem very little; but to the ancient dwellers on earth, who had little else to support them, it was everything: better than their bright beings, their Devas, better than Agni and Indra; because, if once perceived, if once understood, it could never be taken from them.

What we have learnt then from the Veda is this, that the ancestors of our race in India did not only believe in divine powers more or less manifest to their senses, in rivers and mountains, in the sky and the sun, in the thunder and rain, but that their senses likewise suggested to them two of the most essential elements of all religion, the concept of the infinite and the concept of order and law, as revealed before them, the one in the golden sea behind the dawn, the other in the daily path of the sun. These two percepts, which sooner or later must be taken in and minded by every human being, were at first no more than an impulse, but their impulsive force would not rest till it had beaten into the minds of the fathers of our race the deep and indelible impression that "all is right," and filled them with a hope, and more than a hope, that "all will be right."

VI.

HENOTHEISM, POLYTHEISM, MONOTHEISM, AND ATHEISM.

IS MONOTHEISM A PRIMITIVE FORM OF RELIGION?

If you consider how natural, how intelligible, how inevitable, was the origin and growth of the principal deities of the Veda, you will perhaps agree with me that the whole controversy, whether the human race began with monotheism or polytheism, hardly deserves a serious discussion, at least so far as the Indians, or even the Indo-Europeans, are concerned.[1] I doubt whether this question would ever have arisen, unless it had been handed down to us as a legacy of another theory, very prevalent during the Middle Ages, that religion began with a primeval revelation, which primeval revelation could not be conceived at all, except as a revelation of a true and perfect religion, and therefore as monotheism. That primeval monotheism was supposed to have been preserved by the Jews only, while all other nations left it and fell into polytheism and idolatry, from which, at a later time, they worked their way back again

[1] For an able *résumé* of various opinions in favor of or against a primitive monotheism, particularly of Pictet, Pfleiderer, Scherer, Réville, and Roth, see Muir, *Sanskrit Texts*, v. p. 412. I have sometimes been quoted as a supporter of the theory of an original monotheism. In what sense I hold that theory will be seen from the following remarks, particularly page 262, line 3 from bottom.

into the purer light of a religious or philosophical monotheism.

It is curious to see how long it takes before any of these purely gratuitous theories are entirely annihilated. They may have been refuted again and again, the best theologians and scholars may long have admitted that they rest on no solid foundation whatsoever, yet they crop up in places where we should least expect them, in books of reference, and, what is still worse, in popular school-books; and thus the tares are sown broadcast, and spring up everywhere, till they almost choke the wheat.

THE SCIENCE OF LANGUAGE AND THE SCIENCE OF RELIGION.

The science of language offers in this respect many points of similarity with the science of religion. Without any warrant, either from the Bible or from any other source, nay, without being able to connect any clear understanding with such a theory, many mediæval, and even modern, writers have maintained that language too owed its origin to a primeval revelation. The next step was, that this primeval language could only have been Hebrew; the next step again, that all other languages must be derived from Hebrew. It is extraordinary to see the learning and ingenuity expended in voluminous works to prove that Greek and Latin, French and English, were all derived from Hebrew. When, however, no amount of torture could force from Hebrew the confession that she was the mother of all those degenerate children, the very failure of these repeated efforts showed that it was necessary to commence a new trial by an impartial collection of all the evidence that could be brought to bear on the origin and growth of human speech. This, which we call the historical study of language, soon led to a genealogical classification of the principal languages of the world, in which Hebrew at last received its right place, by the side of other Semitic dialects; while the question of the origin of language assumed an altogether new form, viz., What is the origin of roots and radical concepts in every one of the great families of human speech? By following the example of the science of language, the students of the science of religion have arrived at very similar results. Instead of approaching the religions of the world with the preconceived idea that they are either corruptions of the Jewish religion, or descended, in common with the Jewish religion, from some perfect primeval revelation, they have seen that it is their duty first to collect all the evidence of the early history of religious thought that is still accessible in the sacred books of the world, or in the mythology, customs, and even in the languages of various races. Afterwards they have undertaken a genealogical classification of all the materials that have hitherto been collected, and they have then only approached the question of the origin of religion in a new spirit, by trying to find out how the roots of the various religions, the radical concepts which form their foundation, and, before all, the concept of the infinite, could have been developed, taking for granted nothing but sensuous perception on one side, and the world by which we are surrounded on the other.

There is another similarity between these two sciences. As it is well known that there is constant growth and development in language, connected with what is inevitable in all development, viz., a throwing off of whatever is used up and corrupt, the history of religion also has been shown to exhibit a constant growth and development, its very life consisting in a discarding of decayed elements, which is necessary in order to maintain all the better whatever is still sound and vigorous, and at the same time to admit new influences from that inexhaustible source from which all religion springs. A religion that cannot change is like a classical language, that rules supreme for a time, but is swept away violently in the end, by the undercurrent of popular dialects, by the voice of the people, which has often been called the voice of God.

Again, as no one speaks any longer of an innate language, — we hardly know what could be meant by it, — the time will come when the idea of an innate religion too will seem equally unintelligible. Man, we know now, has to conquer everything in the sweat of his face, though we likewise know that wherever he has labored honestly, the ground has not brought forth thorns and thistles only, but enough to support him, though he may be meant to eat his bread in sorrow all the days of his life.

It is easy to understand that, even if a complete grammar and dictionary had suddenly come down from heaven, they would have been useless to beings that had not themselves elaborated their percepts into concepts, and that had not themselves discovered the relation (πτῶσις) in which one concept may stand to another. They would have been a foreign language, and who can learn a foreign language, unless he has a language of his own? We may acquire new languages from without: language and what it implies must come from within. The same with religion.

Ask a missionary whether he can efficiently preach the mysteries of Christianity to people who have no idea of what religion is. All he can do is to discover the few germs of religion which exist even among the lowest savages, though hidden, it may be, beneath deep layers of rubbish; to make them grow again by tearing up the weeds that have choked them, and then to wait patiently till the soil in which alone the natural seeds of religion can grow, may become fit again to receive and to nurture the seeds of a higher religion.

THE PREDICATE OF GOD.

If we approach the study of religion in this spirit, the question whether man began with monotheism or polytheism can never present itself. When man has once arrived at a stage of thought where he can call anything, be it one or many, God, he has achieved more than half of his journey. He has found the predicate God, and he has henceforth to look for the subjects only to which that predicate is truly applicable. What we want to know is, how man first arrived at the concept of the divine, and out of what elements he framed it: afterwards only comes the question how he was able to predicate the divine of this or that, of the One or of the many. Writers on religion[1] speak of "primitive men deifying the

1 "How strong soever may have been the religious feelings of the primitive Aryans, however lively their sense of the supernatural, and however forcibly we may therefore imagine them to have been impelled to *deify* the grand natural objects by which they were surrounded and overawed, it is obvious that the physical impressions made by those objects on their senses would be yet more powerful in proportion as they were more frequent and more obtrusive; and that consequently the sky, earth, sun, etc., even though regarded as *deities*, would naturally be called by names denoting their external characteristics, rather than by other appellations descriptive of the *divine* attributes they were supposed to possess." — J. Muir, *Sanskrit Texts*, v. p. 414.

grand natural objects by which they are surrounded." They might as well speak of primitive men mummifying their dead, before they had *mûm* or wax to embalm them with.

THE NEW MATERIALS SUPPLIED BY THE VEDA.

I am not one of those who hold that the Veda offers the key to this and to all other problems of the science of religion. Nothing could be a greater mistake than to suppose that all nations went through exactly the same religious development which we find in India. On the contrary, the chief interest in these comparative studies in the field of religion consists in our being able to see in how many different ways the same goal could be and has been reached. All I maintain is, that in the Veda we see *one* stream of religious evolution, and a very important stream; and that, if we study that, without bringing to its study any preconceived opinions, the question whether the Aryans of India began with monotheism, in the usual sense of that word, seems to me to convey no meaning at all.

HENOTHEISM.

If we must have a general name for the earliest form of religion among the Vedic Indians, it can be neither *monotheism* nor *polytheism*, but only *henotheism*,[1] that is, a belief and worship of those single objects, whether semi-tangible or intangible, in which man first suspected the presence of the invisible and the infinite, each of which, as we saw, was raised into something more than finite, more than natural, more than conceivable; and thus grew in the end to be an

[1] From εἷς, ἑνός, one, as opposed to μόνος, one only.

Asura, or a living thing; a *Deva*, or a bright being; an *Amartya*, that is, not a mortal, and at last an immortal and eternal being, — in fact, a God, endowed with the highest qualities which the human intellect could conceive at the various stages of its own growth.

This phase of religious thought can nowhere be studied so well as in the Veda; in fact, we should hardly have known of its existence but for the Veda.

THE SUN IN HIS NATURAL ASPECTS.

Let us take the sun as an instance of this transition from natural objects to supernatural, and at last divine powers. The sun has many names, such as Sûrya, Savit*ri*, Mitra, Pûshan, Âditya, and others. It is interesting to watch how each of these names grows by itself into some kind of active personality; and in a study of the Vedic religion, it is most essential to keep each as much as possible distinct from the others. For our purposes, however, it is more important to see how they all branch off from a common source, and were meant originally to express one and the same object, viewed only from different points.

The ordinary descriptions of the sun, whether under his name of Sûrya, Savit*ri*, Mitra, Pûshan, or Âditya, are such that any one, with a poetic feeling for nature, would easily understand them. Sûrya, the sun, is called the son of the sky.[1] The dawn is spoken of both as his wife[2] and as his daughter;[3] and as the

[1] Rig-Veda, X. 37, 1, diva*h* putrâya sûryâya *sam*sata, sing to Sûrya, the son of Dyaus (sky).

[2] Ibid. VII. 75, 5, sûryasya yoshâ, the wife of Sûrya.

[3] Ibid. IV. 43, 2, sûryasya duhitâ, the daughter of Sûrya.

dawn is likewise a daughter of the sky,[1] she might be represented as his sister also. Indra again is sometimes represented as having given birth both to the sun and to the dawn.[2] From another point of view, however, the same dawns are said to have given birth to the sun.[3] Here is at once ample material for the growth of mythology and tragedy: but this does not concern us at present.

In the Veda, as in Greek poetry, Sûrya has a chariot, drawn by one[4] or seven horses,[5] the seven Harits, or bright horses, in which, in spite of all differences, we have to recognize the prototype of the Greek Charites. He is called the face of the gods,[6] and the eye of other more personal gods, such as Mitra, Varu*n*a, and Agni.[7] When he unharnesses his horses, the night spreads out her vesture.[8] All this is solar story, such as we find almost everywhere.

Though Sûrya or the sun is himself called prasavit*ri*,[9] the creator (not, however, in the exclusively Christian sense of the word), yet he assumes under the name of Savit*ri* a more independent and dramatic character. As Savit*ri*, he is represented as standing

1 Rig-Veda, V. 79, 8, duhitâ diva*h*, daughter of the sky.

2 Ibid. II. 12, 7, ya*h* sûryam ya*h* ushasam *g*a*g*âna, he who begat the sun, he who begat the dawn.

3 Ibid. VII. 78, 3, a*g*î*g*anan sûryam ya*g*nam agnim, they produced Sûrya (the sun), the sacrifice, the fire.

4 Ibid. VII. 63, 2, yat etasa*h* vahati.

5 Ibid. I. 115, 3, asvâ*h* harita*h* sûryasya; VII. 60, 3, ayukta sapta harita*h*.

6 Ibid. I. 115, 1, *k*itram devâ*n*âm udagât anîkam, the bright face of the gods rose.

7 Ibid. I. 115, 1, *k*akshu*h* mitrasya varu*n*asya agne*h*, the eye of Mitra, Varu*n*a, Agni.

8 Ibid. I. 115, 4, yadâ it ayukta harita*h* sadhasthât, ât râtrî vâsa*h* tanute simasmai, when he has taken the Harits (horses) from their yoke, then the night spreads out her garment over everybody.

9 Ibid. VII. 63, 2, prasavitâ *g*anâ*n*âm.

on a golden chariot,[1] with yellow hair,[2] with golden arms[3] and hands[4] and eyes,[5] nay, even with a golden tongue,[6] while his jaws are said to be of iron.[7] He puts on armor or a cloak of a brilliant tawny color,[8] and he proceeds on dustless paths.[9]

Mitra again was originally the sun, only in a new light, and therefore with a new name.[10] He is chiefly the bright and cheerful sun of the morning, or the day,[11] sun and day being often used synonymously even in modern languages, such as in yestersun for yesterday. Sometimes a poet says that Savit*ri* is Mitra,[12] or that he at least performs the same work as Mitra. This Mitra is most frequently invoked in conjunction with Varu*n*a. Both stand together on the same chariot, which is golden-colored at the rising of the dawn, and has iron poles at sunset.[13]

1 Rig-Veda, I. 35, 2, hira*n*yayena savitâ rathena.

2 Ibid. X. 139, 1, harikes*a*h.

3 Ibid. I. 35, 10, hira*n*yahasta*h*.

4 Ibid. I. 22, 5, hira*n*yapâni*h*.

5 Ibid. I. 35, 8, hira*n*yâksha*h*.

6 Ibid. VI. 71, 3, hira*n*ya*g*ihva*h*.

7 Ibid. VI. 71, 4, ayohanu*h*.

8 Ibid. IV. 53, 2, pi*s*angam drâpim prati mun*k*ate kavi*h*.

9 Ibid. I. 35, 11, panthâ*h* are*n*ava*h*.

10 Mitra, friend, stands for Mit-tra, and this, as suggested already by native grammarians, must be derived from the root *mid*, to be fat, to make fat, to make shining, to delight, to love. Similar transitions of meaning are to be found in the root snih. From mid we have meda, fat, and medin, one who gladdens, a friend, a companion: cf. Atharva-Veda, X. 1, 33, sûryena medinâ. In the same Veda, V. 20, 8, índramedin occurs in the same sense as índrasakhâ in the Rig-Veda, VII. 37, 24.

11 Atharva-Veda, XIII. 3, 13, sa varu*n*a*h* sâyam agnir bhavati sa mitro bhavati prâtar udyan, sa savitâ bhûtvântariksh*en*a yâti sa indro bhûtvâ tapati madhyato divam; cf. Rig-Veda, V. 3.

12 Rig-Veda, V. 81, 4, uta mitra*h* bhavasi deva dharmabhi*h*.

13 Ibid. V. 62, 8, hira*n*yarûpam ushasa*h* vyush*t*au, aya*h*sthû*n*am uditâ sûryasya. The contrast between hira*n*yarûpa, gold-colored in the morning, and aya*h*sthû*n*a, with iron poles in the evening, seems to indicate that aya*h*, metal, is here intended to indicate the dark iron-like color of the sunset or evening in India. In ayohanu, iron-jawed, ayas, metal or iron, expresses strength.

Again, another name for the sun is Vish*n*u. That he, too, was originally a solar being, is most clearly indicated by his three strides,[1] his position in the morning, at noon, and in the evening. But his physical character soon vanishes behind the splendor of his later divine functions.

Pûshan, on the contrary, always retains a more humble position. He was originally the sun as viewed by shepherds. His horses, if we may say so, in imitation of the Vedic poet, are goats;[2] he carries an ox-goad as his sceptre,[3] and a golden dagger (vâ*s*î).[4] His sister, or his beloved, is Sûrya,[5] the sun or dawn, conceived as a female deity; and, like other solar deities, he too sees everything.[6]

Âditya, in later times a very common name of the sun, is used in the Veda chiefly as a general epithet of a number of solar deities. I call them solar because, though Professor Roth looks upon them as purely ethical conceptions, they clearly reveal their solar antecedents, in some of the Vedic hymns. Thus Sûrya is an Âditya, Savit*ri* is an Âditya, Mitra is an Âditya; and when Âditya occurs by itself, it may often, particularly in later portions of the Rig-Veda, be translated simply by the sun.[7]

All this is intelligible, and familiar to us from other religions and mythologies.

[1] Rig-Veda, I. 22, 17; I. 154.

[2] Ibid. VI. 58, 2, a*g*â*s*va*h*.

[3] Ibid. VI. 53, 9, yâ te ash*t*râ goopa*s*â âgh*rine* pa*s*usâdhanî.

[4] Ibid. I. 42, 6, hira*n*yavâ*s*îmattama.

[5] Ibid. VI. 55, 4, svasu*h* ya*h* *g*âra*h* u*k*yate; VI. 58, 4, yam devâsa*h* adadu*h* sûryâyai.

[6] Ibid. III. 62, 9, ya*h* vi*s*vâ abhi vipa*s*yati, bhuvanâ sam *k*a pa*s*yati; cf. X. 187, 4.

[7] Ibid. I. 50, 13, udagât ayam âditya*h* vi*s*vena sahasâ saha. Grassmann remarks rightly that the last verses of this hymn have rather an Atharva-like character.

THE SUN AS A SUPERNATURAL POWER.

In other places, however, the tone of the Vedic poets changes. The sun is no longer the bright Deva only, who performs his daily task in the sky, but he is supposed to perform much greater work; he is looked upon, in fact, as the ruler, as the establisher, as the creator of the world.

We can follow in the Vedic hymns, step by step, the development which changes the sun from a mere luminary into a creator, preserver, ruler, and rewarder of the world, — in fact, into a divine or supreme being.

The first step leads us from the mere light of the sun to that light which in the morning wakes man from sleep, and seems to give new life not only to man, but to the whole of nature. He who wakes us in the morning, who recalls the whole of nature to new life, is soon called "the giver of daily life."

Secondly, by another and bolder step, the giver of daily light and life becomes the giver of light and life in general. He who brings light and life to-day is the same who brought life and light on the first of days. As light is the beginning of the day, so light was the beginning of creation, and the sun, from being a mere light-bringer or life-giver, becomes a creator, and, if a creator, then soon also a ruler of the world.

Thirdly, as driving away the dreaded darkness of the night, and likewise as fertilizing the earth, the sun is conceived as a defender and kind protector of all living things.

Fourthly, the sun sees everything, both what is good and what is evil; and how natural therefore that both the evil-doer should be told that the sun sees what no human eye may have seen, and that the innocent, when all other help fails him, should appeal to the sun to attest his guiltlessness! "My soul waiteth for the Lord more than they that watch for the morning." (Psalm cxxx. 6.)

Let us examine now a few passages, illustrating every one of these perfectly natural transitions. The very name given to the sun — Savit*ri* — means enlivener, and the sun is called "the enlivener of men," prasavitâ *g*anânâm.[1]

In Rig-Veda, VII. 63, 1, we read: —

> "The sun rises, the bliss-bestowing, the all-seeing,
> The same for all men;
> The eye of Mitra and Varu*n*a,
> The god who has rolled up darkness like a skin."

And again, VII. 63, 4: —

> "The brilliant (sun) rises from the sky, wide shining,
> Going forth to his distant work, full of light;
> Now let men also, enlivened by the sun,
> Go to their places and to their work."

In another hymn (VII. 60, 2) we find the sun invoked as "the protector of everything that moves or stands, of all that exists."

Frequent allusion is made to the sun's power of seeing everything. The stars flee before the all-seeing sun, like thieves.[2] He sees the right and the wrong among men.[3] He who looks upon all the world knows also all the thoughts in men.[4]

As the sun sees everything and knows everything, he is asked to forget and forgive what he alone has seen and knows.

[1] Rig-Veda, VII. 63, 2, ut u eti prasavitâ *g*anânâm.
[2] Ibid. I. 50, 2, apa tye tâyava*h* yathâ nakshatrâ yanti aktubhi*h*.
[3] Ibid. VII. 60, 2, *ri*g*u* marteshu v*ri*g*i*nâ *k*a pasyan.
[4] Ibid. VII. 61, 1, sa*h* manyum martyeshu â *k*iketa.

Thus we read (IV. 54, 3), "Whatever we have committed against the heavenly host through thoughtlessness, through weakness, through pride, through our human nature, let us be guiltless here, O Savitar, before gods and men."

The sun is asked to drive away illness and bad dreams.[1] Other gods also are implored to deliver man from sin, and from the unspeakable (avadya) at the rising of the sun.[2]

Having once and more than once been invoked as the life-bringer, the sun is also called the breath or life of all that moves and rests;[3] and lastly, he becomes the maker of all things, Visvakarman, by whom all the worlds have been brought together,[4] and Pra*g*âpati, which means lord of man and of all living creatures. "Savit*ri*," one poet says,[5] "has fastened the earth with cords; he has established the heaven without a support." He is called the

[1] Rig-Veda, X. 37, 4,

yena sûrya *g*yotishâ bâdhase tama*h*,
*g*agat *k*a visvam udiyarshi bhânunâ,
tena asmat visvâm anirâm anâhutim
apa amîvâm apa du*h*svapnyam suva.

With the light, O Sun, with which thou overcomest darkness, and rousest the whole world in splendor, with that light drive away from us all weakness, all negligence, all illness, and sleeplessness!

[2] Ibid. I. 115, 6, adya devâ*h* uditâ sûryasya ni*h* amhasa*h* piprita ni*h* avadyât.

[3] Ibid. I. 115, 1, sûrya*h* âtmâ *g*agata*h* tasthusha*h* *k*a.

[4] Ibid. X. 170, 4,

vibhrâ*g*an *g*yotishâ sva*h* aga*kkh*a*h* ro*k*anam diva*h*,
yena imâ visvâ bhuvanâni âbh*ri*tâ visvakarmanâ visvadevyavatâ.

Far shining with light thou wentest to the heaven, the brightness of the sky,
Thou by whom all these beings have been brought forth, the maker of all things, endowed with all divine might.

[5] Ibid. X. 149, 1,

savitâ yantrai*h* p*ri*thvîm aramnât
askambhane savitâ dyâm ad*ri*mhat.

upholder of heaven, the Pragâpati of the world,[1] and even then he wears that tawny armor or cloak which seemed to belong more properly to the golden-haired sun-god.

Another poet declares "that the heaven is upheld by the sun, while the earth is upheld by that which is *true*, the Satya, τὸ ὄν.[2] At last the language applied to Sûrya becomes superlative. He is the god among gods;[3] he is the divine leader of all the gods."[4]

The personal and divine elements are still more strongly developed in Savitri. We saw this already in some of the passages quoted before. We shall see it still more clearly in others. Savitri alone rules the whole world.[5] The laws which he has established are firm,[6] and the other gods not only praise him,[7] but have to follow him as their leader.[8] In one passage it is said that he bestowed immortality[9] on the

[1] Rig-Veda, IV. 53, 2, divah dhartâ bhuvanasya pragâpatih.

[2] Ibid. X. 85, 1, satyena uttabhitâ bhûmih sûryena uttabhitâ dyauh.

[3] Ibid. I. 50, 10,

> ut vayam tamasah pari gyotih pasyantah uttaram
> devam devatra sûryam aganma gyotih uttamam.

Seeing the light rising higher and higher above the darkness, we came to the highest light, to Sûrya, the god among gods.

[4] Ibid. VIII. 101, 12, mahnâ devânâm asuryah purohitah.

[5] Ibid. V. 81, 5, uta îsishe prasavasya tvam ekah it.

[6] Ibid. IV. 53, 4,

> adâbhyah bhuvanâni prakâkasat,
> vratâni devah savitâ abhi rakshate.

[7] Ibid. VII. 38, 3,

> api stutah savitâ devah astu,
> yam â kit visve vasavah grinanti.

[8] Ibid. V. 81, 3,

> yasya prayânam anu anye it yayuh
> devâh devasya mahimânam ogasâ.

[9] Ibid. IV. 54, 2,

> devebhyah hi prathamam yagniyebhyah
> amritatvam suvasi bhâgam uttamam,

other gods, and that the lives of men, one succeeding the other, are his gift. This can only mean that both the immortality of the Devas and the life of men were dependent on Savit*ri* as the vivifying sun.[1] Lastly, it should not be forgotten that the most sacred line of the whole Veda is the Gâyatrî verse, addressed to Savit*ri*: "Let us obtain (or, according to the Hindu tradition, let us meditate on) that adorable splendor of Savit*ri*; may he arouse our minds!"[2]

Even Pûshan rises sometimes beyond the limits of a purely pastoral solar deity. Though in one place he is spoken of as only higher than mortals and equal to the gods,[3] he is in other places called the lord of all that rests and moves.[4] Like all solar deities, he sees everything, and, like Savit*ri*, he is also supposed to conduct the souls of the departed to the regions of the blessed.[5]

As to Mitra and Vish*n*u, it is well known that they attained the highest supremacy. Mitra is greater than the earth and the sky,[6] he supports even all the

ât it dâmânam savitar vi ûr*n*ushe
anû*k*înâ *g*îvitâ mânushebhya*h*.

For, first thou givest to the worshipful Devas immortality, as the highest share,
Afterwards thou spreadest thy gifts, O Savit*ri*,
The lives of men, succeeding one another.

1 It is different when we read that Savit*ri* bestowed immortality on the *Ri*bhus, the sons of Sudhanvan, Rig-Veda, I. 110, 3, for these are always represented as having been originally men, and as deified at a later time.

2 Rig-Veda, III. 62, 10, tat savitu*h* vare*n*yam bharga*h* devasya dhîmahi, dhiya*h* ya*h* na*h* pra*k*odayât.

3 Ibid. VI. 48, 19, para*h* hi martyai*h* asi sama*h* devai*h*.

4 Ibid. I. 89, 5, tam îsânam *g*agata*h* tasthusha*h* patim.

5 Ibid. X. 17, 3, pûshâ tvâ ita*h* *k*yavayatu pra vidvân — sa*h* tvâ etebhya*h* pari dadat pit*ri*bhya*h*.

6 Ibid. III. 59, 7, abhi ya*h* mahinâ divam mitra*h* babhûva saprathâ*h*, abhi *s*ravobhi*h* prithivîm.

gods.[1] Vishnu supports all the worlds;[2] he is the companion of Indra in his battles,[3] and no one can reach the limits of his greatness.[4]

THE SUN IN A SECONDARY POSITION.

If we knew nothing else of the religious poetry of the Veda, we might, after reading such praises bestowed upon the sun, feel inclined to say that the old Brahmans worshiped the sun under various names as their supreme deity; and that in that sense they might be said to worship one god only, to be, in fact, monotheists. Nothing, however, could be further from the truth. In this one evolution, no doubt, the sun assumed the character of a supreme deity, but even in the passages which we have quoted there is hardly an assertion of the sun's supremacy that could not be matched in the hymns addressed to other Devas. He is totally different in that respect from *Zeus* and *Jupiter*. Nor do the Vedic poets hesitate for a moment to represent the same deity, the sun, who is at one time the maker and upholder of all things, at another time as the child of the

[1] Rig-Veda, III. 59, 8, sa*h* devân visvân bibharti.

[2] Ibid. I. 154, 4,

ya*h* u tridhâtu p*ri*thivîm uta dyâm, eka*h* dâdhâra bhuvanâni visva,

He who in three places supports the earth and the sky, who alone supports all beings.

[3] Ibid. VI. 69.

[4] Ibid. VII. 99, 2,

na te vish*n*o *g*âyamâna*h* na *g*âta*h*,
deva mahimna*h* param antam âpa,
astabhnâ*h* nâkam *ri*shvam b*ri*hantam,
dâdhartha prâ*k*îm kakubham p*ri*thivyâ*h*.

No one who is now living or who lived formerly reached, O Deva, the farthest end of thy greatness;

Thou hast supported the sky, the bright and great, thou hast holden the eastern point of the earth.

waters, as produced by the dawns, a god among other gods, neither better nor worse.

This is the peculiar character of the ancient Vedic religion which I have tried to characterize as *Henotheism* or *Kathenotheism*, a successive belief in single supreme gods, in order to keep it distinct from that phase of religious thought which we commonly call polytheism, in which the many gods are already subordinated to one supreme god, and by which therefore the craving after the one without a second has been more fully satisfied. In the Veda one god after another is invoked. For the time being, all that can be said of a divine being is ascribed to him. The poet, while addressing him, seems hardly to know of any other gods. But in the same collection of hymns, sometimes even in the same hymn, other gods are mentioned, and they also are truly divine, truly independent, or, it may be, supreme. The vision of the worshiper seems to change suddenly, and the same poet who at one moment saw nothing but the sun, as the ruler of heaven and earth, now sees heaven and earth, as the father and mother of the sun and of all the gods.

It may be difficult for us to enter into this phase of religious thought, but it is a phase perfectly intelligible, nay inevitable, if only we remember that the idea of deity, as we understand it, was not yet fixed and settled, but was only slowly growing towards perfection. The poets ascribed the highest powers to the sun, but they ascribed equally high powers to other natural phenomena likewise. It was their object to praise the mountains, the trees, the rivers, the earth and the sky, the storm and the fire, as high as ever they could be praised. By these superlative praises each became in turn a superlative or supreme power; but to say that they represented each and all as gods or even as devas, involves a mental anachronism; for, when they first uttered those praises, they did not yet possess either that word or that idea. They were looking, no doubt, for something in all these phenomena, which afterwards they called divine. But at first they had to be satisfied with predicating of the various objects of their praise the highest they could predicate. After having done that, nay, while doing it, some of the predicates which were applicable to all or most of the objects of their praise would assume an independent character, and thus supply the first names and conceptions of what we call divine. If the mountains, the rivers, the sky, and the sun were all called living and doing (asura), not-perishing (a*g*ara), immortal (amartya), or bright (deva), then each of these predicates would, after a time, become the name of a class of beings, expressing not only their vital vigor, their freedom from decay or their brilliancy, but everything else that was connoted by these words. To say that Agni or fire belongs to the devas or bright beings would then be something very different from saying that fire is bright. To say that Dyaus, the sky, or Sûrya, the sun, is an asura (a living one) or an amartya (immortal), would imply far more than that the sky does not fade away, or that he is active and moving about. These general predicates, such as asura, vigorous, a*g*ara, imperishable, deva, bright, always predicate one and the same thing of many objects; and if the upholders of an original monotheism mean no more than this, that the predicate god which is looked for and slowly conquered, that the intention of the divine is by its very nature one, there might be something to be said for such a theory.

But what interests us at present is, how that intention was realized; by how many steps, by how many names, the infinite was grasped, the unknown named, and at last the divine reached. Those beings who are called *devas* in the Veda are in many places not yet even the same as the Greek θεοί; for the Greeks, even so early as the time of Homer, had begun to suspect that, whatever the number and nature of the so-called gods might be, there must be something supreme, whether a god or a fate, there must be at least *one* father of gods and men. In some portions of the Veda, too, the same idea breaks through, and we imagine that as in Greece, Italy, Germany, and elsewhere, so in India also, the religious craving after the one would have been satisfied by a monarchical polytheism. But the Indian mind soon went farther, and we shall see how in the end it was driven to a denial of all the devas or gods, and to search for something higher than all the devas, Dyaus himself, or Varu*n*a, or Indra, or Pra*g*âpati not excluded. At present, when dealing with the genesis of the Vedic gods or *devas*, what I want chiefly to show is that, beginning from different beginnings, nothing is more natural than that they should grow up at first side by side, unconcerned about each other, each perfect in his own sphere, and that sphere for a time filling the whole horizon of the vision of their worshipers.

Herein lies the interest and chief value of the Vedic hymns, only that it is almost impossible to exhibit the fullness of those thoughts in modern language. When the poets of the Veda address the mountains to protect them, when they implore the rivers to yield them water, they may speak of rivers and mountains as *devas*, but even then, though *deva* would be more than *bright*, it would as yet be very far from anything we mean by *divine*. How, then, shall we do justice to the old language and its real vagueness by our translation into sharply defined modern terms? To the Vedic poets the rivers and mountains were, no doubt, the same as they are to us, but they were conceived more prominently as active, because everything which in their language was comprehended by a name could only be comprehended as manifesting some activity of which man was conscious in himself; it had no interest, it had no existence in their minds, except when conceived as active. But there is still a long way from this conception of certain parts of nature as active, to what is called personification or deification. Even when the poets spoke of the sun as standing on a chariot, as clad in golden armor, as spreading out his arms, this was no more than a poetical perception of something in nature that reminded them of their own proceedings. What to us is poetry, was to them prose. What to us seems fantastic imagery, arose more often from helplessness in grasping, and poverty in naming the surrounding world, than from any desire of startling or pleasing their hearers. If we could ask Vasish*th*a or Visvâmitra, or any of the old Aryan poets, whether they really thought that the sun, the golden ball which they saw, was a man with legs and arms, with a heart and lungs, they would no doubt laugh at us, and tell us that though we understood their language, we did not understand their thoughts.

A word like Savi*tri*, the sun, meant at first no more than what it said. It was derived from the root *su*, to bring forth, to give life, and therefore, when applied to the sun, it meant just so much of the sun as was perceived of him in his acts of life-giving and fertilizing, and no more. Afterwards only, Savi*tri* became on one hand the name of a mythological being of whom certain stories, applicable to the vivifying sun, might be told; while on the other hand Savi*tri* dwindled away into a traditional and unmeaning word for sun.

The process which we have been watching in the case of the sun, we can watch again and again with regard to most Vedic deities. Not, however, with regard to all. The so-called semi-deities, the rivers, the mountains, the clouds, the sea, others also, such as the dawn, the night, the wind, or the storm, never rise to the rank of supreme deity; but of Agni, the fire, of Varu*n*a, the covering sky, of Indra, Vish*n*u, Rudra, Soma, Par*g*anya, and others, epithets are used and whole descriptions given which, to our mind, would be appropriate to a supreme deity only.

THE SKY AS DYAUS, OR THE ILLUMINATOR.

Let us look at the origin and history of one other god, one of the oldest gods, not only of the Vedic Aryans, but of the whole Aryan race, I mean the Vedic Dyaus, the Greek Ζεύς. Some scholars seem still to doubt the existence of such a deity in the Veda, and there is certainly no trace of Dyaus as a god, nay, even as a masculine noun, in the later literature of India. Dyaus has there become a feminine, and means simply the sky. Now it has always seemed to me one of the most wonderful discoveries made by the students of the Veda that a deity, which was known to have existed in Greece as Ζεὺς πατήρ, in Italy as Ju-piter, in the Edda as Tyr, in German as Zio, and which we know ought to have existed in Sanskrit also, but which did not exist there, should suddenly have come to light in these ancient hymns of the Veda. In the Veda Dyaus occurs, not only as a masculine, but in that close connection with pitâ, father, as Dyaushpitâ, which we find again in the Latin Jupiter. This discovery of Dyaush-pitâ was like finding at last, by means of a powerful telescope, the very star in the very place of the heavens which we had fixed before by calculation.

However, even in the Veda, Dyaus is already a fading star. The meaning of the word is generally given as sky, but its truer meaning would be "the bright or the shining one," for it is derived from the root *div* or *dyu*, to shine, to lighten; and it was this activity of shining and illuminating the world which was embodied in the name of *Dyaus*. Who the shining one was, the word by itself did not declare. He was an asura, a living one; that was all. Afterwards only, Dyaus became the centre of mythological stories, while in the ordinary language it dwindled away, just like Savit*ri*, the life-giver, into one of the many traditional and unmeaning words for sky.

This Dyaus, then, the light, or the illuminator of the sky, was no doubt, from the very first, preëminently fitted to assume some kind of supremacy among the other devas or bright beings; and we know how completely that supremacy was realized in the Greek Ζεύς and the Latin Jupiter. In the Vedic Dyaus, too, we can watch the same tendency; but it was there counteracted by that tendency inherent in almost every deva to assume a superlative character.

Dyaus, the sky, is frequently invoked together with the Earth and with Fire. For instance (Rig-Veda, VI. 51, 5), —

"Dyaus (sky), father, and P*ri*thivî (earth), kind mother, Agni (fire), brother, ye Vasus, ye bright ones, have mercy upon us!"

Dyaus, we see, occupies the first place, and so he does generally in these old invocations. He is constantly called father. For instance (I. 191, 6), "Dyaus is father, P*ri*thivî, the earth, your mother; Soma, your brother; Aditi, your sister." Or again (Rig-Veda, IV. 1, 10), Dyaus, the father, the creator, Dyaush pitâ *g*anitâ, Ζεὺς πατὴρ γενετήρ.

More frequently, however, than by himself, Dyaus (the sky) is invoked together with P*ri*thivî, the earth; and the two words, joined together, form a kind of dual deity in the Veda, called Dyâvâp*ri*thivî, Heaven and Earth.

Now there are many passages in the Veda where Heaven and Earth are invoked as supreme deities. Thus the gods are said to be their sons,[1] more particularly the two most popular deities in the Veda, Indra[2] and Agni,[3] are mentioned as their offspring. It is they, the two parents, who have made the world,[4] who protect it,[5] who support by their power everything, whatsoever exists.[6]

Yet, after heaven and earth have received every

[1] Rig-Veda, I. 159, 1, devâputre. [2] Ibid. IV. 17.

[3] Ibid. X. 2, 7, yam tvâ dyâvâp*ri*thivî yam tvâ âpa*h*, tvash*t*â yam tvâ su*g*animâ *g*a*g*âna.

[4] Ibid. I. 159, 2, suretesâ pitarâ bhûma *k*akratu*h*.

[5] Ibid. I. 160, 2, pitâ mâtâ *k*a bhuvanâni rakshata*h*.

[6] Ibid. I. 185, 1, vis*v*am tmanâ bibh*ri*ta*h* yat ha nâma.

epithet that can be invented to express their imperishableness, their omnipotence, their eternity, we suddenly hear of a clever workman among the gods who made heaven and earth, whether called Dyâvâpri*thivî*[1] or Rodasî.[2] In some places Indra is said to have produced and to support heaven and earth,[3] the same Indra who elsewhere is represented as the son of Dyaus, or as the son of heaven and earth.[4]

STRUGGLE FOR SUPREMACY BETWEEN DYAUS AND INDRA.

In fact we see here for the first time some kind of struggle between two prominent deities, between the old primeval god and goddess, Heaven and Earth, and the more modern and more personal god Indra, originally the rain-giver, the *Jupiter pluvius*, who was raised into an heroic character by his daily and yearly fights against the powers of darkness, of night and of winter, and more particularly against the robbers who carry away the rain-clouds, till Indra conquers them again with thunder and lightning. Of this Indra, though at first the son of Heaven and Earth, it might well be said that at his birth heaven and earth trembled.[5] Then again we read (Rig-Veda, I. 131, 1), "Before Indra the divine Dyaus (heaven) bowed down, before Indra bowed down the great

[1] Rig-Veda, IV. 56, 3, sa*h* it svapâ*h* bhuvaneshu âsa ya*h* ime dyâvâpri-thivî *g*a*g*âna.

[2] Ibid. I. 160, 4, ayam devânâm apasâm apastama*h* ya*h* *g*a*g*âna rodasî visvasambhuvâ.

[3] Ibid. VIII. 36, 4, *g*anitâ diva*h* *g*anitâ prithivyâ*h*; III. 32, 8, dâdhâra ya*h* prithivîm uta dyâm.

[4] *Lectures on the Science of Language*, vol. ii. p. 473, note. Heaven and earth are sometimes replaced by day and night, dyunise, from which Dionysos (dyunisya = Διόνυξος), their child and representative, in his character of λαμπτήρ, νυκτέλιος, and ὕης.

[5] *Lectures on the Science of Language*, vol. ii. p. 473.

Prithivî (earth). Thou, O Indra, shookest the top of heaven."[1] Such expressions, which are physically true, as applied to the god of the thunder-storm, before whom "the earth shall quake, and the heaven shall tremble, the sun and the moon shall be dark, and the stars shall withdraw their shining," would soon be interpreted morally, and then convey the idea of Indra's greatness and supremacy. Thus one poet says,[2] "The greatness of Indra indeed exceeds the heaven (that is, Dyaus), exceeds the earth (that is, Prithivî), and the sky." Another says,[3] "Indra exceeds heaven and earth; they are but as half compared with him."

Next would follow meditations on the relative position of these deities, of father and son, and in the end it would have to be admitted that the son, the valiant Indra, with his thunderbolt and his lightning-arrows, was greater than his father, the serene sky, greater than his mother, the immovable earth, greater also than the other gods. "The other gods," one poet says, "were sent away like (shriveled up) old men; thou, O Indra, becamest the king.[4] We see thus how Indra, too, rose to be another supreme god. "No one is beyond thee," says one poet, "no one is better than thou art, no one is like unto thee."[5] In the majority of the hymns of the Veda he is preëminently the supreme god, yet again not to that extent

[1] Rig-Veda, I. 54, 4.

[2] Ibid. I. 61, 9, asya it eva pra ririke mahitvam divah prithivyâh pari antarikshât.

[3] Ibid. VI. 30, 1; ardham it asya prati rodasî ubhe; X. 119, 7, nahi me rodasî ubhe anyam paksham kana prati.

[4] Ibid. IV. 19, 2, ava asriganta givrayah na devâh bhuvah samrât indra satyayonih.

[5] Ibid. IV. 30, 1, nakih indra tvat uttarah, na gyâyân asti vritrahan, nakih eva yathâ tvam.

that we could compare his position with that of Zeus. Neither are the other gods always subordinate to him, nor can we say that they are all coördinate. Though in some cases certain gods are associated together, and some, particularly Indra, represented as greater than others, yet these other gods, too, have their day, and, when they are asked to bestow their blessings, there is no language too strong to magnify their power and wisdom.

HYMN TO INDRA, AS A SUPREME GOD.

I shall give you the translation of one hymn addressed to Indra, and of another addressed to Varu*n*a, in order to show you what is meant by Henotheism, by a religion in which each god, while he is being invoked, shares in all the attributes of a supreme being. You must not expect anything very poetical, in our own sense of the word. Those ancient poets had no time for poetic ornamentation or mere splendor of words. They labored hard to find the right expression for what they wished to say. Every happy expression was to them a relief, each hymn, however poor it may seem to us, an heroic feat, a true sacrifice. Every one of their words weighs and tells; but when we come to translate them into modern language, we often feel inclined to give it up in despair. Rig-Veda, IV. 17: —

"Thou art great, O Indra! To thee alone has the Earth, has Heaven willingly yielded dominion. When thou hadst struck dewn V*ri*tra with might, thou lettest loose the streams which the dragon had swallowed. (1.)

"At the birth of thy splendor, Heaven trembled, the Earth trembled, from fear of the anger of her own son. The strong mountains danced, the deserts were moistened, the waters flow along. (2.)

"He cleft the mountains, with might whirling thunderbolts, and steadily showing his prowess. Rejoicing he killed V*ri*tra with his bolt, the waters came forth quickly. after their strong keeper had been killed. (3.)

"Thy father, Dyaus, was considered powerful (through thee); he who had made Indra, was the cleverest of all workmen: for he had begotten one who is brilliant, and whose thunderbolt is good, who, like the earth, is not to be moved from his place. (4.)

"Indra, who is invoked by many, who alone can move the earth, the king of the people: all creatures rejoice in him, the only true one; praising the bounty of the powerful god. (5.)

"All libations (somas) always belonged to him; to him, the great one, belonged always the most delightful delights. Thou wast forever the treasurer of treasures; thou, O Indra, settest all people to their share. (6.)

"As soon as thou wast born, O Indra, thou settest all people fearing. Thou, O hero, cuttest asunder with thy thunderbolt the serpent who lay across the down-rushing waters. (7.)

"Praise Indra, the ever-striking, the bold, the wild, the great, the boundless, the manly hero with the good thunderbolt! He kills V*ri*tra, he conquers booty, he gives wealth, the wealthy, the generous. (8.)

"He disperses the hosts that have gathered together, he who alone is renowned as mighty in battle. He brings home the booty which he has conquered; let us be dear to him in his friendship! (9.)

"He is renowned as conquering and killing, he also

brings forth the cattle in the fight. When Indra is serious in his anger, then all that is firm trembles and fears him. (10.)

"Indra conquered the cattle, he conquered gold and horses; he the powerful, who breaks all the strongholds.[1] Rich in men by these his powerful men, he is a divider of treasure and a collector of wealth. (11.)

"How much does Indra mind his mother, or the father who begat him? Indra who rouses his strength in a moment, like the whirlwind rushing along with thundering clouds. (12.)

"He makes homeless him who had a home; he the mighty, stirs up the dust into a cloud. He breaks everything, like Dyaus (the sky), the wielder of the thunderbolt[2]— will he place the singer in the midst of wealth? (13.)

"He drove forth the wheel of the sun, he then stopped Etasa in his march. Turning round, he threw him into the black[3] abyss of night, into the birthplace of this sky. (14.)

"As a ewer is drawn up in a well, thus we poets, wishing for cows, wishing for horses, wishing for booty, wishing for women, bring near to ourselves Indra to be our friend, the strong one who gives us women, and whose help never fails. (16.)

"Be thou our defender, appearing as our friend; look down upon us, thou, the comforter of the sacrificers, the friend, the father, the best of fathers, who gives freedom, and grants life to him who asks for it. (17.)

[1] Grassman reads pûrbhid for pûrvî.

[2] Cf. Rig-Veda, X. 45, 4, stanayan iva dyau*h*.

[3] Even when reading kr*ishn*a instead of kr*ishn*a*h*, the sense remains very obscure.

"Be thou the friend, the protector of all who desire thy friendship. When thou hast been praised, O Indra, give life to him who glorifies thee! Associated together we have sacrificed to thee, magnifying thee, O Indra, by these works. (18.)

"Indra is praised as the powerful, because he, being one, kills many matchless enemies. Neither men nor gods can resist him in whose keeping this his friend and poet stands. (19.)

"May Indra the all-mighty, the powerful, the supporter of men, the invulnerable, make all this true for us indeed! Thou who art the king of all generations, give us what is the mighty glory of the poet." (20.)

HYMN TO VARU*N*A AS A SUPREME GOD.

The next hymn is addressed to Varu*n*a (Rig-Veda, II. 28): —

"This (world) belongs to the wise king Âditya: may he overcome all beings by his might! I seek a hymn of praise for the god who is most gracious to the sacrifices, for the bounteous Varu*n*a. (1.)

"Let us be blessed in thy service, O Varu*n*a, who always think of thee and praise thee; greeting thee day after day, like the fires on the altar, at the approach of the rich dawns. (2.)

"O Varu*n*a, our guide, let us be in thy keeping, thou who art rich in heroes and praised far and wide! And you, unconquered sons of Aditi, deign to accept us as your friends, O gods! (3.)

"Âditya, the ruler, sent forth these rivers; they follow the law of Varu*n*a. They tire not, they cease not; like birds they fly quickly everywhere. (4.)

"Take from me my sin, like a fetter, and we shall

increase, O Varu*n*a, the spring of thy law. Let not the thread be cut, while I weave my song! Let not the form of the workman break before the time! (5.)

"Take far away from me this terror, O Varu*n*a, thou, O righteous king have mercy on me! Like as a rope from a calf remove from me my sin; for away from thee I am not master even of the twinkling of an eye. (6.)

"Do not strike us, Varu*n*a, with weapons which at thy will hurt the evil-doer. Let us not go where the light has vanished! Scatter our enemies that we live. (7.)

"We did formerly, O Varu*n*a, and do now, and shall in future, sing praises to thee, O mighty one! For on thee, unconquerable hero, rest all statutes immovable, as if established on a rock. (8.)

"Move far away from me all self-committed guilt, and may I not, O king, suffer for what others have committed! Many dawns have not yet dawned: grant us to live in them, O Varu*n*a! (9.)

"Whether it be my companion or a friend, who, while I was asleep and trembling, uttered fearful spells against me, whether it be a thief or a wolf who wishes to hurt me, — protect us against them, O Varu*n*a." (10.)

A Greek poet could not say much more in praise of Zeus, yet I could easily give you selections from other hymns in which the same and even stronger language is used of Agni, Mitra, Soma, and other gods.

HENOTHEISM, THE DIALECTIC PERIOD OF RELIGION.

This, then, is what is meant by *henotheism*, a phase of religious thought with which we have become acquainted for the first time through the Veda, though there can be little doubt that other religions also had to pass through it. In a History of Ancient Sanskrit Literature which I published in 1859, I had already called attention to this henotheistic phase of religion. "When these individual gods are invoked," I said (p. 532), "they are not conceived as limited by the power of others, as superior or inferior in rank. Each god is to the mind of the suppliant as good as all the gods. He is felt at the time as a real divinity, as supreme and absolute, in spite of the necessary limitations which, to our mind, a plurality of gods must entail on every single god. All the rest disappear from the vision of the poet, and he only who is to fulfill their desires stands in full light before the eyes of the worshipers. 'Among you, O gods, there is none that is small, and none that is young: you are all great indeed,' is a sentiment which, though perhaps not so distinctly expressed as by the poet Manu Vaivasvata, nevertheless underlies all the poetry of the Veda. Although the gods are sometimes distinctly invoked as the great and the small, the young and the old (Rig-Veda, I. 27, 13), this is only an attempt to find the most comprehensive expression for the divine powers, and nowhere is any one of the gods represented as the slave of others."

It must not be supposed, however, that what I call henotheism, in order to keep it distinct from polytheism, in its ordinary meaning, existed in India only. We see traces of it in Greece, in Italy, in Germany.

We see it most clearly during that period which precedes the formation of nations out of independent tribes. It is, if I may say so, anarchy, as preceding monarchy, a communal as distinct from an imperial form of religion. It is what may best be described as the dialectic period of religion. For as the dialects of a language exist before a language, before what is afterwards called the common language of the people, so it is in the case of religions. They arise round the hearth of every family. When families become united into tribes, the single hearth becomes the altar of a village; and when different tribes combine into a state, the different altars (ædes) become a temple (ædes) or sanctuary of the whole people. This process is natural, and therefore universal. Only we do not see it anywhere so clearly in its very growth as in the Veda.

THE SUPREMACY OF DIFFERENT DEVAS.

A few examples will make this still clearer.[1] In the first hymn of the second Ma*nd*ala, Agni (fire) is called the ruler of the universe, the lord of men, the wise king, the father, the brother, the son, the friend of men; nay, all the powers and names of the other gods are distinctly ascribed to Agni. The hymn belongs, no doubt, to the more modern compositions; yet, though Agni is thus highly exalted in it, nothing is said to disparage the divine character of the other gods.

What could be said of Indra we saw just now in the hymn addressed to him. In the hymns as well as in the later Brâhma*n*as, he is celebrated as the

[1] This subject is treated in my *History on Ancient Sanskrit Literature*, p. 532, and in Muir, *Sanskrit Texts*, iv. p. 113; v. p. 98.

strongest, as the most heroic of gods; and the burden of one of the songs in the tenth book is "Vismasmâd Indra uttarah! Indra is greater than all!"

Of another god, of Soma, it is said that he was born great, and that he conquers every one.[1] He is called the king of the world,[2] he has the power to prolong the life of men,[3] nay, in one sense even the gods are indebted to him for their life and immortality.[4] He is called the king of heaven and earth, of men and gods.[5]

If we read the hymns which are addressed to Varuna (οὐρανός), we perceive again that the god here invoked is, to the mind of the poet, supreme and almighty.

What more could human language achieve, in trying to express the idea of a divine and supreme power, than what our poet says of Varuna, "Thou art lord of all, of heaven and earth" (I. 25, 20); or, as it is said in another hymn (II. 27, 10), "Thou art the king of all, of those who are gods, and of those who are men?" Nor is Varuna represented as the lord of nature only; he knows the order of nature, and upholds it, for this is what is meant by his epithet dhritavrata. The *vratas*, or laws of nature, are not to be shaken; they rest on Varuna, as on a rock. Varuna therefore knows the twelve months, and even the thirteenth; he knows the course of the wind, the birds in the air, and the ships on the sea.

1 Rig-Veda, IX. 59, 4, *g*âyamânah abhavah mahân indo visvân abhi it asi.

2 Ibid. IX. 96, 10, abhisastipâh bhuvanasya râ*g*â.

3 Ibid. VIII. 48, 4, pra nah âyuh *g*ivase soma târih.

4 Ibid. IX. 87, 2, pitâ devânâm *g*anitâ sudakshah vishtambhah divah dharunah prithivyâh.

5 Ibid. IX. 97, 24, râ*g*â devânâm uta martyânâm.

He knows all the wondrous works of nature, and he looks not only into the past, but into the future also. But more than all this, Varu*n*a watches also over the order of the moral world. Thus in one hymn the poet begins with a confession that he has neglected the works of Varu*n*a, that he has offended against his laws. He craves his pardon; he appeals in self-defense to the weakness of human nature; he deprecates death as the reward of sin. He hopes to soothe the god by his prayers, as a horse is soothed by kind words. "Be good," he says, in the end, "let us speak together again." Who can read this without being reminded of the words of the Psalm, "For He knoweth our frame, He remembereth that we are dust?"

But even this Varu*n*a is not supreme; not even he is the One, without a second. He is almost always represented in fellowship with another, Mitra, without any indication that either Varu*n*a is greater than Mitra, or Mitra greater than Varu*n*a.

This is what I call henotheism, a worship of single gods, which must be carefully distinguished both from monotheism, or the worship of one god, involving a distinct denial of all other gods, and from polytheism, the worship of many deities which together form one divine polity, under the control of one supreme god.

FURTHER DEVELOPMENT OF HENOTHEISM.

Let us now see what became of this Vedic henotheism in its further development.

First of all, we find that several of these single deities, having sprung from one and the same source, have a tendency, after a very short career of their own, to run together. Dyaus was the sky as the ever-present light. Varuna was the sky as the all-embracing. Mitra was the sky as lighted up by the light of the morning. Sûrya was the sun as shining in the sky. Savitri was the sun as bringing light and life. Vishnu was the sun as striding with three steps across the sky; Indra appeared in the sky, as the giver of rain; Rudra and the Maruts passed along the sky in thunder-storms; Vâta and Vâyu were the winds of the air; Agni was fire and light, wherever it could be perceived, whether as rising out of darkness in the morning, or sinking into darkness in the evening. The same applies to several of the minor deities.

Hence it happened constantly that what was told of one deity could be told of another likewise; the same epithets are shared by many, the same stories are told of different gods.

And not the solar deities only, such as Sûrya, but Indra, the rain-god, the Maruts, the storm-gods, were all called the sons of Dyaus, or the sky; and as the sky was conceived as the husband of the earth, the earth might become the mother of all the gods.

When the sun rose, it was supposed not only to lighten, but to reveal and spread out heaven and earth; and from that it was but a small step to representing heaven and earth as brought back to us, or made for us, by the sun. The same achievement, however, was likewise ascribed to Indra, to Varuna, and to Agni, who is the light of the sun, and to Vishnu, the god who measures the world with his three steps.

From another point of view, Agni is supposed to bring back the sun, and the same feat is by other poets ascribed to Indra, to Varuna, and to Vishnu.

Though the great battle against darkness and the clouds is chiefly waged by Indra, yet Dyaus also wields the thunderbolt, Agni destroys the demons of darkness, Vishnu, the Maruts, and Parganya, all take part in the same daily or yearly battle.

The old poets saw all this as well as we do, and they often go so far as to declare that one god is identical with others.[1] Thus Agni, really the god of fire, is said to be Indra and Vishnu, Savitri, Pûshan, Rudra, and Aditi; nay, he is said to be all the gods.[2] In a verse of the Atharva-Veda we read (XIII. 3, 13): —

"In the evening Agni becomes Varuna; he becomes Mitra when rising in the morning; having become Savitri he passes through the sky; having become Indra he warms the heaven in the middle."

Sûrya, the sun, is identified with Indra and Agni; Savitri with Mitra and Pûshan; Indra with Varuna; Dyaus, the sky, with Parganya, the rain-god. All this was no doubt very important for helping the Brahmans to reduce the number of independent deities; but it left them still very far removed from monotheism.

Another expedient adopted by the ancient poets, and which seems quite peculiar to the Veda, is the formation of dual deities.[3] The names of two gods who shared certain functions in common were formed into a compound with a dual termination, and this compound became the name of a new deity. Thus

[1] Muir, *Sanskrit Texts*, v. p. 219.

[2] Rig-Veda, V. 3.

[3] The most important of these dual deities are —

Agni-shomau.	Indra-brihaspatî.	Parganya-vâtau.
Indra-vâyû.	Indrâ-varunau.	Mitrâ-varunau.
Indra-agnî.	Indrâ-vishnû.	Somâ-pûshanau.
Indra-pûshanau.	Indrâ-somau.	Somâ-rudrau.

we have hymns not only to Mitra and Varu*n*a, but to Mitrâvaru*n*au as one; nay, sometimes they are called the two Mitras and the two Varu*n*as.

A third expedient was to comprehend all the gods by one common name, to call them Visve Devas, the All-gods, and to address prayers and sacrifices to them in their collective capacity.

Lastly, there was that other expedient, which to us seems to be the most natural of all, in order to bring the craving for one god into harmony with the existence of many gods, viz., the expedient, adopted by the Greeks and Romans, of making one of the gods supreme above all the rest; thus satisfying the desire for a supreme power, the *εἷς κοίρανος ἔστω*, and not breaking entirely with the traditions of the past; and the worship paid to individual manifestations of the divine in nature, such as were Apollon and Athena, or Poseidon and Hades, by the side of Zeus. If it is true, as has sometimes been suggested, that the introduction of a monarchical system among the gods existed only among people whose political system was monarchical,[1] we might argue from the absence of a king of gods in ancient India to the absence of kingly government in that country.

TENDENCY TOWARDS MONOTHEISM.

Attempts, however, were made by the Vedic Aryans also to establish some kind of supremacy among their gods, though not with the success which these attempts had in Greece and elsewhere.

We saw already that certain gods, such as Savit*ri*,

[1] *Aristotelis Politica*, i. 2, 7: "And therefore all people say that the gods also had a king, because they themselves had kings either formerly or now; for men create the gods after their own image, not only with regard to their form, but also with regard to their manner of life."

the sun, Varuna, and others, were conceived not only as having revealed the world by their light, but as having spread out heaven and earth, as having measured, and at last as having made them.[1] They thus received the epithets not only of visvakakshas, all-seeing, visvavyakas, all-embracing, visvavedas, all-knowing, but also of visvakarman,[2] maker of all things, Pragâpati, lord of all men; and these two epithets, after a time, were raised apparently into names of new deities. There are a few hymns addressed to Visvakarman, the Creator, and Pragâpati, the Lord, in which there are but small traces left of the solar germ from whence they sprang. Some of them remind us of the language of the Psalms, and one imagines that a deity such as Pragâpati or Visvakarman would really have satisfied the monotheistic yearnings, and constituted the last goal in the growth of the religious sentiment of the ancient Aryans of India. But this, as we shall see, was not to be.

VISVAKARMAN, THE MAKER OF ALL THINGS.

I shall read you a few extracts from the Rig-Veda, taken from some of these so-called later hymns, in which the idea of the *one* God, the creator and ruler of the world, is very clearly expressed.

And first some verses addressed to Visvakarman:[3]—

"What was the place, what was the support, and where was it, from whence the all-seeing Visvakarman (the maker of all things), when producing the earth, displayed the heaven by his might? (2.)

[1] Rig-Veda, V. 85, 5, mânena iva tasthivân antarikshe ni yah mame prithivîm sûryena, he who standing in the sky measured out the earth with the sun, as with a measure.

[2] Indra also is visvakarman, Rig-Veda, VIII. 98, 2.

[3] Rig-Veda, X. 81, 2.

"He, the *one* God, whose eyes are everywhere, whose mouth, whose arms, whose feet are everywhere; he, when producing heaven and earth, forges them together with his arms and with the wings. (3.)

"What was the forest, what was the tree,[1] from which they cut out heaven and earth? Ye wise, seek in your mind that place on which he stood when supporting the worlds. (4.)

"Let us invoke to-day, for our protection in battle, the lord of speech, Visvakarman, the maker of all things, who inspires our mind. May he accept all our offerings, he who is a blessing to everybody, and who performs good deeds for our safety!" (7.)

In another hymn, equally addressed to Visvakarman,[2] we read: —

"He who is the father that begat us, the ruler who knows the laws, and all the worlds, he who alone gave names to the gods, all other creatures go to ask of him. (3.)

"Beyond the sky, beyond the earth, beyond the Devas and the Asuras,[3] what was the first germ which the waters bore, wherein all gods were seen? (5.)

"The waters bore that first germ in which all the gods came together. That *one* thing in which all creatures rested was placed in the lap of the unborn. (6.)

"You will never know him who created these things; something else stands between you and him. Enveloped in mist and with faltering voice, the poets walk along, rejoicing in life." (7.)

1 We say ὕλη or *materies*, matter; Rig-Veda, X. 81, 7.

2 Rig-Veda, X. 82.

3 Or, it may be, "beyond the living gods."

PRAGÂPATI, THE LORD OF CREATURES.

The next deity we have to consider is Pra*g*âpati, the lord of all creatures, in many respects identical with Visvakarman, the maker of all things,[1] yet enjoying a greater individuality than Visvakarman, particularly in the Brâhma*n*as. In some of the hymns of the Veda, Pra*g*âpati occurs still as a mere epithet of Savit*ri*, the sun, *e. g.*: —

"The supporter of heaven, the Pra*g*âpati of the world, the sage puts on his brilliant armor; shining forth, spreading and filling the wide space, Savit*ri* creates the highest happiness."[2] (1.)

He is also invoked as bestowing progeny, and there is one hymn (Rig-Veda, X. 121) where he is celebrated as the creator of the universe, as the first of all gods, also called Hira*n*yagarbha, the golden germ, or the golden egg.

"In the beginning there arose Hira*n*yagarbha (the golden germ); he was the one born lord of all this. He established the earth and this sky: — Who is the god to whom we shall offer our sacrifice? (1.)

"He who gives breath, he who gives strength; whose command all the bright gods revere; whose shadow is immortality, whose shadow is death: — Who is the god to whom we shall offer our sacrifice? (2.)

"He who through his power became the sole king of the breathing and slumbering world, he who governs all, man and beast: — Who is the god to whom we shall offer our sacrifice? (3.)

"He through whose power these snowy mountains

[1] *S*atapatha Brâhma*n*a, VIII. 2, 1, 10, Pra*g*âpatir vai Visvakarmâ.
[2] Rig-Veda, IV. 53, 2.

are, and the sea, they say, with the distant river (the Rasâ): he of whom these regions are the two arms: — Who is the god to whom we shall offer our sacrifice? (4.)

"He through whom the sky is bright and the earth firm, he through whom the heaven was established, nay, the highest heaven; he who measured the space in the sky: — Who is the god to whom we shall offer our sacrifice? (5.)

"He to whom heaven and earth,[1] standing firm by his will, look up, trembling in their mind; he over whom the rising sun shines forth: — Who is the god to whom we shall offer our sacrifice? (6.)

"When the great waters went everywhere, holding the seed, and generating the fire, thence arose he who is the sole life of the gods: — Who is the god to whom we shall offer our sacrifice? (7.)

"He who by his might looked even over the waters which held power and generated the sacrificial fire, he who *alone is God above all gods*:[2] — Who is the god to whom we shall offer our sacrifice? (8.)

"May he not hurt us, he who is the creator of the earth, or he, the righteous, who created the heaven; he who also created the bright and mighty waters: — Who is the god to whom we shall offer our sacrifice? (9.)

"Pra*g*âpati, no other than thou embraces all these created things. May that be ours which we desire when sacrificing to thee: may we be lords of wealth!" (10.)

With such ideas as these springing up in the minds of the Vedic poets, we should have thought

[1] Read rodasî for krandasî.

[2] τὸν ἐπὶ πᾶσι θεόν. Froude, Celsus: *Fraser's Magazine*, 1878, p. 131.

that the natural development of their old religion could only have been towards monotheism, towards the worship of one personal god, and that thus in India also the highest form would have been reached which man feels inclined to give to the Infinite, after all other forms and names have failed. But it was not so. Hymns like those I have quoted are few in number in the Rig-Veda, and they do not lead to anything much more definite and solid in the next period, that of the Brâhma*n*as. In the Brâhma*n*as, Pra*g*âpati, the lord of living creatures, the father both of Devas and Asuras,[1] has, no doubt, a more prominent part assigned to him than in the hymns, but even there his mythological character breaks out occasionally very strongly, as, for instance, when he appears[2] as the father of Agni, Vâyu, Âditya (the sun), *K*andramas (the moon), and Ushas (the dawn); and in the story of his love for his daughter, who was originally the Dawn, chased by the sun, a story which afterwards became a great stumbling-block to the worshipers of Pra*g*âpati.

Now and then, in reading certain chapters of the Brâhma*n*as, one imagines that the craving after one supreme personal God had at last found its satisfaction in Pra*g*âpati, the lord of all living things, and that all the other gods would vanish before this new radiance. Thus we read: —

"Pra*g*âpati alone was all this in the beginning.[3] Pra*g*âpati is Bharata, the supporter, for he supports all this.[4] Pra*g*âpati created living creatures. From his higher vital breath he created the gods; from his

[1] Taittirîya Brâhma*n*a, I. 4, 1, 1.
[2] Sânkhâyana Brâhma*n*a, VI. 1. Muir, iv. p. 343.
[3] Satapatha Brâhma*n*a, II. 2, 4, 1. Muir, iv. p. 28.
[4] Satapatha Brâhma*n*a, VI. 8, 1, 14.

lower vital breath he created men. Afterwards he created death as one who should be a devourer for all living creatures. Of that Pra*g*âpati one half was mortal, the other immortal, and with that half which was mortal he was afraid of death.[1]

TENDENCY TOWARDS ATHEISM.

Here we see that even the authors of the Brâhma*n*as perceived that there was something mortal in Pra*g*âpati, and there is another passage where they go so far as to declare that he at last fell to pieces, and that all the gods went away from him, with one exception, viz., Manyu.[2]

And so it was indeed, though in a different sense from that intended by his worshipers.

The Hindu mind had grown, and was growing, stronger and stronger. In its search after the infinite it had been satisfied for a time by resting on the mountains and rivers, by asking their protection, praising their endless grandeur, though feeling all the time that they were but signs of something else that was sought for. Our Aryan ancestors had then learnt to look up to the sky, the sun, and the dawn, and there to see the presence of a living power, half-revealed, and half-hidden from their senses, those senses which were always postulating something beyond what they could grasp.

They went farther still. In the bright sky they perceived an illuminator; in the all-encircling firmament an embracer; in the roar of thunder and in the violence of the storm they felt the presence of a shouter and of furious strikers; and out of the rain they created an Indra, or giver of rain.

[1] *S*atapatha Brâhma*n*a, X. 1, 3, 1.

[2] *S*atapatha Brâhma*n*a, IX. 1, 1, 6. Muir, iv. p. 348.

With these last steps, however, came also the first reaction, the first doubt. So long as the thoughts of the ancient Aryan worshipers had something manifest or tangible to rest on, they might, no doubt, in their religious aspirations, far exceed the limits of actual observation; still no one could ever question the existence or the sensuous foreground of what they chose to call their Devas or their gods. The mountains and rivers were always there to speak for themselves; and if the praises bestowed upon them seemed to be excessive, they might be toned down, without calling in question the very existence of these beings. The same applied to the sky, the sun, and the dawn. They also were always there; and though they might be called mere visions and appearances, yet the human mind is so made that it admits of no appearance without admitting at the same time something that appears, some reality or substance. But when we come to the third class of Devas or gods, not only intangible but invisible, the case is different. Indra, as the giver of rain, Rudra, as the thunderer, were completely creations of the human mind. All that was given was the rain and the thunder, but there was nothing in nature that could be called an appearance of the god himself. Thunder and rain were not considered divine, but only as the work of beings who themselves never assumed a visible shape.

Man saw their work, but that was all; no one could point to the sky or the sun or the dawn or anything else visible to attest the existence of Indra and Rudra in their original meaning and character. It is something like the difference between being able to use a human skull or only a chipped flint in order to prove the presence of human life and human activity in distant periods of history. We saw before that Indra, for the very reason that there was nothing in nature to which he clung, nothing visible that could arrest his growth in the mind of his worshipers, developed more than other gods into a personal, dramatic, and mythological being. More battles are recorded, more stories are told, of Indra than of any other Vedic god, and this helps us to understand how it was that he seemed even to the ancient poets to have ousted Dyaus, the Indian Zeus, from his supremacy. But a Nemesis was to come.

This very god who seemed for a time to have thrown all the others into the shade, whom many would call, if not the supreme, at least the most popular deity of the Veda, was the first god whose very existence was called in question.

FAITH IN INDRA, DOUBTS ABOUT INDRA.

It sounds strange that for Indra more than for any other god, *faith* (sraddhâ) is required in the Vedic hymns. "When the fiery Indra hurls down the thunderbolt, then people put *faith* in him," we read.[1] Again: "Look at this his great and mighty work, and believe in the power of Indra."[2] "Do not, O Indra, hurt our nearest kin, for we believe in thy great power."[3] "Sun and moon move in regular

[1] Rig-Veda, I. 55, 5, adha *k*ana *s*rat dadhati tvishimate indrâya va*g*ram nighanighnate vadham. "Alte tonantem credidimus Jovem." Cf. Rig-Veda, I. 104, 7.

[2] Ibid. I. 103, 5, tat asya idam pasyata bhûri push*t*am, *s*rat indrasya dhattana vîryâya.

[3] Ibid. I. 104, 6, mâ antaram bhu*g*am â ririsha*h* na*h*, *s*raddhitam te mahate indriyâya.

succession, that we may have faith, O Indra."[1] Such appeals sound almost like a theological argument, and we should hardly expect to meet with it at so early a time. But in the history of the human mind, too, we may learn the lesson that everything new is old, and everything old new. Think how closely the world and the thoughts of men hang together. The word here used for the first time for faith, sraddhâ, is the very same word which meets us again in the Latin *credo*, and still lives in our own *creed*. Where the Romans said *credidi*, the Brahmans said sraddadhau; where the Romans said *creditum*, the Brahmins said sraddhitam. That word and that thought, therefore, must have existed before the Aryan family broke up, before Sanskrit was Sanskrit and before Latin was Latin. Even at that early time people believed what neither their senses could apprehend nor their reason comprehend. They believed; and they did not only believe, as a fact, but they had formed a word for belief, that is, they were conscious of what they were doing in thus believing, and they consecrated that mental function by calling it *srad-dhâ*.[2] I cannot enter into all that is implied by this coincidence; I can only here

[1] Rig-Veda, I. 102, 2, asme sûryâ*k*andramase abhi*k*akshe sraddhe kam indra *k*arata*h* vitarturam.

[2] The original meaning of srat in srad-dhâ is not clear to me. I cannot adopt one of the latest conjectures, that it stands for Sk. hard or h*ri*d, heart, and that sraddhâ meant originally to take to heart; not on account of phonetic difficulties, but because we have in the Veda also srat k*ri*; Rig-Veda, VIII. 75, 2, srat visvâ vâryâ k*ri*dhi, make all wishes true! I believe with Benfey that srat is connected with sru, to hear, and that the original conception was to hold a thing as heard, as known, as true. But I cannot as yet offer any satisfactory explanation of its etymology. If srat is a contraction of sravat, then sravat may stand for sravas, as ushat, etc., for ushas. Contraction before dhâ is common, but we should expect srot or sros rather than srat.

call your attention to the endless *vista* which that one word opens before our eyes far beyond the Alps and the Caucasus to the Himalayan mountains.

This very god, however — Indra — who was to be, before all others, believed in, while most of the other gods were simply taken for granted, was also the first god that roused the skepticism of his worshipers. Thus we read:[1] —

"Offer praise to Indra, if you desire booty; true praise, if he truly exists. One and the other says, There is no Indra. Who has seen him? Whom shall we praise?"

In this hymn the poet turns round, and introducing Indra himself, makes him say: —

"Here I am, O worshiper! behold me here. In might I overcome all creatures."[2]

But we read again in another hymn:[3] —

"The terrible one of whom they ask where he is, and of whom they say he that he is not: he takes away the riches of his enemy, like the stakes at a game. Believe in him, ye men, for he is indeed Indra."

When we thus see the old god Dyaus antiquated by Indra, Indra himself denied, and Pra*g*âpati falling to pieces, and when another poet declares in so many words that all the gods are but names, we might imagine that the stream of religious thought, which sprang from a trust in mountains and rivers, then proceeded to an adoration of the sky and the sun,

[1] Rig-Veda, VIII. 100, 3, pra su stomam bharata vâ*g*ayanta*h* indrâya satyam yadi satyam asti, na indra*h* asti iti nema*h* u tva*h* âha, ka*h* îm dadarsa kam abhi stavâma.

[2] Ayam asmi *g*arita*h* pasya mâ iha visvâ *g*âtâni abhi asmi mahnâ.

[3] Ibid. II. 12, 5, yam sma p*rikkh*anti kuha sa*h* iti ghoram, uta îm âhu*h* na esha*h* asti iti enam, sa*h* araya*h* push*t*î*h* vi*g*a*h* ivâ â minâti, srat asmai dhatta sa*h* *g*anâsa*h* indra*h*.

then grew into a worship of invisible gods, such as the sender of thunder-storms and the giver of rain, had well-nigh finished its course. We might expect in India the same catastrophe which in Iceland the poets of the Edda always predicted — the twilight of the gods, preceding the destruction of the world. We seem to have reached the stage when henotheism, after trying in vain to grow into an organized polytheism on the one side, or into an exclusive monotheism on the other, would by necessity end in atheism, or a denial of all the gods or Devas.

DIFFERENCE BETWEEN HONEST AND VULGAR ATHEISM.

And so it did. Yet atheism is not the last word of Indian religion, though it seemed to be so for a time in some of the phases of Buddhism. The word itself, atheism, is perhaps out of place, as applied to the religion of India. The ancient Hindus had neither the *θεοί* of the Homeric singers, nor the *θεός* of the Eleatic philosophers. Their atheism, such as it was, would more correctly be called *Adevism*, or a denial of the old Devas. Such a denial, however, of what was once believed, but could be honestly believed no longer, so far from being the destruction, is in reality the vital principle of all religion. The ancient Aryans felt from the begining, ay, it may be, more in the beginning than afterwards, the presence of a Beyond, of an Infinite, of a Divine, or whatever else we may call it now; and they tried to grasp and comprehend it, as we all do, by giving to it name after name. They thought they had found it in the mountains and rivers, in the dawn, in the sun, in the sky, in the heaven, and the Heaven-Father. But after every name, there came the No! What they looked for was *like* the mountains, *like* the rivers, *like* the dawn, *like* the sky, *like* the father; but it was *not* the mountains, *not* the rivers, *not* the dawn, *not* the sky, it was *not* the father. It was something of all that, but it was also more, it was beyond all that. Even such general names as *Asura* or *Deva* could no longer satisfy them. There may be Devas and Asuras, they said; but we want more, we want a higher word, a purer thought. They forsook the bright Devas, not because they believed or desired less, but because they believed and desired more than the bright Devas.

There was a new conception working in their mind; and the cries of despair were but the harbingers of a new birth.

So it has been, so it always will be. There is an atheism which is unto death, there is another atheism which is the very life-blood of all true faith. It is the power of giving up what, in our best, our most honest moments, we know to be no longer true; it is the readiness to replace the less perfect, however dear, however sacred it may have been to us, by the more perfect, however much it may be detested, as yet, by the world. It is the true self-surrender, the true self-sacrifice, the truest trust in truth, the truest faith. Without that atheism religion would long ago have become a petrified hypocrisy; without that atheism no new religion, no reform, no reformation, no resuscitation would ever have been possible; without that atheism no new life is possible for any one of us.

Let us look at the history of religion. How many men in all countries and all ages have been called atheists, not because they denied that there existed anything beyond the visible and the finite, or because they declared that the world, such as it was, could be explained without a cause, without a purpose, without a God, but often because they differed only from the traditional conception of the Deity prevalent at the time, and were yearning after a higher and purer conception of God than what they had learnt in their childhood.

In the eyes of the Brahmans, Buddha was an atheist. Now, some of the Buddhist schools of philosophy were certainly atheistical, but whether Gautama *S*âkyamuni, the Buddha, was himself an atheist, is at least doubtful, and his denial of the popular Devas would certainly not make him so.[1]

In the eyes of his Athenian judges, Sokrates was an atheist; yet he did not even deny the gods of Greece, but simply claimed the right to believe in something higher and more truly divine than Hephaistos and Aphrodite.

In the eyes of the Jews, whoever called himself the son of God was a blasphemer, and whoever worshiped the God of his fathers after "that new way" was a heretic. The very name for the Christians among Greeks and Romans was atheists, ἄθεοι.[2]

Nor did the same abuse of language cease altogether among the Christians themselves. In the eyes of Athanasius, the Arians were "devils, antichrists, maniacs, Jews, polytheists, *atheists*,"[3] and we need not

[1] In the Rúpnáth Inscription (221 B. C.) Asoka takes credit "that those gods who during this time were considered to be true in *G*ambudvîpa, have now been abjured." See G. Bühler, *Three New Edicts of Asoka* (Bombay, 1877), p. 29.

[2] *Eusebii Smyrnensis Epist. de St. Polycarpi martyrio*, 3, 9.

[3] Dr. Stanley in his *Eastern Church*, p. 246, quotes the following string

wonder if Arius did not take a much more charitable view of the Athanasians. Yet both Athanasius and Arius were only striving to realize the highest ideal of Deity, each in his own way, Arius fearing that Gentile, Athanasius that Jewish errors might detract from its truth and majesty.[1]

Nay, even in later times the same thoughtlessness of expression has continued in theological warfare. In the sixteenth century Servetus called Calvin a trinitarian and atheist,[2] while Calvin considered Servetus worthy of the stake (1553), because his view of the Deity differed from his own.

In the next century, to quote only one case which has lately been more carefully reëxamined, Vanini was condemned to have his tongue torn out, and to be burnt alive (1619 A. D.), because, as his own judge declared, though many considered him an heresiarch only, he condemned him as an atheist. As some recent writers, who ought to have known better, have joined in Grammont's condemnation of Vanini, it is but right that we should hear what that atheist said of God.

"You ask me what God is," he writes. "If I knew it, I should be God, for no one knows God, except God Himself. Though we may in a certain way discover Him in his works, like the sun through the clouds: yet we should not comprehend Him bet-

of epithets applied by Athanasius to Arius and the Arians, as collected in Athanasius's *Historical Treatises* (Newman's ed., ii. p. 34): "Devils, antichrists, maniacs, Jews, polytheists, atheists, dogs, wolves, lions, hares, chameleons, hydras, eels, cuttle-fish, gnats, beetles, leeches."

[1] Gregory of Nyssa, *Logos katecheticos*, cap. 3; Pfleiderer, *Religionsphilosophie*, p. 381.

[2] "Item — il appelle ceux qui croyent en la Trinité, trinitaires et athéistes." *Procès contre Michel Servet.*

ter by that means. Let us say, however, that He is the greatest good, the first Being, the whole, just, compassionate, blessed, calm; the creator, preserver, moderator, omniscient, omnipotent; the father, king, lord, rewarder, ruler; the beginning, the end, the middle, eternal; the author, life-giver, observer, the artificer, providence, the benefactor. He alone is all in all."[1]

The man who wrote this was burnt as an atheist. Such was in fact the confusion of ideas during the seventeenth century with regard to the true meaning of atheism, that so late as 1696 the Parliament at Edinburgh passed an Act[2] "against the Atheistical opinions of the Deists," and that men, such as Spinoza and Archbishop Tillotson,[3] though they could no longer be burnt, were both branded indiscriminately as atheists.

Nor has even the eighteenth century been quite free from similar blots. Many men were called atheists even then, not because they dreamt of denying the existence of a God, but because they wished to purify the idea of the Godhead from what seemed to them human exaggeration and human error.

In our own time we have learnt too well what atheism does mean, to use the word thus lightly and thoughtlessly. Yet it is well that whoever dares to be honest towards himself and towards others, be he layman or clergyman, should always remember what men they were who, before him, have been called blasphemers, heretics, or atheists.

[1] G. C. Vanini, da R. Palumbo (Napoli, 1878), p. 27.

[2] Macaulay, *History of England*, chap. xxii.; Cunningham, *History of the Church of Scotland*, ii. p. 313.

[3] Macaulay, *History of England*, chap. xvii.: "He was an Arian, a Socinian, a Deist, an Atheist."

There are moments in our life when those who seek most earnestly after God think they are forsaken of God; when they hardly venture to ask themselves, Do I then believe in God, or do I not?

Let them not despair, and let us not judge harshly of them; their despair may be better than many creeds.

Let me quote, in conclusion, the words of a great divine, lately deceased, whose honesty and piety have never been questioned. "*God*," he says, "is a *great* word. He who feels and understands that, will judge more mildly and more justly of those who confess that they dare not say that they believe in God."

Now I know perfectly well that what I have said just now will be misunderstood, will possibly be misinterpreted. I know I shall be accused of having defended and glorified atheism, and of having represented it as the last and highest point which man can reach in an evolution of religious thought. Let it be so! If there are but a few here present who understand what I mean by honest atheism, and who know how it differs from vulgar atheism, ay, from dishonest theism, I shall feel satisfied, for I know that to understand that distinction will often help us in the hour of our sorest need. It will teach us that while the old leaves, the leaves of a bright and happy spring, are falling, and all seems wintry, frozen, and dead within and around us, there is and there must be a new spring in store for every warm and honest heart. It will teach us that honest doubt is the deepest spring of honest faith; and that he only who has lost can find.

How the Indian mind, having arrived at this stage, grappled with this, the last and greatest of all religious problems, how it shook off, like another Laokoon, the coils of atheism, we shall see in our next and last lecture.

VII.

PHILOSOPHY AND RELIGION.

COLLAPSE OF THE GODS.

WHEN the Aryan settlers in India had arrived at the conviction that all their Devas or gods were mere names, we might imagine that they would have turned away in despair and disgust from what for ages they had adored and worshiped. Whether they had been deceived or had deceived themselves, the discovery that their old gods, their Indra, and Agni, and Varu*n*a, were names and nothing but names, was most likely to have produced on them the same impression as when the Greeks saw the temples of their gods demolished, or when the Germans stood by to see their sacred oaks felled, neither Apollo nor Odin appearing to avenge the sacrilege. But the result was totally different from what we should have expected. With the Greeks and Romans and Germans we know that their ancient gods, when their course was run, disappeared either altogether, or, if their existence could not be entirely annihilated, they were degraded into evil and mischievous spirits; while there was at the same time a new religion, namely Christianity, ready at hand, and capable of supplying those cravings of the heart which can never be entirely suppressed.

In India there was no such religion coming, as it

were, from outside, in which the Brahmans, after they had lost their old gods and protectors, could have taken refuge. So, instead of turning aside and making a new start, like the Greeks and Romans and Germans, they toiled on, on their own track, trusting that it would lead them right, if they fainted not in their search after what had been present to their minds from the first awakening of their senses, but what they had never been able to grasp firmly, to comprehend, or to name.

They threw away the old names, but they did not throw away their belief in that which they had tried to name. After destroying the altars of their old gods, they built out of the scattered bricks a new altar to the Unknown God — unknown, unnamed, and yet omnipresent; seen no more in the mountains and rivers, in the sky and the sun, in the rain and the thunder, but present even then, and, it may be, nearer to them, and encirling them, no longer like Varu*n*a, the encircling and all-embracing ether, but more closely and more intimately, being, as they called it themselves, the very ether in their heart: it may be, the still small voice.

THE OBJECT OF DIVINE APPELLATION.

Let us remember, first, that the old poets of the Veda did not say that Mitra, Varu*n*a, and Agni were names and names only. They said:[1] "They speak of Mitra, Varu*n*a, Agni; then he is the heavenly bird Garutmat; *that which is, and is one*, the poets

[1] Rig-Veda, I. 164, 46,
indram mitram varu*n*am agnim âhu*h*
atho divya*h* sa*h* supar*n*a*h* garutmân,
ekam sat viprâ*h* bahudhâ vadanti,
agnim yamam mâtarisvânam âhu*h*.

call in various ways; they speak of Yama, Agni, Mâtarisvan."

Here then we see three things: first, that the poets never doubted that there was something real (sat), of which Agni, Indra, and Varuna, and all the rest, were but names.

Secondly, that that something real was with them one, and one only.

Thirdly, that it must not be called one, as a masculine, such as Pra*g*âpati was, and other gods, but as a neuter.

NEUTER NAMES HIGHER THAN MASCULINE OR FEMININE.

Now this, no doubt, jars on our ears. *We* cannot bear the neuter as a name of the divine. With us the neuter generally conveys the idea of something purely material, dead, or impersonal. But it was not so in ancient language, that is, in ancient thought: it is not so even now in some of our modern languages. On the contrary, in choosing the neuter the ancient sages tried to express something that should be neither male nor female, that should be in fact as far removed from weak human nature as weak human language could well express it; something that should be higher than masculine or feminine, not lower. They wanted a sex-less, by no means a life-less, or what some, without perceiving the contradiction in terms, would call an impersonal God.

There are other passages where, though the poets speak of one God, with many names, they still speak of him in the masculine. Thus we read in a hymn addressed to the sun, and where the sun is likened to a bird:[1] "Wise poets represent by their words the bird, who is *one*, in many ways." This is to us pure mythology.

Less mythologically, but still very anthropomorphously, the supreme Being is represented in the following verse:[2] —

"Who saw Him, when he was first born, when he who has no bones bore him who has bones?

"Where was the breath, the blood, the self of the world? Who went to ask this from any that knew it?"

Every one of these words is pregnant with thought. "He who has no bones" is an expression used to convey what we should express by saying, "He who has no form;" while "he who has bones" is meant for that which has assumed consistency and form. "The breath and blood of the world," again, are attempts at expressing the unknown or invisible power which supports the world. "Breath" is in fact the nearest approach to what we should now call the essence or substance of the world.

ÂTMAN, THE SUBJECTIVE SELF.

This word, *breath*, in Sanskrit *âtman*, which is generally translated by *self*, is a word which, as we shall see, had a great future before it. Originally it meant breath, then life, sometimes body; but far more frequently, the essence or the self. It became

[1] Rig-Veda X. 114, 5,
suparnam viprâh kavayah .vakobhih
ekam santam bahudhâ kalpayanti.

[2] Rig-Veda, I. 164, 4,
kah dadarsa prathamam gâyamânam
asthanvantam yat anasthâ bibharti,
bhûmyâh asuh asrik âtmâ kva svit
kah vidvâmsam upa gât prashtum etat.

in fact a reflexive pronoun, like *αὐτός*, *ipse*, or *self*. It was not, however, entirely restricted to this grammatical category, but entered upon a new career as the name of one of the highest philosophical abstractions in India, or anywhere else. It was used to express, not simply the *Ego* or the I, for that *Ego*, the *Aham*, the I, was too much made up of the fleeting elements of this life. No, it expressed what was beyond the Ego, what supported the Ego for a time; but, after a time, freed itself from the fetters and conditions of the human Ego, and became again the pure Self.

Âtman differs from words which in other languages, after originally expressing breath, came to mean life, spirit, and soul. It lost its meaning of breath at a very early time, and after it had been divested of its physical meaning, after it had served as a mere pronoun, it became the vehicle of an abstraction more abstract even than ψυχή or πνεῦμα in Greek, *anima* or *animus* in Latin, asu or prâ*n*a in Sanskrit. In the Upanishads a belief in prâ*n*a, breath or spirit, as the true principle of existence, marks professedly a lower stage of philosophical knowledge than a belief in Âtman, the Self. As with us the Self transcends the I, the Âtman with the Hindus transcended the prâ*n*a, and finally absorbed it.

This is the way in which, at a later time, the ancient Indian philosophers discovered the Infinite that supported their own being, the inward Self, as far beyond the *Ego*.

ÂTMAN, THE OBJECTIVE SELF.

Let us now see how they tried to discover the infinite in the outward or objective world.

The poets had rested for a time in the One, whom they conceived as the one god, but who was still masculine, active, slightly mythological; who was in fact a divine *Ego*, not yet a divine *Self*. Suddenly, however, we light on passages of a different character. We seem to be moving in a new world. All that is dramatic and mythological, every form and every name, is surrendered, and there remains only "the One," or that which exists, as a neuter, as a last attempt to grasp the infinite.

The Vedic poets no longer glorify the sky or the dawn, they do not celebrate the prowess of Indra, or the wisdom of Visvakarman and Pra*g*âpati. They move about, as they say themselves, "as if enveloped in mist and idle speech."[1] Another says:[2] "My ears vanish, my eyes vanish, and the light also which dwells in my heart; my mind with its far-off longing leaves me; what shall I say, and what shall I think?"

Or again, "Knowing nothing myself, I ask the seers here, who know; ignorant myself, that I may learn; He who established the six worlds, is he that One which exists in the form of the unborn Being?"[3]

These are the storms that announce a brighter sky, and a new spring.

At last,[4] the existence of that One, the Self, is

[1] Rig-Veda, X. 82, 7,
nîhârena prâv*ri*tâ*h* *g*alpyâ *k*a asut*ri*pa*h* ukthasâsa*h* *k*aranti.

[2] Ibid. VI. 9, 6,
vi me kar*n*â patayata*h*, vi *k*akshu*h*
vi idam *g*yoti*h* h*ri*daye âhitam yat;
vi me mana*h* *k*arati duraâdhî*h*
kim svit vakshyâmi kim u nu manishye.

[3] Ibid. I. 164, 6,
a*k*ikitvân *k*ikitusha*h* *k*it atra kavîn p*rikkh*âmi vidmane na vidvân
vi ya*h* tastambha sha*t* imâ ra*g*âmsi a*g*asya rûpe kim api svit ekam.

[4] Rig-Veda, X. 129, 2.

boldly asserted, as existing by itself, existing before all created things, existing so long before the gods that even they, the gods, do not know from whence this creation sprang.

"Before there was anything," we are told, "before there was either death or immortality, before there was any distinction between day and night, there was that One. It breathed breathless by itself. Other than it there nothing since has been. There was darkness then, everything in the beginning was hidden in gloom — all was like the ocean, without a light. Then that germ which was covered by the husk, the One, was brought forth by the power of heat." So the poet goes on brooding on the problem of the beginning of all things, how the One became many, how the unknown became known or named, how the infinite became finite; and he finally breaks off with these lines: —

"Who knows the secret? who proclaimed it here?
Whence, whence this manifold creation sprang?
The gods themselves came later into being —
Who knows from whence this great creation sprang?
He from whom all this great creation came, —
Whether his will created or was mute, —
The most high seer, that is in highest heaven,
He knows it, or perchance even he knows not."

These ideas which in the hymns of the Rig-Veda appear only like the first dim stars, become more numerous, and more brilliant as time goes on, till at last they form a perfect galaxy in what is called the Upanishads, the last literary compositions which still belong to the Vedic period, but which extend their influence far beyond its limits.

THE PHILOSOPHY OF THE UPANISHADS.

You remember that, next to what we call the age of the hymns, followed the age of the Brâhma*n*as, ancient prose works intended to describe and to illustrate the ancient sacrifices.

At the end of the Brâhma*n*as we generally find what is called an Âra*n*yaka, a forest book, a book intended for those who have left their house to dwell in the solitude of the forest.

And at the end of the Âra*n*yakas again or incorporated within them, we find the oldest Upanishads, literally *Sessions*, or assemblies of pupils round their master; and in those Upanishads all the religious philosophy of the Vedic age is gathered up.

In order to give you an idea of the wealth of thought collected in these Upanishads, I may tell you that it was at first my intention to devote the whole of these lectures to an exposition of the doctrines of the Upanishads. I should have found ample material in them; while now I can only give you the slightest sketch of them in the short time that is still left to me.

There is not what could be called a philosophical system in these Upanishads. They are, in the true sense of the word, guesses at truth, frequently contradicting each other, yet all tending in one direction. The key-note of the old Upanishads is "Know thy Self," but with a much deeper meaning than that of the Γνῶθι σεαυτόν of the Delphic oracle. The "Know thy Self" of the Upanishads means, know thy true Self, that which underlies thine Ego, and find it and know it in the highest, the eternal Self, the One without a Second, which underlies the whole world.

This was the final solution of the search after the Infinite, the Invisible, the Unknown, the Divine, a search begun in the simplest hymns of the Veda, and ended in the Upanishads, or, as they were afterwards called, the Vedânta, the end or the highest object of the Veda.

I can do no more than read you some extracts from these works, which stand unrivaled in the literature of India, nay, in the literature of the world.

PRA*G*APATI AND INDRA.

The first extract is from the *Kh*ândogya Upanishad (VIII. 7–12). It is a story representing Indra as the chief of the Devas or gods, and Viro*k*ana as the chief of the Asuras, seeking instruction from Pra*g*âpati. This, no doubt, sounds modern, if compared with the hymns of the Rig-Veda, yet it is anything but modern, if compared with all the rest of Indian literature. The opposition between Devas and Asuras is, no doubt, secondary, but traces of it begin to show themselves in the Rig-Veda, particularly in the last book. "Asura," living, was originally an epithet of certain powers of nature, particularly of the sky. In some passages one feels inclined to translate devâ asurâ*h* by the living gods. After a time asura is used as an epithet of certain evil spirits also, and at last it occurs in the plural as the name of the evil spirits, opposed to the Devas, the bright, kind, and good spirits. In the Brâhma*n*as that distinction is firmly established, and nearly everything is settled there by battles between Devas and Asuras.

That Indra should represent the Devas is natural. Viro*k*ana, however, is of later date; the name does not occur in the hymns. He appears first in the

Taittirîya Brâhma*n*a, I. 5, 9, 1, where he is introduced as the son of Phrahrâda and Kayâdhû. Pra*g*âpati has assumed in this story his later character, as a kind of supreme god; he is even represented as father of Indra in the Taittirîya Brâhma*n*a, I. 5, 9, 1.

The object of our legend is evidently to show the different stages by which we are to arrive at a knowledge of the true Self in man. Pra*g*âpati speaks at first in an equivocal way, saying that the person seen in the eye is the Self. He means the seer, as independent of the eye, but his pupils misunderstand him, the Asura supposing that the small body seen in the pupil of the eye as in a mirror is the Self, the Deva imagining that the shadow or the image in the mirror or in the water is the Self. But while Viro*k*ana is satisfied, Indra is not, and he is then led on to seek the Self, first in the person who, freed from the impressions of the senses, is dreaming; then in the person who has ceased to dream and is quite unconscious. Dissatisfied, however, with this, which seems to him utter annihilation, Indra is at last allowed to see that the Self is he who uses the senses, but is distinct from them, the person, in fact, seen in the eye, *i. e.*, perceived in the eye, as the seer; or again, he who knows that he is the knower, while the mind, the divine eye, as it is called, is but his instrument. We find here the highest expression of the truth as seen by the dwellers in the forest, the highest goal reached by them in their search after the infinite.

SEVENTH KHA*ND*A.

"Pra*g*âpati said: 'The Self which is free from sin, free from old age, from death and grief, from hunger and thirst, which desires nothing but what it ought to desire, and imagines nothing but what it ought to imagine, that it is which we must search out, that it is which we must try to understand. He who has searched out that Self and understands it, obtains all worlds and all desires.'" 1.

"The Devas (gods) and Asuras (demons) both heard these words, and said: 'Well, let us search for that Self by which if one has searched it out, all worlds and all desires are obtained.'

"Thus saying Indra went from the Devas, Viro*k*ana from the Asuras, and both, without having communicated with each other, approached Pra*g*âpati, holding fuel in their hands, as is the custom for pupils approaching their master." 2.

"They dwelt there as pupils for thirty-two years. Then Pra*g*âpati asked them: 'For what purpose have you both dwelt here?'

"They replied: 'A saying of yours is being repeated, viz., "the Self which is free from sin, free from old age, from death and grief, from hunger and thirst, which desires nothing but what it ought to desire, and imagines nothing but what it ought to imagine, that it is which which we must search out, that it is which we must try to understand. He who has searched out that Self and understands it, obtains all worlds and all desires." Now we both have dwelt here because we wish for that Self.'" 3.

"Pra*g*âpati said to them: 'The person that is seen in the eye,[1] that is the Self. This is what I

[1] The commentator explains this rightly. Pra*g*âpati means the person that is seen in the eye, that is, the real agent of seeing, who is seen by sages even with their eyes shut. His pupils, however misunderstand him. They think of the person that is seen, not of the person that sees. The person seen in the eye is to them the small figure imaged in the eye, and

have said. This is the immortal, the fearless, this is Brahman.'

"They asked: 'Sir, he who is perceived in the water, and he who is perceived in a mirror, who is he?'

"He replied: 'He himself alone is seen in all these.'"[1] 4.

EIGHTH KHA*N*D*A*.

"Look at your Self in a pan of water, and whatever you do not understand of your Self,[2] come and tell me.

"They looked in the water-pan. Then Pra*g*âpati said to them: 'What do you see?'

"They said: 'We both see the Self thus altogether, a picture even to the very hairs and nails.'" 1.

"Pra*g*âpati said to them: 'After you have adorned yourselves, have put on your best clothes and cleaned yourselves, look again into the water-pan.'

"They, after having adorned themselves, having put on their best clothes, and cleaned themselves, looked into the water-pan.

"Pra*g*âpati said: 'What do you see?'" 2.

"They said: 'Just as we are, well adorned, with our best clothes and clean, thus we are both there, Sir, well adorned, with our best clothes and clean."

"Pra*g*âpati said: 'That is the Self, this is the immortal, the fearless, this is Brahman.'

"Then both went away satisfied in their hearts.

they go on therefore to ask, whether the image in the water or in a mirror is not the Self.

[1] The commentators are at great pains to explain that Pra*g*âpati told no falsehood. He meant by purusha the personal element in the highest sense, and it was not his fault that his pupils took purusha for man or body.

[2] I take âtmana*h* as a genitive, governed by yad, not as an accusative plural.

"And Pra*g*âpati, looking after them, said: 'They both go away without having perceived and without having known the Self, and whoever of these two,[1] whether Devas or Asuras, will follow this doctrine (upanishad), will perish.'

"Now Viro*k*ana satisfied in his heart went to the Asuras and preached that doctrine to them, that the Self (the body) alone is to be worshiped, that the Self (the body) alone is to be served, and that he who worships the Self and serves the Self, gains both worlds, this and the next." 4.

"Therefore they call even now a man who does not give alms here, who has no faith, and offers no sacrifices, an Âsura, for this is the doctrine (upanishad) of the Asuras. They deck out the body of the dead with perfumes, flowers, and fine raiment by way of ornament, and think they will thus conquer that world." 5.

NINTH KHA*ND*A.

"But Indra, before he had returned to the Devas, saw this difficulty. As this Self (the shadow in the water)[2] is well adorned when the body is well adorned, well dressed when the body is well dressed, well cleaned if the body is well cleaned, that Self will also be blind if the body is blind, lame if the body is lame,[3] crippled if the body is crippled, and will perish in fact as soon as the body perishes. Therefore I see no good in this (doctrine)." 1.

[1] The commentator reads yatare for yata*h*.

[2] The commentator remarks that though both Indra and Viro*k*ana had mistaken the true import of what Pra*g*âpati said, yet while Viro*k*ana took the body to be the Self, Indra thought that the Self was the shadow of the body.

[3] Srâma, lame, is explained by the commentator as one-eyed ekanetra.

"Taking fuel in his hand he came again as a pupil to Pra*g*âpati. Pra*g*âpati said to him: 'Maghavat (Indra), as you went away with Viro*k*ana, satisfied in your heart, for what purpose did you come back?'

"He said: 'Sir, as this Self (the shadow) is well adorned when the body is well adorned, well dressed when the body is well dressed, well cleaned if the body is well cleaned, that Self will also be blind if the body is blind, lame if the body is lame, crippled if the body is crippled, and will perish in fact as soon as the body perishes. Therefore I see no good in this (doctrine).'" 2.

"'So it is indeed, Maghavat,' replied Pra*g*âpati; 'but I shall explain him (the true Self) further to you. Live with me another thirty-two years.'

"He lived with him another thirty-two years, and then Pra*g*âpati said: 3.

TENTH KHA*N*DA.

"'He who moves about happy in dreams, he is the Self, this is the immortal, the fearless, this is Brahman.'

"Then Indra went away satisfied in his heart. But before he had returned to the Devas, he saw this difficulty. Now although it is true that that Self is not blind even if the body is blind, nor lame, if the body is lame, though it is true that that Self is not rendered faulty by the faults of it (the body), nor struck when it (the body) is struck, nor lamed when it is lamed, yet it is as if they struck him (the Self) in dreams, as if they drove him away. He becomes even conscious, as it were, of pain, and sheds tears. Therefore I see no good in this." 1.

"Taking fuel in his hands, he went again as a pupil to Pra*g*âpati. Pra*g*âpati said to him: 'Maghavat, as you went away satisfied in your heart, for what purpose did you come back?'

"He said: 'Sir, although it is true that that Self is not blind even if the body is blind, nor lame if the body is lame, though it is true that that Self is not rendered faulty by the faults of it (the body), nor struck when it (the body) is struck, nor lamed when it is lamed, yet it is as if they struck him (the Self) in dreams, as if they drove him away. He becomes even conscious, as it were of pain, and sheds tears. Therefore I see no good in this.'" 1.

"'So it is indeed, Maghavat,' replied Pra*g*âpati; 'but I shall explain him (the true Self) further to you. Live with me another thirty-two years.'

"He lived with him another thirty-two years. Then Pra*g*âpati said: 4.

ELEVENTH KHA*ND*A.

"'When a man being asleep, reposing, and at perfect rest,[1] sees no dreams, that is the Self, this is the immortal, the fearless, this is Brahman.'

"Then Indra went away satisfied in his heart. But before he had returned to the Devas, he saw this difficulty. In truth he thus does not know himself (his self) that he is I, nor does he know anything that exists. He is gone to utter annihilation. I see no good in this." 1.

"Taking fuel in his hand he went again as a pupil to Pra*g*âpati. Pra*g*âpati said to him: 'Maghavat, as you went away satisfied in your heart, for what purpose did you come back?'

"He said: 'Sir, in that way he does not know

[1] See *Kh*ândogya Upanishad, VIII. 6, 3.

himself (his self) that he is I, nor does he know anything that exists. He is gone to utter annihilation. I see no good in this.'

"'So it is indeed, Maghavat,' replied Pra*g*âpati; 'but I shall explain him (the true Self) further to you, and nothing more than this.[1] Live here other five years.'

"He lived there other five years. This made in all one hundred and one years, and therefore it is said that Indra Maghavat lived one hundred and one years as a pupil with Pra*g*âpati. Pra*g*âpati said to him:

TWELFTH KHA*ND*A.

"'Maghavat, this body is mortal and always held by death. It is the abode of that Self which is immortal and without body.[2] When in the body (by thinking this body is I and I am this body) the Self is held by pleasure and pain. So long as he is in the body, he cannot get free from pleasure and pain. But when he is free of the body (when he knows himself different from the body), then neither pleasure nor pain touches him.'"[3] 1.

"'The wind is without body, the cloud, lightning, and thunder are without body (without hands, feet, etc.). Now as these, arising from this heavenly ether (space), appear in their own form, as soon as they have approached the highest light, 2.

"'Thus does that serene soul, arising from this body, appear in its own form, as soon as it has ap-

[1] *S*ankara explains this as meaning, the real Self, not anything different from the Self.

[2] According to some, the body is the result of the Self, the elements of the body, light, water, and earth springing from the Self, and the Self afterwards entering them.

[3] Ordinary, worldly pleasure. Comm.

proached the highest light (the knowledge of Self).[1] He (in that state) is the highest person (uttama pûrusha). He moves about there laughing (or eating), playing, and rejoicing (in his mind), be it with women, carriages, or relatives, never minding that body into which he was born.[2]

"'Like as a horse attached to a cart, so is the spirit[3] (prâna, pragnâtman) attached to this body.'" 3.

"'Now where the sight has entered into the void (the open space, the black pupil of the eye), there is the person of the eye, the eye itself is the instrument of seeing. He who knows, let me smell this, he is the Self, the nose is the instrument of smelling. He who knows, let me say this, he is the Self, the tongue is the instrument of saying. He who knows, let me hear this, he is the Self, the ear is the instrument of hearing.'" 4.

"'He who knows, let me think this, he is the Self, the mind in his divine eye.[4] He, the Self, seeing

[1] The simile is not so striking as most of those old similes are. The wind is compared with the Self on account of its being for a time lost in the ether (space), as the Self is in the body, and then rising again out of the ether and assuming its own form as wind. The chief stress is laid on the highest light, which in the one case is the sun of summer, in the other the light of knowledge.

[2] These are pleasures which seem hardly compatible with the state of perfect peace which the Self is supposed to have attained. The passage may be interpolated, or put in on purpose to show that the Self enjoys such pleasures as an inward spectator only, without identifying himself with either pleasure or pain. He sees them, as he says afterwards, with his divine eye. The Self perceives in all things his Self only, nothing else. In his commentary on the Taittirîya Upanishad (p. 45) Sankara refers this passage to Brahman as an effect, not to Brahman as a cause.

[3] The spirit is not identical with the body, but only joined to it, like a horse, or driving it, like a charioteer. In other passages the senses are the horses, *buddhi*, reason, the charioteer, *manas*, the mind, the reins. The spirit is attached to the cart by the *k*etana: cf. Ânanda*g*nânagiri.

[4] Because it perceives not only what is present, but also what is past and future.

these pleasures (which to others are hidden like a buried treasure of gold) through his divine eye, *i. e.*, the mind, rejoices.

"'The Devas who are in the world of Brahman worship that Self (as taught by Pra*g*âpati to Indra, and by Indra to the Devas). There all worlds are held by them, and all pleasures. He who knows that Self and understands it, obtains all worlds and all desires.' Thus said Pra*g*âpati, thus said Pra*g*âpati."

YÂ*G*NAVALKYA AND MAITREYÎ.

The next extract is taken from the B*ri*hadâra*n*yaka, where it is repeated twice, with slight differences, the first time in the second, the second time in the fourth Adhyâya:[1]—

"Yâ*g*navalkya[2] had two wives, Maitreyî and Kâtyâyanî. Of these Maitreyî was conversant with Brahman, but Kâtyâyanî possessed such knowledge only as women possess.

"Now when Yâ*g*navalkya was going to enter upon another state, he said: 'Maitreyî, verily I am going away from this my house (into the forest).[3] Forsooth, let me make a settlement between thee and that Kâtyâyanî (my other wife).'" 1.

"Maitreyî said: 'My Lord, if this whole earth full of wealth belonged to me, tell me, should I be immortal by it?'[4]

"'No,' replied Yâ*g*navalkya; 'like the life of rich people will be thy life. But there is no hope of immortality by wealth.'" 2.

[1] The variations of the second recension are marked by B.

[2] This introductory paragraph occurs in the second version only.

[3] Instead of udyâsyan, B. gives pravra*g*ishyan, the more technical term.

[4] Should I be immortal by it, or no? B.

"And Maitreyî said: "What should I do with that by which I do not become immortal? What my Lord knoweth (of immortality), tell that to me.'"[1] 3.

"Yâ*g*navalkya replied: 'Thou who art truly dear to me, thou speakest dear words. Come, sit down,[2] I will explain it to thee, and mark well what I say.'" 4.

"And he said: 'Verily, a husband is not dear, that you may love the husband; but that you may love the Self, therefore a husband is dear.

"'Verily, a wife is not dear, that you may love the wife; but that you may love the Self, therefore a wife is dear.

"'Verily, sons are not dear, not that you may love the sons; but that you may love the Self, therefore sons are dear.

"'Verily, wealth is not dear, that you may love wealth; but that you may love the Self, therefore wealth is dear.[3]

"'Verily, the Brahman-class is not dear, that you may love the Brahman-class; but that you may love the Self, therefore the Brahman-class is dear.

"'Verily, the Kshattra-class is not dear, that you may love the Kshattra-class; but that you may love the Self, therefore the Kshattra-class is dear.

"'Verily, the worlds are not dear, that you may love the worlds; but that you may love the Self, therefore the worlds are dear.

"'Verily, the Devas are not dear, that you may

1 Tell that clearly to me. B.

2 Thou who art dear to me, thou art dearer to me still. Therefore sit down. B.

3 B. adds, Verily, cattle are not dear, etc.

love the Devas; but that you may love the Self, therefore the Devas are dear.[1]

"'Verily, creatures are not dear, that you may love the creatures; but that you may love the Self, therefore are creatures dear.

"'Verily, everything is not dear that you may love everything; but that you may love the Self, therefore everything is dear.

"'Verily, the Self is to be seen, to be heard, to be perceived, to be marked, O Maitreyî! When we see, hear, perceive, and know the Self,[2] then all this is known.'" 5.

"'Whosoever looks for the Brahman-class elsewhere than in the Self, should be abandoned by the Brahman-class. Whosoever looks for the Kshattra-class elsewhere than in the Self, should be abandoned by the Kshattra-class. Whosoever looks for the worlds elsewhere than in the Self, should be abandoned by the worlds. Whosoever looks for the Devas elsewhere than in the Self, should be abandoned by the Devas.[3] Whosoever looks for creatures elsewhere than in the Self, should be abandoned by the creatures. Whosoever looks for everything elsewhere than in the Self, should be abandoned by everything. This Brahman-class, this Kshattra-class, these worlds, these Devas,[4] these creatures, this everything, all is that Self.'" 6.

"'Now as[5] the sounds of a drum when beaten cannot be seized externally by themselves, but the

[1] B. inserts, Verily the Vedas are not dear, etc.

[2] When the Self has been seen, heard, perceived, and known. B.

[3] B. inserts, Whosoever looks for the Vedas, etc.

[4] These Vedas, B.

[5] I construe sa yathâ with evam vai in § 12, looking upon § 11 as probably a later insertion.

sound is seized when the drum is seized or the beater of the drum;'" 7.

"'And as the sounds of a conch-shell when blown, cannot be seized externally (by themselves), but the sound is seized when the shell is seized or the blower of the shell;'" 8.

"'And as the sounds of a lute when played cannot be seized externally by themselves, but the sound is seized when the lute is seized or the player of the lute;'" 9.

"'As clouds of smoke proceed by themselves out of a lighted fire kindled with damp fuel, thus verily, O Maitreyî, has been breathed forth from this great Being what we have as *Ri*gveda, Ya*g*urveda, Sâmaveda, Atharvângirasa*h*, Itihâsa (legends), Purâ*n*a (cosmogonies), Vidyâ (knowledge), the Upanishads, *S*lokas (verses), Sûtras (prose rules), Anuvyâkhyânas (glosses), Vyâkhyânas (commentaries).[1] From him alone all these were breathed forth.'" 10.

"'As all waters find their centre in the sea, all touches in the skin, all tastes in the tongue, all smells in the nose, all colors in the eye, all sounds in the ear, all percepts in the mind, all knowledge in the heart, all actions in the hands, all movements in the feet, and all the Vedas in speech,'" 11.

"'As a lump of salt, when thrown into water, becomes dissolved into water, and could not be taken out again, but wherever we taste (the water), it is salt, thus verily, O Maitreyî, does this great Being, endless, unlimited, consisting of nothing but knowledge,[2] rise from out these elements, and vanish again

[1] B. adds, sacrifice, offering, food, drink, this world and the other world, and all creatures.

[2] As solid salt, compact, pure, and entire is nothing but taste, thus, verily, O beloved, this Self, compact, pure, and entire, is nothing but knowledge. B.

in them. When he has departed, there is no more knowledge, I say, O Maitreyî.' Thus spoke Yâgnavalkya." 12.

"Then Maitreyî said: 'Here thou hast bewildered me, Sir, when thou sayst that having departed, there is no more knowledge.' [1]

"But Yâgnavalkya replied: 'O Maitreyî, I have said nothing that is bewildering. This is enough, O beloved, for wisdom.'" [2] 13.

"'For when there is as it were duality, then one sees the other, one smells the other, one hears the other,[3] one salutes the other,[4] one perceives the other,[5] one knows the other; but when the Self only is all this, how should he smell another,[6] how should he see [7] another [8], how should he hear [9] another, how should he salute [10] another, how should he perceive another,[11] how should he know another? How should he know him by whom he knows all this? How, O beloved, should he know (himself) the Knower?'" [12]

YAMA AND NAKIKETAS.

One of the best known among the Upanishads is

[1] "Here, Sir, thou hast brought me into bewilderment; I do not understand him." B.

[2] Verily, beloved, that Self is imperishable, and of an indestructible nature. B.

[3] One tastes the other. B.

[4] B. inserts, one hears the other. B.

[5] B. inserts, one touches the other. B.

[6] See. B.

[7] Smell.

[8] B. inserts taste.

[9] Salute.

[10] Hear.

[11] B. inserts, how should he touch another?

[12] Instead of the last line B. adds (IV. 5, 15): "That Self is to be described by No, No! He is incomprehensible, for he is not comprehended: free from decay, for he does not decay; free from contact, for he is not touched; unfettered, he does not tremble, he does not fail. How, O beloved, should he know the knower? Thus, O Maitreyî, thou hast been instructed. Thus far goes immortality." Having said so, Yâgnavalkya went away (into the forest). 15.

the Ka*th*a Upanishad. It was first introduced to the knowledge of European scholars by Ram Mohun Roy, one of the most enlightened benefactors of his own country, and, it may still turn out, one of the most enlightened benefactors of mankind. It has since been frequently translated and discussed, and it certainly deserves the most careful consideration of all who are interested in the growth of religious and philosophical ideas. It does not seem likely that we possess it in its original form, for there are clear traces of later additions in it. There is in fact the same story told in the Taittirîya Brâhma*n*a, III. 11, 8, only with this difference, that in the Brâhma*n*a freedom from death and birth is obtained by a peculiar performance of a sacrifice, while in the Upanishad it is obtained by knowledge only.

The Upanishad consists of a dialogue between a young child, called Na*k*iketas, and Yama, the ruler of departed spirits. The father of Na*k*iketas had offered what is called an All-sacrifice, which requires a man to give away all that he possesses. His son, hearing of his father's vow, asks him whether he does or does not mean to fulfill his vow without reserve. At first the father hesitates; at last, becoming angry, he says: "Yes, I shall give thee also unto death."

The father, having once said so, was bound to fulfill his vow, and to sacrifice his son to death. The son is quite willing to go, in order to redeem his father's rash promise.

"I go," he says, "at the first, at the head of many (who have still to die); I go in the midst of many (who are now dying). What Yama (the ruler of the departed) has to do, that he will do unto me today.

"Look back, how it was with those who came before; look forward, how it will be with those who come hereafter. A mortal ripens like corn;—like corn they spring up again."

When Na*k*iketas entered the abode of the departed, their ruler, Yama, was absent, and his new guest was left for three days without receiving due hospitality. In order to make up for this neglect, Yama, when he returns, grants him three boons to choose.

The first boon which Na*k*iketas chooses is, that his father may not be angry with him any more.[1]

The second boon is, that Yama may teach him some peculiar form of sacrifice.[2]

Then comes the third boon:—

"Na*k*iketas says:[3] 'There is that doubt, when man is dead, some saying that he is, others that he is not: this I should like to know, taught by thee. This is the third of my boons.'" 20.

"Death replied: 'On this point even the Devas have doubted formerly; it is not easy to understand. That subject is subtle. Choose another boon, O Na*k*iketas. Do not force me, let me off that boon!'" 21.

"'Whatever desires are difficult to attain for mortals, ask for them according to thy wish! These fair maidens with their chariots and musical instruments, such as are not indeed to be obtained by men, be

[1] In the Taittirîya Brâhma*n*a the first boon is that he should return to his father alive.

[2] In the Taittirîya Brâhma*n*a the second boon is that his good works should not perish, whereupon Yama told him a peculiar sacrifice, henceforth to be called by the name of Na*k*iketas.

[3] In the Taittirîya Brâhma*n*a the third boon is that Yama should tell him how to conquer death, whereupon Yama tells him again the Nâ*k*iketa sacrifice, only, according to the commentary, with this modification, that the meditation (upâsana) should be the principal, the performing of the sacrifice (*k*ayana) the secondary part.

waited on by them! I give them to thee. But do not ask me about dying."

"Na*k*iketas said: 'They last till to-morrow, O Death, they wear out the vigor of all the senses. Even the whole of life is short! Keep thy horses, keep dance and song to thyself. No man can be made happy by wealth. Shall we possess wealth, when we see thee, O Death! No, that on which there is doubt, O Death, tell us, what there is in that great future. Na*k*iketas does not choose another boon but that which enters into the hidden world.'" 29.

At last, much against his will, Yama is obliged to reveal his knowledge of the Self: —

"Fools," he says, "dwelling in ignorance, wise in their own sight, and puffed up with vain knowledge, go round and round, staggering to and fro, like blind men led by the blind. II. 5.

"The future never rises before the eyes of the careless child, deluded by the delusion of wealth. *This* is the world, he thinks; there is no other; thus he falls again and again under my sway." 6.

"The wise, who by means of meditating on his Self, recognizes the Old, who is difficult to be seen, who has entered into darkness, who is hidden in the cave, who dwells in the abyss, as God, he indeed leaves joy and sorrow far behind." 12.

"The knowing Self is not born, it dies not; it came from nothing, it became nothing.[1] The Old is unborn, from everlasting to everlasting, he is not killed, though the body is killed." 18.

"The Self is smaller than small, greater than great; hidden in the heart of the creature. A man

1 Nothing sprang from it. Comm.

who has no more desires and no more griefs, sees the majesty of the Self by the grace of the creator." 20.

"Though sitting still, he walks far; though lying down, he goes everywhere. Who save myself is able to know that God who rejoices and rejoices not?" 21.

"That Self cannot be gained by the Veda; nor by understanding, nor by much learning. He whom the Self chooses, by him alone the Self can be gained. The Self chooses him as his own." 23.

"But he who has not first turned away from his wickedness, who is not tranquil and subdued, or whose mind is not at rest, he can never obtain the Self, even by knowledge." 24.

"No mortal lives by the breath that goes up and by the breath that goes down. We live by another, in whom these two repose." V. 5.

"Well then, I shall tell thee this mystery, the eternal Brahman, and what happens to the Self, after reaching death." 6.

"Some are born again, as living beings, others enter into stocks and stones, according to their work and according to their knowledge." 7.

"But he, the highest Person, who wakes in us while we are asleep, shaping one lovely sight after another, he indeed is called the Bright, he is called Brahman, he alone is called the Immortal. All worlds are founded on it, and no one goes beyond. This is that." 8.

"As the one fire, after it has entered the world, though one becomes different according to whatever it burns, thus the one Self within all things, becomes different, according to whatever it enters, and exists also apart." 9.

"As the sun, the eye of the world, is not contaminated by the external impurities seen by the eye, thus the one Self within all things, is never contaminated by the suffering of the world, being himself apart." 11.

"There is one eternal thinker, thinking non-eternal thoughts; he, though one, fulfills the desires of many. The wise who perceive him within their Self, to them belongs eternal peace." 13.

"Whatever there is, the whole world, when gone forth (from Brahman) trembles in his breath. That Brahman is a great terror, like a drawn sword. Those who know it, become immortal." VI. 2.

"He (the Brahman) cannot be reached by speech, by mind, or by the eye. He cannot be apprehended, except by him who says: *He is.*" 12.

"When all desires that dwell in the heart cease, then the mortal becomes immortal, and obtains Brahman." 14.

"When all the fetters of the heart here on earth are broken, then the mortal becomes immortal — here ends my teaching." 15.

RELIGION OF THE UPANISHADS.

It will probably be said that this teaching of the Upanishads can no longer be called religion, but that it is philosophy, though not yet reduced to a strictly systematic form. This shows again how much we are the slaves of language. A distinction has been made for us between religion and philosophy, and, so far as form and object are concerned, I do not deny that such a distinction may be useful. But when we look to the subjects with which religion is concerned, they are, and always have been, the very subjects on which philosophy has dwelt, nay, from which philosophy has sprung. If religion depends for its very life on the sentiment or the perception of the infinite within the finite and beyond the finite, who is to determine the legitimacy of that sentiment or of that perception, if not the philosopher? Who is to determine the powers which man possesses for apprehending the finite by his senses, for working up his single and therefore finite impressions into concepts by his reason, if not the philosopher? And who, if not the philosopher, is to find out whether man can claim the right of asserting the existence of the infinite, in spite of the constant opposition of sense and reason, taking these words in their usual meaning? We should damnify religion if we separated it from philosophy; we should ruin philosophy if we divorced it from religion.

The old Brahmans, who displayed greater ingenuity then even the Fathers of our church in drawing a sharp line between profane and sacred writing, and in establishing the sacred and revealed character of their Scriptures, always included the Upanishads in their sacred code. The Upanishads belong to the *S*ruti or revelation, in contradistinction to the Sm*ri*ti and all the rest of their literature, including their sacred laws, their epic poetry, their modern Purâ*n*as. The philosophy of the ancient *Ri*shis was to them as sacred ground as sacrifice and hymns of praise.

Whatever occurs in the Upanishads, even though one doctrine seems to contradict the other, is to them, according to the principles of their most orthodox theology, absolute truth; and it is curious to see how later systems of philosophy, which are opposed to each other on very essential points, always try to find some kind of warrant for their doctrines in one or the other passage of the Upanishads.

EVOLUTION IN VEDIC RELIGION.

But there is another point which deserves our careful attention in the final establishment of the ancient Hindu religion.

There can be no doubt that, even in the Sa*m*hitâs, in the collections of the Sacred Hymns, we can observe the palpable traces of historical development. I tried to show this in some of my former lectures, though I remarked at the same time that it seemed to me almost useless to apply a chronological measurement to these phases of thought. We must always make allowance for individual genius, which is independent of years, and even of centuries, nor must we forget that Berkeley, who often reminds us of the most advanced Hindu philosophers, was a contemporary of Watts, the pious poet.

In ancient times, however, and during a period of incipient literature, such as the Vedic period seems to have been, we have a right to say that, generally speaking, hymns celebrating the dawn and the sun were earlier than hymns addressed to Aditi; that these again were earlier than songs in honor of Pra*g*âpati, the one lord of all living things; and that such odes as I tried to translate just now, in which the poet speaks of "the One breathing breathless by itself," came later still.

There is an historical, or, as it is now called, an evolutionary succession to be observed in all the hymns of the Veda, and that is far more important, and far more instructive than any merely chronological succession. All these hymns, the most ancient and the most modern, existed before what we now call the collection (sa*m*hitâ) of the hymns of the Veda was closed; and if we put that collection at about 1000 B. C., we shall not, I believe, expose ourselves to any damaging criticism.

The final collection of the hymns must have preceded the composition of the Brâhma*n*as. In the hymns, and still more in the Brâhma*n*as, the theological treatises which belong to the next period, the highest rewards are promised to all who conscientiously perform the ancient sacrifices. The gods to whom the sacrifices are addressed are in the main the gods who are celebrated in the hymns, though we can clearly perceive how gods, such as Pra*g*âpati for instance, representing more abstract concepts of deity, come more and more into the foreground in the later Brâhma*n*as.

Next follow the Âra*n*yakas which, not only by the position which they occupy at the end of the Brâhma*n*as, but also by their character, seem to be of a later age again. Their object is to show how sacrifices may be performed by people living in the forest, without any of the pomp described in the Brâhma*n*as and the later Sûtras; by a mere mental effort. The worshiper had only to imagine the sacrifice, to go through it in his memory, and he thus acquired the same merit as the performer of tedious rites.

Lastly come the Upanishads; and what is their object? To show the utter uselessness, nay, the mischievousness of all ritual performances; to condemn every sacrificial act which has for its motive a desire or hope of reward; to deny, if not the existence, at least the exceptional and exalted character of the Devas, and to teach that there is no hope of salvation and deliverance except by the individual Self recognizing the true and universal Self, and finding rest there, where alone rest can be found.

How these various thoughts were reached, how one followed naturally upon the other, how those who discovered them were guided by the sole love of truth, and spared no human effort to reach the truth — all this I have tried to explain, as well as it could be explained within the limits of a few lectures.

And now you will no doubt ask, as many have asked before, How was it possible to maintain a religion, so full not only of different shades of thought, but containing elements of the most decidedly antagonistic character? How could people live together as members of one and the same religious community, if some of them held that there were Devas or gods, and others that there were no Devas or no gods; if some of them spent all their substance in sacrifices, and others declared every sacrifice a deception and a snare? How could books containing opinions mutually destructive be held as sacred in their entirety, revealed, in the strictest sense of the word, nay, as beyond the reach of any other test of truth?

Yet so it was thousands of years ago, and, in spite of all the changes that have intervened, so it is still, wherever the old Vedic religion is maintained. The fact is there; all we have to do is to try to understand it, and perhaps to derive a lesson from it.

THE FOUR CASTES.

Before the ancient language and literature of India had been made accessible to European scholarship, it was the fashion to represent the Brahmans as a sect of priests jealously guarding the treasures of their sacred wisdom from the members of all the other castes, and thus maintaining their ascendency over an ignorant people. It requires but the slightest acquaintance with Sanskrit literature to see the utter groundlessness of such a charge. One caste only, the *S*ûdras, were prohibited from knowing the Veda. With the other castes, the military and civil classes, a knowledge of the Veda, so far from being prohibited, was a sacred duty. All had to learn the Veda, the only privilege of the Brahmans was that they alone were allowed to teach it.

It was not even the intention of the Brahmans that only the traditional forms of faith and the purely ritual observances should be communicated to the lower castes, and a kind of esoteric religion, that of the Upanishads, be reserved for the Brahmans. On the contrary, there are many indications to show that these esoteric doctrines emanated from the second rather than from the first caste.

In fact, the system of castes, in the ordinary sense of the word, did not exist during the Vedic age. What we may call castes in the Veda is very different even from what we find in the laws of Manu, still more from what exists at the present day. We find the old Indian society divided, first of all, into two classes, the *Âryas* or nobles born, and the *Sûdras*, the servants or slaves. Secondly, we find that the Âryas consist of *Brâhmanas*, the spiritual nobility, the *Kshatriyas* or *Râganyas*, the military nobility, and the *Vaisyas*, the citizens. The duties and rights assigned to each of these divisions are much the same as in other countries, and need not detain us at present.

THE FOUR STAGES OR ÂSRAMAS.

A much more important feature, however, of the ancient Vedic society than the four castes, consists in the four Âsramas or stages.

A Brâhma*n*a, as a rule, passes through four,[1] a nobleman through three, a citizen through two, a *S*ûdra through one of these stages. The whole course of life was traced out in India for every child that was born into the world; and, making every allowance for human nature, which never submits entirely to rules, we have no reason to doubt that, during the ancient periods of Indian history, this course of life, as sanctioned by their sacred books and their codes of law, was in the main adhered to.

As soon as the child of an Ârya is born, nay, even before his birth, his parents have to perform certain sacramental rites (sa*m*skâras), without which the child would not be fit to become a member of society; or, what was the same thing with the old Brahmans, a member of the church. As many as twenty-five sa*m*skâras are mentioned, sometimes even more. *S*û-dras[2] only were not admitted to these rites; while Âryas who omitted to perform them were considered no better than *S*ûdras.

FIRST STAGE, STUDENTSHIP.

The first stage of life to the son of an Ârya, that is of a Brâhma*n*a, or a Kshatriya, or a Vaisya, begins when he is from about seven to eleven years of age.[3]

[1] Âryavidyâ-sudhânidhi, p. 153.

[2] According to Yama, *S*ûdras also may receive these sacraments up to the Upanaya, apprenticeship, but unaccompanied by Vedic verses.

[3] Âryavidyâ-sudhânidhi, p. 101. Âpastamba-sûtras, I. 1, 18, ed. Bühler, "Let him initiate a Brahman in spring, a Kshatriya in summer, a Vai*s*ya

He is then sent away from home, and handed over to a master to be educated. The chief object of his education is to learn the Veda or the Vedas by heart. The Veda being called Brahman, he is called a Brahma*k*âriu, a student of the Veda. The shortest time assigned to an effective study is twelve years, the longest forty-eight.[1] While the young student stays in his master's house, he has to submit to the strictest discipline. He has to say his prayers twice a day, at sunrise and sunset (sandhyopâsana). Every morning and evening he has to go round the village begging, and whatever is given him he has to hand over to his master. He is himself to eat nothing except what his master gives him. He has to fetch water, to gather fuel for the altar, to sweep the ground round the hearth, and to wait on his master day and night. In return for this, his master teaches him the Veda, so that he can say it by heart, and whatever else may be required to fit him to enter upon his second stage, and to become a married man and a householder (*gri*hastha). The pupil may attend additional lessons of other teachers (upâdhyâyas), but his initiation, and what is called his second birth, he receives from his spiritual guide or â*k*ârya only.[2]

When his apprenticeship is finished, the pupil, after paying his master his proper fee, is allowed to

in autumn; a Brahman in the eighth year after his conception, a Kshatriya in the eleventh year after his conception, a Vaisya in the twelfth year after his conception."

[1] Âpastamba-sûtras, I. 2, 12, "He who has been initiated shall dwell as a religious student in the house of his teacher, for forty-eight years (if he learns all the Vedas), for thirty-six years, for twenty-four years, for eighteen years. Twelve years should be the shortest time."

[2] More details are to be found in the old Dharma-sûtras, the sources of the Laws of Manu and other later law-books. A translation of several of these Dharma-sûtras, by Dr. G. Bühler, of Bombay, will soon be published in the *Sacred Books of the East*.

return to his paternal home. He is then called a *Snâtaka*,[1] one who has bathed, or *Samâvritta*, one who has returned. We should say he had taken his degree.

Some students (naishthika) stay all their life at their master's house, never marrying; others, if moved by the spirit, enter at once, after serving their apprenticeship, upon the life of an anchorite (sannyâsin). But the general rule is that the young Ârya, who is now, at the lowest estimate, nineteen or twenty-two years[2] of age, should marry.[3]

SECOND STAGE, MARRIED LIFE.

This is the second stage of life, during which he is called a Grihastha, or Grihamedhin, a householder. The most minute rules are given as to the choice of a wife and the marriage ceremonies. What interests us, however, most, is his religion. He has by that time learnt the hymns of the Veda by heart, and we may therefore suppose that he believes in Agni, Indra, Varuna, Pragâpati, and the other Vedic deities. He has also learnt the Brâhmanas, and he is bound to perform a constant succession of sacrifices, as either prescribed or at least sanctioned by those sacred codes. He has also learnt some of the Âranyakas and Upanishads[4] by heart, and if he has understood them, we

1 The name of Snâtaka does not apply to him from the time only of his leaving his master to the time of his marriage, but belongs to him through life. Cf. Âryavidyâ-sudhânidhi, p. 131.

2 He may begin his apprenticeship at seven; the shortest study of the Veda takes twelve years, and, according to some, the study of the Mahânâmnî and other Vratas another three years. See Âsvalâyana Grihya-sûtra, I. 22, 3. Comment.

3 Manu says that the right age for a man to marry is 30, for a woman 12; but that the law allows a man to marry at 24, and a woman at 8.

4 Âpastamba-sûtras, XI. 2, 5, 1. *S*atapatha-brâhmana, X. 3, 5, 12, tasya vâ etasya yagusho rasa evopanishat.

may suppose that his mind has been opened, and that he knows that this second stage of active life is only a preparation for a third and higher stage which is to follow. No one, however, is allowed to enter on that higher stage who has not passed through the first and second stages. This at least is the general rule, though here too it is well known that exceptions occurred.[1] While a married man, the householder has to perform the five daily sacrifices; they are: —

(1.) The study or teaching of the Veda;

(2.) Offering oblations to the Manes or his ancestors;

(3.) Offering oblations to the gods;

(4.) Offering food to living creatures;

(5.) Receiving guests.

Nothing can be more perfect than the daily life mapped out for the householder in the so-called Domestic Rules (G*ri*hya-sûtras). It may have been an ideal only, but even as an ideal it shows a view of life such as we find nowhere else.

It was, for instance, a very old conception of life in India, that each man is born a debtor, that he owes a debt first to the sages, the founders and

[1] The question of the four Â*s*ramas is fully discussed in the Vedânta-sûtras, III. 4. The general rule is: brahma*k*aryam samâpya g*ri*hî bhavet, g*ri*hî bhûtvâ vanî bhavet, vanî bhûtvâ pravra*g*et, "let a man become a householder after he has completed the studentship, let him be a dweller in the forest after he has been a householder, and let him wander away after he has been a dweller in the forest." But it is added: yadi vetarathâ brahma*k*aryâd eva pravra*g*ed, g*ri*hâd vâ, vanâd vâ, "or otherwise let him wander forth even from his studentship, from the house, or from the forest." (*G*âbâlopanishad, 4.) There is a quotation in Govindânanda's gloss to Vedânta-sûtra, III. 4, 49, mentioning four kinds in each of the four Â*s*ramas: gâyatra*h*, brâhma*h*, prâ*g*âpatya*h*, brahan (b*ri*han?) iti brahma*k*ârî *k*aturvidha*h*; g*ri*hastho 'pi vârtâv*ri*tti*h*, sâtînav*ri*tti*h*, yâyâvarah, ghorasannyâsî iti *k*aturvidha*h*; vânaprastha*s* *k*a vaikhânasa-udumbara-vâlakhilya-phenapa-prabhedai*s* *k*aturvidha*h*; tathâ parivrâ*d* api kuṭî*k*aka-bahûdaka-ha*m*sa-paramaha*m*sa-prabhedai*s* *k*aturvidha*h*.

fathers of his religion; secondly to the gods; thirdly to his parents.[1] The debt he owes to the sages he repays as a student by a careful study of the Veda. The debt he owes to the gods he repays as a householder, through a number of sacrifices, small or great. The debt he owes to his parents he repays by offerings to the Manes, and by becoming himself the father of children.

After having paid these three debts, a man is considered free of this world.

But besides all these duties, which each faithful Ârya is bound to discharge, there are a great many other sacrifices which he is expected to perform, if he can afford it: some of them being daily sacrifices, others fortnightly, others connected with the three seasons, with the time of harvest, or with the return of each half-year or year. The performance of these sacrifices required the assistance of professional priests, and must in many cases have been very expensive. They had to be performed for the benefit of the three upper classes, the Âryas only, and during these great sacrifices, a Kshatriya and a Vaisya were both considered, for the time being, as good as a Brâhma*n*a. The actual performance of the sacrifices, however, and the benefits derived from that service were strictly reserved to the Brâhma*n*as. Some of the sacrifices, such as the horse-sacrifice and the Râ*g*asûya, could be performed for the benefit of Kshatriyas

[1] Manu, VI. 35. "When he has paid his three debts (to the sages, the manes, and the gods), let him apply his mind to final beatitude; but low shall he fall who presumes to seek beatitude without having discharged those debts. After he has read the Vedas in the form prescribed by law, has legally begotten a son, and has performed sacrifices to the best of his power, he (has paid his three debts, and) may then apply his heart to eternal bliss." See, also, Manu, XI. 66. Sometimes the number is raised to four and five. See Boehtlingk and Roth, Sanskrit Dictionary, s. v.

only. *S*ûdras were at first entirely excluded from sacrifices, though in later times we hear of certain exceptions, provided that no sacred hymns were employed during their performance.

From what we know of the ancient times of India, between about 1000 and 500 before our era, we find that for almost every hour of the day and even the night, the life of a Brâhma*n*a was under the strictest discipline from one end of the year to the other. The slightest neglect of his sacred duties entailed severe penance and loss of caste, to say nothing of threatened punishments in another life; while a careful observance of his prayers and sacrifices carried the promise, not only of a long and prosperous life on earth, but of the highest happiness in heaven.

THIRD STAGE, RETIREMENT.

But now we come to the most important and most instructive features in the life of the ancient Indians. When the father of a family perceived his hair growing gray, or when he had seen the child of his child, he knew that he was quit of this world, he was to give up all that belonged to him to his sons, leave his house, and repair to the forest. He was then called a Vânaprastha. It was free to his wife to follow him or not, as she chose. There is in fact on this and on some other points connected with the forest-life considerable difference of opinion among ancient authorities, which deserves much greater attention than it has hitherto received. The chief difficulty is how to determine whether these different authorities represent local and contemporaneous usages, or successive historical stages in the development of Indian society. Wherever, for instance, retirement from the world was strictly enforced, it is clear that the law of inheritance must have been considerably affected by it, while the option left to a wife of following her husband or not, as she pleased, would have greatly influenced the domestic arrangements of Indian families. But in spite of all differences, one thing is quite certain, that, from the moment a man entered the forest, he enjoyed the most perfect freedom of thought and action. He might for a time perform certain ceremonies, but in many cases that performance was purely mental. He thought the sacrifice through as we might hum a symphony to ourselves, and thus he had done all that could be required of him. But after a time that occupation also came to an end. We read of the Vânaprasthas subjecting themselves to several kinds of austerities, comprehended under the general name of tapas, but the idea that every act inspired by selfish interests, and particularly by a hope of rewards in another life, was not only useless, but even hurtful, became more and more prevalent, and the only occupation left was self-inspection, in the true sense of the word, that is, recognizing the true and intimate relation between the individual and the eternal Self.

Many questions of the highest interest to the student of Indian history are connected with a true appreciation of the forest-life. On these we cannot dwell at present.

Two points only must be noticed. *First*, that there was, after the third stage, a fourth and final stage, that of the *Sannyâsin*, who retired from all human society, and after solitary wanderings in the wilderness, threw himself into the arms of death. It is not always easy to distinguish the Sannyâsin, also called by different authorities bhikshu, yati, parivrâ*g*, and muni, from the Vânaprastha, though originally there was this very important difference, that the members of the three former âsramas aspired to rewards in another life (traya*h* pu*n*yalokabhâ*g*a*h*), while the Sannyâsin, who had thrown off all works, aspired to true immortality in Brahman (eko 'm*ri*tatvabhâk, brahmasa*m*stha*h*), that the dweller in the forest continued to belong to the parishad or *commune*, while the Sannyâsin shrank from any intercourse with the world.

Secondly, we must remember that the third stage, the forest-life, which is so characteristic a feature in the ancient literature of India, and fully recognized even in such late works as the Laws of Manu and the epic poems, was afterwards abolished,[1] possibly as affording too great a support to what we are accustomed to call Buddhism,[2] but what in many respects might be called a complete realization and extension of the forest-life and the final retirement from the world, as sanctioned by the old Brahmanic law. The orthodox scheme of the Brahmans was simple enough, so long as they could persuade men to pass through it step by step, and not to anticipate

1 *Nârada*: "The procreation of a son by a brother (of the deceased), the slaughter of cattle in the entertainment of a guest, the repast on flesh meat at funeral obsequies, and the order of a hermit (are forbidden or obsolete in the fourth age).

Âditya Purâna: "What was a duty in the first age, must not (in all cases) be done in the fourth; since, in the Kali age, both men and women are addicted to sin: such are a studentship continued for a very long time, and the necessity of carrying a water-pot, marriage with a paternal kinswoman, or with a near maternal relation, and the sacrifice of a bull."

2 According to the Âpastamba-sûtras, I. 6, 18, 31, a person who has become a hermit without (being authorized thereto) by the rules of the law (avidhinâ pravra*g*ita) is to be avoided. The Commentator explains this by *S*âkyâdaya*h*, *S*âkyas, *i. e.*, Buddhists, and the rest.

the freedom of the forest or the blessings of complete solitude without first having fulfilled the duties of the student and the householder. That difficulty is well illustrated by the dialogue between a father and his son in the Mahâbhârata (*S*ântiparva, Adhy. 175). The father advises the son to follow the traditions of the elders, first to learn the Veda, observing all the rules of studentship, then to marry and to have children, to erect the altars, and perform the appropriate sacrifices, then to go into the forest, and at last to try to become a Muni. The son, however, rejects his advice, and declares the life of a householder, wife, children, sacrifices and all the rest, as worse than useless. "The enjoyment of a man who lives in the village," he says, "is the jaws of death; the forest is the abode of the gods, so the scripture teaches. The enjoyment of a man who lives in the village is a rope to bind him; the good cut it asunder and are free, the bad never cut it. There is no such treasure for a Brahman as solitude, equanimity, truth, virtue, steadiness, kindness, righteousness, and abstaining from works. What does wealth profit thee, or relatives, or a wife, O Brâhma*n*a, when thou art going to die? Seek for the Self that is hidden in the heart. Whither are thy grandfathers gone and thy father?"

All this may sound fanciful, poetical, imaginary, but it represents the real life of ancient India. That in the ancient history of India this forest-life was no mere fiction, we know, not only from the ancient literature of India, but also from the Greek writers, to whom nothing was so surprising as to find, by the side of the busy life of towns and villages, these large settlements of contemplative sages, the ὑλόβιοι, as they called them, in the forests of India.

To us this forest-life is interesting, chiefly as a new conception of man's existence on earth. No doubt it offers some points of resemblance with the life of Christian hermits in the fourth century, only that the Indian hermitages seem to be pervaded by a much fresher air, both in an intellectual and bodily sense, than the caves and places of refuge chosen by Christian sages. How far the idea of retirement from the world and living in the desert may first have been suggested to Christian hermits by Buddhist pilgrims, who were themselves the lineal descendants of Indian forest-sages or Vânaprasthas ; whether some of those extraordinary similarities which exist between the Buddhist customs and ceremonial and the customs and ceremonial of the Roman Catholic church (I will only mention tonsure, rosaries, cloisters, nunneries, confession (though public), and clerical celibacy) could have arisen at the same time — these are questions that cannot, as yet, be answered satisfactorily. But with the exception of those Christian hermits, the Indians seem to have been the only civilized people who perceived that there was a time in a man's life when it is well for him to make room for younger men, and by an undisturbed contemplation of the great problems of our existence here and hereafter, to prepare himself for death. In order to appreciate the wisdom of such a philosophy of life, we must not forget that we are speaking of India, not of Europe. In India the struggle of life was a very easy one. The earth, without much labor, supplied all that was wanted, and the climate was such that life in a forest was not only possible, but delightful. Several of the names given to the forest by the Aryans meant originally delight or bliss. While in European countries the old people had still to struggle on, and maintain their position in society as a *Senatus*, a collection of elders, guiding, moderating, sometimes also needlessly checking the generous impulses of the succeeding generation, in India the elders gladly made room for their children, when they had themselves become fathers, and tried to enjoy the rest of their lives in peace and quietness.

LIFE IN THE FOREST.

Do not let us suppose that those ancient Aryans were less wise than we are. They knew, as well as we do, that a man may live in the forests and yet have his heart darkened by passions and desires: they also knew, as well as we do, that a man, in the very thick of a busy life, may have in his heart a quiet hermitage where he can always be alone with himself and his truest Self.

We read in the Laws of Yâ*g*navalkya, III. 65: —

"The hermitage is not the cause of virtue; virtue arises only when practiced. Therefore let no man do to others what is painful to himself."

A similar sentiment occurs in Manu, VI. 66 (translated by Sir W. Jones): —

"Equal-minded towards all creatures, in whatsoever order he may be placed, let him fully discharge his duty, though he bear not the visible mark of his order. The visible mark of his order is by no means an effective discharge of duty."

In the Mahâbhârata the same sentiments occur again and again: —

"O Bhârata,[1] what need has a self-controlled man

[1] *S*ântiparva, 5961,
dântasya kimara*n*yena tathâdântasya bhârata
yatraiva nivased dântas tadara*n*yam sa *k*âsrama*h*.

of the forest, and what use is the forest to an uncontrolled man? Wherever a self-controlled man dwells, that is a forest, that is an hermitage.

"A sage, even though he remains in his house, dressed in fine apparel, if only always pure, and full of love, as long as life lasts, becomes freed from all evils.[1]

"Carrying the three staves, observing silence, wearing platted hair, shaving the head, clothing one's self in dresses of bark or skins, performing vows and ablution, the agnihotra-sacrifice, dwelling in the forest, and emaciating the body, all these are vain, if the heart is not pure."[2]

Such ideas became in time more and more prevalent, and contributed no doubt to the victory of Buddhism, in which all external works and marks had ceased to be considered as of any value. Thus we read in the Buddhist aphorisms of the Dhammapada,[3] Nos. 141, 142: —

"Not nakedness, not platted hair, not dirt, not fasting, nor lying on the earth, not rubbing with dust, nor sitting motionless, can purify a mortal who has not overcome desires.

"He who, though dressed in fine apparel, exercises tranquillity, is quiet, subdued, restrained, chaste, and has ceased to find fault with all other beings,[4] he indeed is a Brâhma*n*a, a *S*rama*n*a (ascetic), a Bhikshu (a friar)."

[1] Vanaparva, 13450,
tish*th*an g*ri*he *k*aiva munir nityam su*k*ir alaṅk*ri*ta*h*
yâva*gg*îvam dayâvâ*ms* *k*a sarvapâpai*h* pramu*k*yate.

[2] Vanaparva, 13445,
tridâ*nd*adhâra*n*am maunam *gat*âbhâro 'tha mu*nd*anam,
valkalâ*g*inasa*m*vesh*t*am vrata*k*aryâbhishe*k*anam,
agnihotram vanevâsa*h* *s*arîraparisosha*n*am,
sarvâny etâni mithyâ syur yadi bhâvo na nirmala*h*.

[3] Buddhaghosha's *Parables*, ed. M. M., 1870, p. xcviii.

[4] da*nd*anidhâna is explained by vâṅmana*h*kâyair hi*m*sâtyâga*h*, in the commentary on the Mahâbhârata, *S*ântiparva, 175, v. 37.

All these thoughts had passed again and again through the minds of Indian thinkers as they pass through our own, and had received simple and beautiful expression in their religious and epic poetry. I need only mention here from the Mahâbhârata[1] the curious dialogue between king *G*anaka and Sulabhâ, who, in the guise of a beautiful woman, convicts him of deceiving himself in imagining that he can be at the same time a king and a sage, living in the world, yet being not of the world. This is the same king *G*anaka of Videha who gloried in saying that if his capital Mithilâ were in flames, nothing belonging to him would be burnt.[2]

Still the ancient Brahmans retained their conviction that, after the first and second stages of life were passed, when a man was fifty — what we in our insatiable love of work call the very best years of a man's life — he had a right to rest, to look inward and backward and forward, before it was too late.

It would be out of place here to enter into any historical disquisitions as to the advantages of these two systems in retarding or accelerating the real progress, the real civilization, and the attainment of the real objects of human life. Only let us not, as we are so apt to do, condemn what seems strange to us, or exalt what seems familiar. Our senators and elders have, no doubt, rendered important services; but their authority and influence have many a time been used in history to check and chill the liberal and generous tendencies of younger hearts. It may be a true saying that young men imagine that old men are fools,

1 Mahâbhârata, *S*ântiparva, Adhyâya 320; ed. Bombay, vol. v. p. 227 *seq.* Muir, *Religious and Moral Sentiments*, p. 126.

2 Dhammapada, translated by M. M., p. cxv.

and that old men know that young men are; but is it not equally true of many a man eminent in Church and State, that, in exact proportion as the vigor of his mind and the freshness of his sentiments decrease, his authority and influence increase for evil rather than for good?

And remember, this life in the forest was not an involuntary exile; it was looked upon as a privilege, and no one was admitted to it who had not conscientiously fulfilled all the duties of the student and the householder. That previous discipline was considered essential to subdue the unruly passions of the human heart. During that period of probation and preparation, that is, during the best part of a man's life, little freedom was allowed in thought or deed. As the student had been taught, so he had to believe, so he had to pray, so he had to sacrifice to the gods. The Vedas were his sacred books, and their claims to a supernatural origin, to be considered as revelation, were more carefully and minutely guarded in the apologetic literature of India than in any other theological literature which I know.

And yet, on a sudden, as soon as a man entered upon the third stage or the forest-life, he was emancipated from all these fetters. He might carry on some outward observances for a time, he might say his prayers, he might repeat the scriptures which he had acquired as a boy, but his chief object was to concentrate his thoughts on the eternal Self, such as it was revealed in the Upanishads. The more he found his true home there, and could give up all that he had formerly called his own, divesting himself of his *Ego*, and all that was personal and transient, and recovering his true Self in the eternal Self, the more all fetters of law, of custom, and caste, of tradition and outward religion fell from him. The Vedas now became to him the *lower* knowledge only; the sacrifices were looked upon as hindrances; the old gods, Agni and Indra, Mitra and Varu*n*a, Visvakarman also and Pra*g*âpati, all vanished as mere names. There remained only the *Âtman*, the subjective, and Brahman, the objective Self, and the highest knowledge was expressed in the words *tat tvam*, *thou art it;* thou thyself, thy own true Self, that which can never be taken from thee, when everything else that seemed to be thine for a time disappears; when all that was created vanishes again like a dream, thy own true Self belongs to the eternal Self; the Âtman or Self within thee is the true Brahman,[1] from whom thou

[1] I have avoided to use the word Brahman instead of Âtman, because, though its later development is clear, I must confess that I have not been able as yet to gain a clear conception of its real roots. As for all other abstract conceptions, there must be for brahman also something tangible from which it sprang, but what this was seems to me still very doubtful.

There can be little doubt that the root from which brahman was derived is b*ri*h or v*ri*h. The meanings ascribed to this root by native grammarians are to erect, to strive, and to grow. These three meanings may be reduced to one, viz., to push, which, if used intransitively, would mean to spring up, to grow; if transitively, to make spring up, to erect.

Between these meanings, however, and the meanings assigned to Brahman by the oldest exegetes, there seems little connection. Yâska explains brahman as meaning either food or wealth. Sâya*n*a adopts these meanings and adds to them some others, such as hymn, hymn of praise, sacrifice, also great (b*ri*hat). (See Haug, *Über die ursprünglich Bedeutung des Wortes Brahma*, 1868, p. 4.) Professor Roth gives as the first meaning of brahmán, (1) pious meditation appearing as an impulse and fullness of the mind, and striving towards the gods, every pious manifestation at divine service, (2) sacred formula, (3) sacred word, word of God, (4) sacred wisdom, theology, theosophy, (5) sacred life, chastity, (6) the highest object of theosophy, the impersonal god, the absolute, (7) the clergy. Professor Haug, on the contrary, thinks that brahmán meant originally a small broom made of Ku*s*a grass, which during a sacrifice is handed round, and is also called veda, *i. e.*, tied together, a bundle. He identifies it, as Benfey before him, with the Zend baresman, always used at the Izeshne ceremony, which is a reflex of the Vedic Soma-sacrifice. The original meaning of brahman and baresman he supposes to have been sprouts or shoots (Lat.

wast estranged for a time through birth and death, but who receives thee back again as soon as thou returnest to Him, or to It.

THE END.

Here is the end of the long journey which we undertook to trace; here the infinite, which had been seen as behind a veil in the mountains and rivers, in the sun and the sky, in the endless dawn, in the heavenly father, in Visvakarman, the maker of all things, in Pra*g*âpati, the lord of all living creatures, was seen at last in the highest and purest form which

virga), then growth, prosperity. As the prosperity of a sacrifice depended on the hymns and prayers, these too were called brahman, the sacrifice was called brahman, and at last this prosperity was conceived as the first cause of all being.

Neither of these biographies seems to me altogether satisfactory. Without attempting to explain here my own view of the origin and growth of brahman, I shall only say that there is a third meaning assigned to the root b*ri*h, to sound or to speak. Speech, in its most general meaning, may have been conceived as what springs forth and grows, then also as what not only develops itself, but develops its objects also, more particularly the gods, who are named and praised in words. From the root v*ri*h, determined in that direction, we have, I believe, the Latin *verb-um* and the Gothic *vaurd*, word (cf. *barba* and O. N. *barð-r*, *urbs* and Sanskrit *ardha*, etc.; Ascoli in Kuhn's *Zeitschrift*, xvii. 334). How far the Indians retained the consciousness of the original meaning of brih and brahma, is difficult to say, but it is curious to see how they use B*ri*has-pati and Vâ*k*aspati, as synonyms of the same deity. In the B*ri*hadâra*n*yaka, I. 3, 20, we read: esha u eva b*ri*haspatir, vâg vai b*ri*hatî, tasyâ esha patis, tasmâd u b*ri*haspati*h*; esha u eva brahma*n*aspatir, vâg vai brahma, tasyâ esha patis, tasmâd u brahma*n*aspati*h*. Here the identity of vâk, speech, with b*ri*hatî (or b*ri*h) and brahman is clearly asserted. From the root v*ri*h, in the sense of growing, we have in Sanskrit *barhis*, shoots, grass, bundle of grass, in Latin *virga*. The Latin *verbenae*, also, the sacred branches, borne by the fetiales and possibly the *verbera* (verberibus caedere), may come from the same root. Without attempting to trace the further ramifications of brahman, word, hymn of praise, prayer, sacrifice, I shall only guard at once against the idea that we have in it some kind of Logos. Though brahman comes in the end to mean the cause of the universe, and is frequently identified with the highest Âtman or Self, its development was different from that of the Alexandrian Logos, and historically, at all events, these two streams of thought are entirely unconnected.

the Indian intellect could reach. Can we define him, they said, or comprehend him? No, they replied; all we can say of him, is No, no! He is not this. He is not that; he is not the maker, not the father, not the sky or the sun, not the rivers or the mountains. Whatever we have called him, that he is not. We cannot comprehend or name him, but we can feel him; we cannot know him, but we can apprehend him; and if we have once found him, we can never escape from him. We are at rest, we are free, we are blessed. They waited patiently for the few years before death would release them: they did nothing to prolong their old age, but at the same time they thought it wrong to put an end to their life themselves.[1] They had reached what was to them eternal life on earth, and they felt convinced that no new birth and death could separate them again from that eternal Self which they had found, or which had found them.

And yet they did not believe in the annihilation of their own Self. Remember the dialogue in which Indra was introduced as patiently acquiring a knowledge of the Self. He first looks for the Self in the shadow in the water; then in the soul while dreaming; then in the soul when in deepest sleep. But he is dissatisfied even then, and says: "No, this cannot be; for he, the sleeper, does not know himself (his self) that he is I, nor does he know anything that exists. He is gone to utter annihilation. I see no good in this."

But what does his teacher reply? "This body is mortal," he says, "and always held by death, but it is

[1] Manu, VI. 45, "Let him not wish for death, let him not wish for life; let him expect the appointed time, as an hired servant expects his wages."

the abode of the Self, which is immortal and without a body. When embodied (when thinking this body is I, and I am this body) the Self is held by pleasure and pain. So long as he is thus embodied, he cannot get rid of pleasure and pain. But when the Self is disembodied (when he knows himself to be different from the body), then neither pleasure nor pain can touch him any more.

Yet this Self, the serene soul, or the highest person, does not perish, it only comes to himself again; it rejoices even, it laughs and plays, but as a spectator only, never remembering the body of his birth. He is the Self of the eye, the eye itself is but an instrument: He who knows I will say this, I will hear this, I will think this, he is the Self; the tongue, the ear, the mind are but instruments. The mind is his divine eye, and through that divine eye the Self sees all that is beautiful, and rejoices.

Here we see that annihilation was certainly not the last and highest goal to which the philosophy or the religion of the Indian dwellers in the forest looked forward. The true Self was to remain, after it had recovered himself. We cease to be what we seemed to be; we are what we know ourselves to be. If the child of a king is exposed and brought up as the son of an outcast, he is an outcast. But as soon as some friend tells him who he is, he not only knows himself to be a prince, but he is a prince, and succeeds to the throne of his father. So it is with us. So long as we do not know our Self, we are what we appear to be. But when a kind friend comes to us and tells us what we really are, then we are changed as in the twinkling of an eye: we come to our Self, we know our Self, we are our Self, as the young prince knew his father, and thus became himself a king.

PHASES OF RELIGIOUS THOUGHT.

We have seen a religion growing up from stage to stage, from the simplest childish prayers to the highest metaphysical abstractions. In the majority of the hymns of the Veda we might recognize the childhood; in the Brâhma*n*as and their sacrificial, domestic, and moral ordinances the busy manhood; in the Upanishads the old age of the Vedic religion. We could have well understood if, with the historical progress of the Indian mind, they had discarded the purely childish prayers as soon as they had arrived at the maturity of the Brâhma*n*as; and if, when the vanity of sacrifices and the real character of the old gods had once been recognized, they would have been superseded by the more exalted religion of the Upanishads. But it was not so. Every religious thought that had once found expression in India, that had once been handed down as a sacred heir-loom, was preserved, and the thoughts of the three historical periods, the childhood, the manhood, and the old age of the Indian nation, were made to do permanent service in the three stages of the life of every individual. Thus alone can we explain how the same sacred code, the Veda, contains not only the records of different phases of religious thought, but of doctrines which we may call almost diametrically opposed to each other. Those who are gods in the simple hymns of the Veda, are hardly what we should call gods when Pra*g*âpati, the one lord of living creatures, had been introduced in the Brâhma*n*as; and they ceased altogether to be gods when, as in the Upanishads, Brahman had been recognized as the cause of all things, and the individual self had been discovered a mere spark of the eternal Self.

For hundreds, nay, for thousands of years this ancient religion has held its ground, or, if it lost it for a time, has recovered it again. It has accommodated itself to times and seasons, it has admitted many strange and incongruous elements. But to the present day there are still Brahmanic families who regulate their life, as well as may be, according to the spirit of the *S*ruti, the revelation contained in the old Veda, and according to the laws of the Sm*ri*ti, or their time-honored tradition.

There are still Brahmanic families in which the son learns by heart the ancient hymns, and the father performs day by day his sacred duties and sacrifices, while the grandfather, even though remaining in the village, looks upon all ceremonies and sacrifices as vanity, sees even in the Vedic gods nothing but names of what he knows to be beyond all names, and seeks rest in the highest knowledge only, which has become to him the highest religion, viz., the so-called Vedânta, the end and fulfillment of the whole Veda.

The three generations have learnt to live together in peace. The grandfather, though more enlightened, does not look down with contempt on his son or grandson, least of all does he suspect them of hypocrisy. He knows that the time of their deliverance will come, and he does not wish that they should anticipate it. Nor does the son, though bound fast by the formulas of his faith, and strictly performing the minutest rules of the old ritual, speak unkindly of his father. He knows he has passed through the narrower path, and he does not grudge him his freedom and the wider horizon of his views.

Is not here, too, one of the many lessons which an historical study of religion teaches us?

When we see how in India those who in the earliest times worshiped Agni, the fire, lived side by side with others who worshiped Indra, the giver of rain ; when we see how those who invoked Pra*g*âpati, the one lord of living creatures, did not therefore despise others who still offered sacrifices to the minor Devas ; when we see how those who had learnt that all the Devas were merely names of the one, the highest Self, did not therefore curse the names or break the altars of the gods whom they had formerly adored: may we not learn something even from the old Vedic Indians, though in many respects we may be far better, wiser, and more enlightened than they were or ever could have been ?

I do not mean that we should slavishly follow the example of the Brahmans, and that we should attempt to reintroduce the successive stages of life, the four Âsramas, and the successive stages of religious faith. Our modern life is beyond such strict control. No one would submit to remain a mere ritualist for a time, and then only to be allowed to become a true believer. Our education has ceased to be so uniform as it was in India, and the principle of individual liberty, which is the greatest pride of modern society, would render such spiritual legislation as India accepted from its ancient lawgivers utterly impossible with us. Even in India we only know the laws, we do not know how they were obeyed ; nay, even in India, history teaches us that the galling fetters of the old Brahmanic law were at last broken, for there can be little doubt that we have to recognize in Buddhism an assertion of the rights of individual liberty, and, more particularly, of the right of rising above the trammels of society, of going, as it were, into the forest, and of living a life of perfect spiritual freedom, whenever a desire for such freedom arose. One of the principal charges brought by the orthodox Brahmans against the followers of Buddha was that "they went forth" (pravra*g*), that they shook off the fetters of the law, before the appointed time, and without having observed the old rules enjoining a full course of previous discipline in traditional lore and ritualistic observances.

But though we need not mimic the ideal life of the ancient Aryans of India, though the circumstances of modern life do not allow us to retire into the forest when we are tired of this busy life, nay, though, in our state of society, it may sometimes be honorable "to die in harness," as it is called, we can yet learn a lesson even from the old dwellers in Indian forests; not the lesson of cold indifference, but the lesson of viewing objectively, within it, yet above it, the life which surrounds us in the market-place; the lesson of toleration, of human sympathy, of pity, as it was called in Sanskrit, of love, as we call it in English, though seldom conscious of the unfathomable depth of that sacred word. Though living in the *forum*, and not in the forest, we may yet learn to agree to differ with our neighbor, to love those who hate us on account of our religious convictions, or, at all events, unlearn to hate and persecute those whose own convictions, whose hopes and fears, nay, even whose moral principles differ from our own. That, too, is forest-life, a life worthy of a true forest-sage, of a man who knows what man is, what life is, and who has learnt to keep silence in the presence of the Eternal and the Infinite.

It is easy, no doubt, to find names for condemning

such a state of mind. Some call it shallow indifference, others call it dishonesty to tolerate a difference of religion for the different Âsramas, the different stages of life, for our childhood, our manhood, and our old age; still more, to allow any such differences for the educated and the uneducated classes of our society.

But let us look at the facts, such as they are around us and within us, such as they are and as they always must be. Is the religion of Bishop Berkeley, or even of Newton, the same as that of a ploughboy? In some points, Yes; in all points, No. Surely Matthew Arnold would have pleaded in vain if people, particularly here in England, had not yet learnt that culture has something to do with religion, and with the very life and soul of religion. Bishop Berkeley would not have declined to worship in the same place with the most obtuse and illiterate of ploughboys, but the ideas which that great philosopher connected with such words as God the Father, God the Son, and God the Holy Ghost were surely as different from those of the ploughboy by his side as two ideas can well be that are expressed by the same words.

And let us not think of others only, but for ourselves; not of the different phases of society, but of the different phases through which we pass ourselves in our journey from childhood to old age. Who, if he is honest towards himself, could say that the religion of his manhood was the same as that of his childhood, or the religion of his old age the same as the religion of his manhood? It is easy to deceive ourselves, and to say that the most perfect faith is a childlike faith. Nothing can be truer, and the older we grow the more we learn to understand the wisdom of a childlike faith. But before we can learn that, we have first to learn another lesson, namely, to put away childish things. There is the same glow about the setting sun as there is about the rising sun: but there lies between the two a whole world, a journey through the whole sky, over the whole earth.

The question, therefore, is not, whether there exist these great differences of religion in the different stages of each life, and in the different ranks of society, but whether we shall frankly recognize the fact, as the ancient Brahmans recognized it, and try to determine accordingly our position, not only towards those who use the same words in religion which we use, though with greatly varying meanings, but also towards those who do not even use the same words?

But then it is asked, Is it really indifferent whether we use the same words or not, whether we use one name for the Divine or many? Is Agni as good a name as Pra*g*âpati, as Baal as good as Jehovah, or Ormazd as good as Allah? However ignorant we may be as to the real attributes of the Deity, are there not some at least which we know to be absolutely wrong? However helpless we may feel as to how to worship God worthily, are there not certain forms of worship which we know must be rejected?

Some answers to these questions there are which everybody would be ready to accept, though not everybody might see their full purport:—

"Of a truth I perceive that God is no respecter of persons: but in every nation, he that feareth Him, and worketh righteousness, is accepted with Him." (Acts x. 34, 35.)

"Not every one that saith unto me, Lord, Lord,

shall enter into the kingdom of heaven; but he that doeth the will of my Father which is in heaven." (St. Matthew vii. 21.)

But if such testimony is not enough, let us try a similitude which, as applied to the Deity, has, better than any other similitude, helped us, as it has helped others before us, to solve many of our difficulties. Let us think of God as a father, let us think of men, of all men, as his children.

Does a father mind by what strange, by what hardly intelligible a name his child may call him, when for the first time trying to call him by any name? Is not the faintest faltering voice of a child, if we only know that it is meant for us, received with rejoicing? Is there any name or title, however grand or honorable, which we like to hear better?

And if one child calls us by one name and another by another, do we blame them? Do we insist on uniformity? Do we not rather like to hear each child calling us in his own peculiar childish way?

So much about names. And what about thoughts? When children begin to think, and to form their own ideas about father and mother, if they believe their parents can do anything, give them everything, the very stars from the sky, take away all their little aches, forgive them all their little sins, does a father mind it? Does he always correct them? Is a father angry, even if his children think him too severe? Is a mother displeased if her children believe her to be kinder, more indulgent, more in fact a child herself than she really is? True, young children cannot understand their parents' motives nor appreciate their purposes, but as long as they trust and love their parents in their own peculiar childish way, what more do we demand?

And as to acts of worship, no doubt the very idea of pleasing the Eternal by killing an ox is repulsive to us. But, however repulsive it may seem to all around, what mother is there who would decline to accept the sweet morsel which her child offers her out of its own mouth and, it may be, with fingers anything but clean? Even if she does not eat it, would she not wish the child to think that she had eaten it, and that it was very good? No, we do not mind in our children either mistaken names, or mistaken thoughts, or mistaken acts of kindness, as long as they spring from a pure and simple heart.

What we do mind in children, even in little children, is their using words which they do not fully understand; their saying things which they do not fully mean; and, above all, their saying unkind things one of another.

All this can only be a similitude, and the distance which separates us from the Divine is, as we all know, quite incommensurate with that which separates children from their parents. We cannot feel that too much; but, after we have felt it, and only *after* we have felt it, we cannot, I believe, in our relation to the Divine, and in our hopes of another life, be too much what we are, we cannot be too true to ourselves, too childlike, too human, or, as it is now called, too anthropomorphous in our thoughts.

Let us know by all means that human nature is a very imperfect mirror to reflect the Divine, but instead of breaking that dark glass, let us rather try to keep it as bright as we can. Imperfect as that mirror is, to us it is the most perfect, and we cannot go far wrong in trusting to it for a little while.

And let us remember, so long as we speak of possibilities only, that it is perfectly possible, and perfectly conceivable, that the likenesses and likelihoods which we project upon the unseen and the unknown may be true, in spite of all that we now call human weakness and narrowness of sight. The old Brahmans believed that as perfect or as imperfect as the human heart could conceive and desire the future to be, so it would be. It was to them according to their faith. Those, they thought, whose whole desire was set on earthly things, would meet with earthly things: those who could lift their hearts to higher concepts and higher desires, would thus create to themselves a higher world.

But even if we resign ourselves to the thought that the likenesses and likelihoods which we project upon the unseen and the unknown, nay, that the hope of our meeting again as we once met on earth, need not be fulfilled exactly as we shape them to ourselves, where is the argument to make us believe that the real fulfillment can be less perfect than what even a weak human heart devises and desires? This trust that whatever is will be best, is what is meant by faith, true, because inevitable faith. We see traces of it in many places and in many religions, but I doubt whether anywhere that faith is more simply and more powerfully expressed than in the Old and the New Testaments: —

"For since the beginning of the world men have not heard, nor perceived by the ear, neither hath the eye seen O God, beside thee, what he hath prepared for him that waiteth for him." (Isaiah lxiv. 4.)

"But, as it is written, Eye hath not seen, nor ear heard, neither have entered into the heart of man, the things which God hath prepared for them that love him." (1 Cor. ii. 9.)

We may do what we like, the highest which man can comprehend is man. One step only he may go beyond, and say that what is beyond may be different, but it cannot be less perfect than the present: the future cannot be worse than the past. Man has believed in pessimism, he has hardly ever believed in pejorism, and that much decried philosophy of evolution, if it teaches us anything, teaches us a firm belief in a better future, and in a higher perfection which man is destined to reach.

The Divine, if it is to reveal itself at all to us, will best reveal itself in our own human form. However far the human may be from the Divine, nothing on earth is nearer to God than man, nothing on earth more godlike than man. And as man grows from childhood to old age, the idea of the Divine must grow with us from the cradle to the grave, from âsrama to âsrama, from grace to grace. A religion which is not able thus to grow and live with us as we grow and live, is dead already. Definite and unvarying uniformity, so far from being a sign of honesty and life, is always a sign of dishonesty and death. Every religion, if it is to be a bond of union between the wise and the foolish, the old and the young, must be pliant, must be high, and deep, and broad; bearing all things, believing all things, hoping all things, enduring all things. The more it is so, the greater its vitality, the greater the strength and warmth of its embrace.

It was exactly because the doctrine of Christ, more than that of the founders of any other religion, offered in the beginning an expression of the highest truths in which Jewish carpenters, Roman publicans, and Greek philosophers could join without dishonesty, that it has conquered the best part of the world. It was because attempts were made from very early times to narrow and stiffen the outward signs and expressions of our faith, to put narrow dogma in the place of trust and love, that the Christian Church has often lost those who might have been its best defenders, and that the religion of Christ has almost ceased to be what, before all things, it was meant to be, a religion of world-wide love and charity.

RETROSPECT.

Let us look back once more on the path on which we have traveled together, the old path on which our Aryan forefathers, who settled in the land of the Seven Rivers, it may be not more than a few thousand years ago, have traveled in their search after the infinite, the invisible, the Divine.

They did not start, as was imagined, with a worship of fetishes. Fetish worship comes in in later times, where we expect it: in the earliest documents of religious thought in India there is no trace of it; nay, we may go farther and say, there is no room for it, as little as there is room for lias before or within the granite.

Nor did we find in their sacred books any traces of what is commonly meant by a primeval revelation. All is natural, all is intelligible, and only in that sense truly revealed. As to a separate religious instinct, apart from sense and reason, we saw no necessity for admitting it, and even if we had wished to do so, our opponents, who, here as elsewhere, prove always our best friends, would not have allowed it. In explaining religion by a religious instinct or faculty, we should only have explained the known by the less known. The real religious instinct or impulse is the perception of the infinite.

We therefore claimed no more for the ancient Aryans than what we claim for ourselves, and what no adversaries can dispute — our senses and our reason; or, in other words, our power of apprehending, as manifested in the senses, and our power of comprehending, as manifested in words. Man has no more, and he gains nothing by imagining that he has more.

We saw, however, that our senses, while they supply us with a knowledge of finite things, are constantly brought in contact with what is not finite, or, at least, not finite yet; that their chief object is, in fact, to elaborate the finite out of the infinite, the seen out of the unseen, the natural out of the supernatural, the phaenomenal world out of the universe which is not yet phaenomenal.

From this permanent contact of the senses with the infinite sprang the first impulse to religion, the first suspicion of something existing beyond what the senses could apprehend, beyond what our reason and language could comprehend.

Here was the deepest foundation of all religion, and the explanation of that which before everything — before fetishism, and figurism, and animism, and anthropomorphism — needs explanation: why man should not have been satisfied with a knowledge of finite sensuous objects; why the idea should ever have entered into his mind, that there is or can be anything in the world besides what he can touch, or hear, or see, call it powers, spirits, or gods.

When our excavations among the ruins of the Vedic literature had once carried us to that solid rock, we went on digging, in order to see whether some at least of the oldest pillars erected on that rock might still be discovered, and some of the vaults and arches laid free which supported the later temples of the religions of India. We saw how, after the idea had once laid hold of man, that there was something beyond the finite, the Hindu looked for it everywhere in nature, trying to grasp and to name it: at first, among semi-tangible, then among intangible, and at last among invisible objects.

When laying hold of a semi-tangible object, man's senses told him that they could grasp it in part only: — yet it was there.

When laying hold of an intangible, and at last of an invisible object, his senses told him that they could grasp it hardly, or not at all: — and yet it was there.

A new world thus grew up peopled by semi-tangible, intangible, and invisible objects, all manifesting certain activities, such as could be compared with the activities of human beings, and named with names that belonged to these human activities.

Of such names some were applied to more than one of those invisible objects; they became, in fact, general epithets, such as *Asura*, living things, *Deva*, bright beings, *Deva asura*, living gods,[1] *Amartya*, Immortals, best known to us through the Greek θεοὶ ἀθάνατοι, the Italian *Dii Immortales*, the old German immortal gods.

We also saw how other ideas, which are truly religious, and which seem the most abstract ideas that man can form, were nevertheless, like all abstract ideas, abstracted, deduced, derived from sensuous im-

[1] Rig-Veda, X. 82, 5.

pressions, even the ideas of law, virtue, infinitude, and immortality.

Here I should have much liked to have had some more lectures at my disposal, if only to show the influence which the first conscious contact with death exercised on the mind of man; and again to watch the slow, yet irresistible growth of those ideas which we now comprehend under the names of Faith and Revelation.

In India also, whatever may have been said to the contrary, the thoughts and feelings about those whom death had separated from us for a time supplied some of the earliest and most important elements of religion, and faith drew its first support from those hopes and imaginings of a future life and of our meeting again, which proved their truth to the fathers of our race, as they still do to us, by their very irresistibility.

Lastly, we found how, by a perfectly natural and intelligible process, a belief in single supreme beings, or Devas — *Henotheism*, tended to become a belief in *one* God, presiding over the other, no longer supreme gods — *Polytheism;* or a belief in one god, excluding the very possibility of other gods — *Monotheism.*

Still further, we saw that all the old Devas or gods were found out to be but names; but that discovery, though in some cases it led to *Atheism* and some kind of *Buddhism*, led in others to a new start, and to a new belief in one being, which is the Self of everything, which is not only beyond and beneath all finite things, as apprehended by the senses, but also beneath and beyond our own finite Ego, the Self of all Selfs.

Here for the present we had to leave our excavations, satisfied with having laid free that lowest stratum of solid rock on which in India all the temples rest that were erected in later times for worship or sacrifice.

I thought it right to warn you again and again, against supposing that the foundations which we discovered beneath the oldest Indian temples must be the same for all the temples erected by human hands. In concluding, I must do so once more.

No doubt the solid rock, the human heart, must be the same everywhere: some of the pillars even, and the ancient vaults, may be the same everywhere, wherever there is religion, faith, or worship.

But beyond this we must not go, at least not for the present.

I hope the time will come when the subterraneous area of human religion will be rendered more and more accessible. I trust that these Lectures, which I have had the great privilege to inaugurate, will in future supply for that work abler and stronger laborers than I can pretend to be; and that the Science of Religion, which at present is but a desire and a seed, will in time become a fulfillment and a plenteous harvest.

When that time of harvest has come, when the deepest foundations of all the religions of the world have been laid free and restored, who knows but that those very foundations may serve once more, like the catacombs, or like the crypts beneath our old cathedrals, as a place of refuge for those who, to whatever creed they may belong, long for something better, purer, older, and truer than what they can find in the statutable sacrifices, services, and sermons of the days in which their lot on earth has been cast; some who have learnt to put away childish things, call them genealogies, legends, miracles, or oracles, but who cannot part with the childlike faith of their heart.

Though leaving much behind of what is worshiped or preached in Hindu temples, in Buddhist vihâras, in Mohammedan mosques, in Jewish synagogues, and Christian churches, each believer may bring down with him into that quiet crypt what he values most — his own pearl of great price :

The Hindu his innate disbelief in this world, his unhesitating belief in another world ;

The Buddhist his perception of an eternal law, his submission to it, his gentleness, his pity ;

The Mohammedan, if nothing else, at least his sobriety ;

The Jew his clinging, through good and evil days, to the One God, who loveth righteousness, and whose name is "I am" ;

The Christian, that which is better than all, if those who doubt it would only try it — our love of God, call Him what you like, the infinite, the invisible, the immortal, the father, the highest Self, above all, and through all, and in all, — manifested in our love of man, our love of the living, our love of the dead, our living and undying love.

That crypt, though as yet but small and dark, is visited even now by those few who shun the noise of many voices, the glare of many lights, the conflict of many opinions. Who knows but that in time it will grow wider and brighter, and that the Crypt of the Past may become the Church of the Future.

INDEX.

ABIPONES, their idea of numbers, 69.
Abraham, his perception of the unity of the Godhead, 64.
Abyssinian or Nubian tribes, 66.
— of Semitic race, 66.
Accents in the Veda, 160.
— not marked in later Sanskrit, 138.
— of Zeus and Dyaus alike, 138.
Active, everything named as, 180.
— does not mean human, 181.
— natural objects as, 264.
Adhyâya or lecture, 154.
Aditi, the infinite, 218.
— not a modern deity, 220.
— natural origin of, 220.
— the oldest, 221.
— the place of, taken by *Ri*ta, 231.
Aditi and Diti, 221.
Âditya, the sun, 251, 254.
Âdityas, sons of Aditi, 219.
— seven or eight, 222.
Adonai, 175.
Adu*h*spr*i*sh*t*â Samhitâ, 159, *note*.
Africa, full of animal fables, 112.
African religion, higher elements in, 103.
— Waitz on, 102.
— many-sidedness of, 113.
African savages, Portuguese sailors on, 55.
African tribes, classified by Waitz, 66.
A*g*ara, a general predicate of deities, not decaying, 190, 262.
Agni, ignis, 199.
— supreme, 276.
— becomes Varu*n*a, 280.
— Mitra, 280.
— Savit*ri*, 280.
— Indra, 280.
Agni, same as Indra and Vish*n*u, 280.
Agnihotris, or sacrificers, 161.
Ahu, Zend, conscience, world, Sanskrit asu, breath, 185, *note*.
Ahu in Zend, lord, 185, *note*.
Ahura-mazda, 185, *note*.
Aistheton, the infinite as, 45.
A*k*ârya, or spiritual guide, 332.
Akesines, river, 194.
Akra, people of, worship the sun, 106.
— their god Jongmaa, 106.
Akwapim, one word for God and weather, 108.
All-Father, Charles Kingsley on the, 208, 209.
All-gods, Visve Devas, 281.
Amarta, not dying, 190.
Amartya, an immortal, 251.
American ethnologists, their excuse for slavery, 88.
Ammon, 175.
Anadhyâya, or non-reading days, holidays, 156.
Anchorite, sannyâsin, 333.
Ancient and modern belief, difference between, 8.
Ancient and modern literature in India, Buddhism the barrier between, 129.
Ancient mythology, how produced, 186.
Ancients, testimonies of the, as to the character of their gods, 174.
Anima, breath, 85.
Animal fables in Africa, 112.
Animism, 120, 180.
Animus, mind, 85.
Anirbhu*g*a Sa*m*hitâ, 159, *note*.
Annihilation of Self, 347.
An*ri*ta, untrue, 235.
Anthropology, Waitz's book on, 102.
— theology begins with, 36.
Anthropomorphism, 120, 180.
Anthropopathism, 120, 180.
Antinomies of human reason, discussed by Kant, 34.
Antiquity of religion, 4.
Anustara*n*î, the, in burning the dead, 79.
Âpastamba Sûtra, the, translated by Bühler, 157.
Apprehension of the Infinite, religion

as a subjective faculty for the, 21, 33.
Arabic, green, black, and brown confounded in, 39.
Âranyakas, or forest books, 144, 306.
Argikîyâ, river, 194.
Aristotle on the tricolored rainbow, 37.
— men create gods after their own image, 281, *note*.
Arius, 295.
Arnold, Matthew, 353.
Artemis Patroa, image of, 99.
Aryan language, testimony of the undivided, 176.
Âryas, or nobles born, 330.
AS, to breathe, 185.
Asha in Zend is *Ri*ta, 240.
Ashanti or Odji, name for the Supreme Being in, 104.
— word Kla, life, 112.
Asiknî, Akesines, river, 194.
Asoka, 130, *note*; 294, *note*.
— his great council, 130, *note*.
— two inscriptions by, 130, *note*.
— patron of Buddha, 131.
Âsrâmas, or the four stages, 330.
— discussed in the Vedânta-sûtras, 334, *note*.
Astronomy, indigenous in India, 142.
As-u, breath, 185.
Asura, from asu, breath, 191.
— living, 262.
— a living thing, 251.
— the living gods, 185.
— applied alike to beneficial and malignant powers, 191.
Asuras and Devas, battles between, 307.
— Viro*k*ana, chief of the, 307.
Âsura, a man who has no faith, 311.
Asvinau, the twins, day and night, 201, 205.
Athanasius and Arius, 295.
Atharva-Veda and Rig-Veda compared, 147.
— fetishes in, 191.
Atharva-vedis, in Bombay, 160.
Atheism, 207, 362.
— tendency towards, 287.
— difference between honest and vulgar, 292.
Atheistical, opinions of the Deists, 296.
Atheists, those who have been called, 294.
Âtman, Self, 302.
— the objective Self, 303.
Atom, something that cannot be cut asunder, 36.
Attention, *religio*, 10.
Atua or Akua, Polynesian word for God, 86.
— derivation of, 87.
Audible objects among the Vedic deities, 202.
Augustus, punishing Neptune, 99.
Australia, first used by De Brosses, 54.
Auxiliary verbs, 184.
Avagraha, dissolves compounds, 160.
Avam or Om, 81.
Avesta, dualism of good and evil in the, 78.
Ayas, metal or iron, 253.

BAMBA, great fetish of, 98.
Banâras, study of the Veda at, 157.
Baresman, Zend = brahman, 346, *note*.
Bastian, on the word fetish, 97, *note*.
Being, the Unborn, 304.
Belief, ancient and modern, differences between, 8.
Belief or οἴησις, 8.
Belief in closer community with the Gods, 164.
Benedictine missionaries, 92.
Benin negroes regard their shadows as their souls, 85.
Berber and Copt tribes, 66.
Berkeley, 327, 353.
Bhandarkar, Professor, on native learning, 157.
Bhavabhûti, 140.
Bhikshu, mendicant friar, 337, 342.
Bhikshuka, Brahmans, 157.
Bhû, to grow, to be, 185.
Bindusâra, 130, *note*.
Black, 39.
— and blue, no distinct words for among savages, 39.
— and blue, to beat, 39.
— confounded with brown and green in Arabic, 39.
— Ya*g*ush, the, 157.
Blakkr, black in old Norse, 39.
Bláman and blá-maðr, old Norse, 39.
Blár, blá, blátt, blue in Norse, 39.
Blavus and blavius, 39.
Bleak, A. S. blac, blæc, 40.
Blue, a late idea, 37.
Blue sky, not mentioned by the ancients, 38.

Bombay, Atharva-vedis in, 160.
Book religions, 125.
Brahma*k*ârin, students of the Veda, 332.
Brahmán, Zend Baresman, 346, *note*.
Brahman and Âtman, 345, *note*.
Brahman and the objective Self, 345.
Brâhma*n*a period, 144.
Brahmaya*g*na, the, 158.
Bread, worshiped as Demeter, 175.
Breath and shadow, 86.
— essence of the world, 302.
B*ri*haspati, quoted, 136.
— his heretical doctrines, 135.
— his follower, *K*árvâka, 135.
Bronze period, 225.
Brown confounded with black and green in Arabic, 39.
Buddha, his denial of any devas or gods, 13.
— an atheist, 294.
Buddhism, its date, 131.
— the frontier between ancient and modern literature in India, 129.
— and the third stage, 338.
— an assertion of the rights of individual liberty, 351.
— 362.
Buddhist stories in metre and prose, 73, *note*.
— and Roman Catholic ceremonies, 340.
Buddhists deny the authority of the Veda, 132.
Buddhists, 338, *note*.
Buffon instigates de Brosses' investigations, 54.
Bühler, Dr., publication of Asoka's inscriptions, 130, *note*.
Burning of the dead, hymn on, 78.
— of widows, 80.
Burton, on the Dahomans, 69, *note*.

CABUL river, 194.
Caesar, on the religion of the Germans, 175.
Caesar and Tacitus, opposite reports on the Germans, 88.
Caesius, 39.
Calvin and Servetus, 295.
Calx, the heel, 183.
— stone, 183.
Carmichael, account of mission in Western Australia, 15.
Castes, the four, 329.
Caucasian, Sanskrit in, 128.
Celsus, worship of the genii, 107.
Celsus, on various names for God, 174, 175.
— on the Persian religion, 175.
— defense of Greek polytheism, 196, *note*.
Cerebration, unconscious, 227.
Ceremonies, domestic, in the Sûtras, 143.
Chando, Santhal name for sun, 201.
Charites, Greek, same as harits, 252.
Charme, or Carmen, 60.
Chave, feitiça, a false key, 60.
Child of a king, the son of an outcast, 348.
Childhood, manhood, and old age of the Indian religion, 349.
Children and dolls, 119.
— their surroundings, 120.
— contrasted with savages, 120.
China, five colors known in, 39.
Chinese, tones in, 178.
Christians, as atheists, 294.
Cicero, 228.
— his derivation of *religio*, 10.
— on man's possession of religion, 32.
Cienga, the author of evil, 16.
Clerical celibacy, 340.
Cloisters, 340.
Clouds, the cows, 231, *note*.
Codrington, Rev. R. H., on the religion of the Melanesians, 51.
— Norfolk Island, 70, *note*.
— on Mota word for soul, 85.
— on the confusion in communications between natives and English, 92.
Collapse of the gods, 299.
Colors, 37.
— four known to Demokritos, 38.
— five known in China, 39.
Comte and Feuerbach, 19.
Concept of gods, 197.
— of the divine, 249.
Concepts, serial, 27.
— correlative, 27.
— early, 179.
Confession, 340.
Conscious perception, impossible without language, 38.
Consciousness of dependence, Schleiermacher's view of religion, 18.
Contact with death, its influence, 362.
Copula, sentences impossible without the, 184.
Correlative concepts, 27.
Council of Ephesus, 65.

Cousin, on Indian philosophy, 143.
Cows, days, 231.
— the clouds, 231, *note*.
Created beings, certain gods in the Veda looked on as, 82.
Credo, 290.
Cromlechs, 94.
Cruickshank, negroes of the Gold Coast, 104.
Cultus, Kant's view of, 17.
Cunningham, his discovery of inscriptions by Asoka, 130, *note*.
— date he fixes for Buddha's death, 130, *note*.
Curtius, E. Über die Bedeutung von Delphi, 6, *note*.
Cyrillus, 65.

DÂ, to bind, diti derived from root, 219.
DÂ, in Zend = Sk. dâ and dhâ, 289.
Dahomey, the sun as supreme in, 108.
Daily sacrifices, five, 334, 335.
Dakshinâ, fee, alms, 157.
Darkness and sin, 222.
Dasagranthas, or ten books of a Rig-Veda-Sâkhâ, 155.
Dawn, the, 201, 220.
— golden-colored chariot of the, 221.
— wife and daughter of the sun, 251.
Dawns, the, as parents of the sun, 251.
Days, cows, 231.
Dead, hymn accompanying the burning of, 78.
— body casts no shadow, 86.
— bodies devoured by wolves, 110.
Death, influence of contact with, 362.
De Brosses, the inventor of fetishism, 54.
— his idea of a fetish, 61.
— 1709-1777, 54.
— his Histoire des Navigations aux Terres Australes, 54.
— his Traité de la Formation mécanique des Langues, 54.
Debts, the three, 334, *note*.
Defining religion, difficulty of, 20.
Definitions, necessity of, 9.
Definitions of religion, 9.
— of religion by Kant and Fichte, 13.
— by Schleiermacher (dependence) and by Hegel (freedom), 18.
Deification of parts of nature, 264.
Deists, atheistical opinions of the, 296.
Deities, 205.
— or intangible objects, 17.
— dual, 280.
Deity, idea of, slowly perfected, 262.
Delians, ignorant of geometry, 143, *note*.
Demeter, bread worshiped as, 175.
Demokritos, knew of four colors, 38.
Departing souls as small shooting-stars in Fiji, 83.
Dependence, Schleiermacher's definition of religion, 18.
Deva, 189.
— derivation of, 4.
— meaning bright, 5, 206, 262.
— shining one, 266.
— meaning God, 4.
— its meaning is its history, 190.
— a bright thing, 251.
— more than bright yet very far from divine, 264.
— nature only a, 207.
— meaning forces or faculties, 196, *note*.
Devas, the, 206.
— and Asuras, battles between, 307.
Devatâ, deity, 189.
— object of the hymn, 189.
Dialectic period of religion, Henotheism, 275.
Difference between ancient and modern belief, 8.
Difficulty of defining religion, 20.
Dî-ligo, to gather, 10, *note*.
Dionysos, wine worshiped as, 175.
— (Sk. dyunisya), 268, *note*.
Dioskuroi, the, 201.
Dis, or the Most High, 175.
Discovery of Sanskrit literature, 129.
Dispersonifying, difficulty in, 182.
Diti, root Dâ, to bind, 219.
Divine, concept of the, 249.
— deva very far from, 264.
Dolls and children, 119.
Dolmen, 94.
Dual Deities, 280.
Dualism of good and evil in the Avesta, 78.
Duallahs, name for Great Spirit, 106.
Duty, sense of, 47.
Dyaus, same word as Ζεύς, 139.
— Zeus, 265.

Dyaus, has the acute in the nominative and circumflex in the vocative like Ζεύς, 138.
— the sky, 220.
— the illuminator, the sky as, 265.
— invoked with the earth and fire, 267.
— identified with Parganya, 280.
Dyaush-pita, 209.
Dyaushpitâ, Jupiter, 266.
Dyâvâprithivî, 205.
— heaven and earth, 267.
— maker of heaven and earth, 268.
Dyu-patar, 209.

EARLY concepts, 179.
Earth, the, 171.
— fire, and Dyaus, invoked together, 267.
— mother of all the gods, 279.
— sky as husband of, 279.
East, the abode of *R*ita, 231.
Edda, mention of rainbow in, 37.
Edîyahs of Fernando Po, name for Supreme Being, 106.
Ego, the I, 303.
Eight and nine, expressed as ten minus one or two, 70, *note*.
Elephants, as natural fetishes, 110.
Enquizi, word for fetish, 97, *note*.
Ephesus, council of, 65.
— time of Herakleitos and of Cyrillus, 64, 65.
Ephod, the, 57.
Epicharmos on the gods, 174.
Epikouros, 6.
Epithets, standing, 188.
Erinnys, the, 228.
Eros, Thespian image of, 99.
Eternal part, unborn part, the, 78.
Eternal life on earth, 347.
Eternity, the snake as emblem of, 112.
Etymological meaning of *religio*, 10.
Evidence of religion, never entirely sensuous, 162.
Evil spirit, a supreme, 105.
Evolution in Vedic religion, 327.
External revelation, 163.

FABLES of animals in Africa, 112.
Facultas occulta, 24.
Faculties, Locke on, 23, *note*.
Faculty, objections to the word, 22.
Faith, as a religious faculty in man, 21.
— and revelation, slow yet sure growth of the ideas of, 361.
Faith, sense, and reason, three functions of, 24.
— sraddhâ, 289.
Famine in India, the late, 149.
Fate, Greek moira, 228.
Father, God as, 215.
— God, not a, like a, 214.
— few nations who do not apply this name to God, 215.
Fatum, etymon of feitiço, 60.
Fée, a fairy, from fata, 61.
Feitiçero, a, 60.
Feitiço, Latin factitius, 60.
— derived from fatum, 60.
Feminines, introduction of, 183.
Festus, 167.
Fétichisme, 56.
Fetish, native words for, 97.
— Schultze, F., on the word, 97, *note*.
— Bastian, 97, *note*.
— of Bamba, the great, 98.
— origin of the name, 58.
— whence the supernatural predicate of a, 117.
— wide extension of the meaning of, 94.
— worship considered as degrading, 108.
— worship distinct from idolatry, 61.
— worshipers, the Jews never were, 57.
— wrong extension of the name, 60.
Fetishes, De Brosses' idea of, 61.
— national, 62.
— private, 62.
— elephants as, 110.
— in the Atharva-Veda, 191.
— instruments never become, 192, *note*.
—sellers of, despised, 91.
— believers in, called infidels, 91.
Fetishism, De Brosses the inventor of, 54.
— first used 1760, 54.
— accidental origin of, 118.
— and tangible objects, 174.
— antecedents of, 95.
— ubiquity of, 98.
— a parisitical development, 113.
— no religion consists of it only, 101.
— not a primary form of religion, 122.
— proper, 61.
— supposed psychological necessity of, 115.
— the original form of all religion, 53.
— universal primeval, 93.

Feuerbach, definition of religion, 2.
— and Comte, 19.
— views on religion same as Greek philosophers, 5.
Fichte and Kant, definitions of religion, 13.
— religion is knowledge, 14.
Figurism, 120, 180.
— of Platonic philosophy, 55.
Fiji, religion of, 83.
Finite, can it apprehend the infinite, 28.
— none without an infinite, 43.
Fire invoked, 193, 198.
— worshiped as Hephæstos, 175.
First impulse to the perception of the infinite, 50.
Fist, 167.
Flavus, from flagvus, 39.
Flesh, eating of, commanded, 137.
Forest, life in the, 341.
Formation mécanique des Langues, De Brosses', 1765, 54.
Fortnightly sacrifices, 335.
Four expressed as two-two, 70.
— stages or Âsramas, 330.
— steps, the, 121.
— strata of Vedic literature, 140.
Freedom, Hegel's definition of religion, 18.
Froude, Origen and Celsus, 196, *note*.
Fulahs, 66.
Functions of sense, reason, and faith, 24.
Future life, Greek belief in, 77.
— earliest imaginings of, 228.
Fustis, a cudgel, 167.

GÂBÂLOPANISHAD, 334, *note*.
Gaimini, 149, *note*.
Ganaka of Videha, 343.
— and Sulabhâ, 343.
Gangâ, Ganges, 194.
Garutmat, 300.
Gatâ text of the Veda, 156, 158–160.
Gate of reason, 212.
— of the senses, 212.
Gâthâs, older elements in, 126.
Gâyatrî addressed to Savitri, 158, 259.
Geiger, L., Über den Farbensinn der Urzeit, 38, *note*.
— Über Ursprung und Entwickelung der menschlichen Sprache, 49.
Gender, grammatical, 182.
Genesis, the snake in, 111.
Genii, Celsus on the worship of, 107.
Geometry, indigenous in India, 142.
Germans, Cæsar on the religion of, 175.
— opposite accounts of Cæsar and Tacitus, 88.
Ghana, text of the Veda, 156, 158–160.
Gill, Rev. W. W., on the word atua, God, 87.
Goblet, d'Alviella, 61; De la supériorité du Brahmanisme, sur le Catholicisme, 58, *note*.
God, as a Father, 355.
— few nations who do not apply the name father to, 215.
— *not* a father, *like* a father, a father, 214.
— Polynesian word for, 86.
— predicate of 249.
— whence the predicate, 118.
— predicate of, slowly conquered, 262.
— the Unknown, 300.
— words for in Akwapim and Bonny and among the Makuas, 108.
Gods, belief in closer community with the, 164.
— concept of, 197.
— earth mother of all, 279.
— Pausanias on the rude images of the, 98.
— testimony of the ancients as to the character of their, 174.
Gold, color of the morning, and iron color of the evening, 23, *note*.
Golden-colored chariot of the dawn, 221.
Goldziher, Mythology among the Hebrews, 236, *note*.
Gomal, river, 194.
Gomatî, Gomal river, 194.
Good and evil, dualism of, in the Avesta, 78.
Grammatical gender, 182.
Granthârthaparîkshâ, construction of passages, 156.
Gravity, not a thing by itself, 23.
Great, the infinitely, 33.
Greek, belief in a future life, 77.
— moira or fate, 228.
— philosophers on religion, 5.
Green, confounded with black and brown in Arabic, 39.
Grigri, native word for fetish, 97.
Grihastha, or Grihamedhin, a householder, 333.
Grihasthas, Bramans, 157.
Grihya and Dharma-sûtras, 143.
Growth of the idea of the Infinite, 40.

Grugru, native word for fetish, 59, 97.
Guilt, deliverance from, 197.
Gujarât, study of the Veda in, 157.

HALF-YEARLY sacrifices, 335.
Hamilton, Sir W., 213.
— on the origin of the idea of the infinite, 35.
Harits, one or seven, horses of the sun, 252.
— same as Greek Charites, 252.
Harvest sacrifices, 335.
Heaven-father, 209.
Hebrews, Goldziher, Mythology among, 236, *note*.
Hegel, definition of religion (freedom), 18, 19.
Helios will not overstep the bounds, 228.
Henotheism or kathenotheism, 261, 362.
— the dialectic period of religion, 275.
— further development of, 278.
— in Greece, Italy, and Germany, 275.
Hephæstos, fire worshiped as, 175.
Herakleitos, religion a disease, 6.
— blames the singers, 6, 8.
— 64, 226, 228, 233.
Herakles, statue of, at Hyettos, 99.
Herder, on religious tradition, 4.
Hermeias or Hermes, identified with Sârameya, 232.
Hermits, Christian, of the fourth century, 340.
Herodotus avoids naming Osiris, 82.
— on the Persian religion, 175.
Hesiod, theogony of, 190.
Hidatsa, or Grosventre Indians, 16.
Hindus, despised history, 74.
Hira*n*yagarbha, golden germ, 284.
Hira*n*yarûpa, gold color of the morning, contrasted with aya*h*sthû*n*a, the iron poles of the evening, 253, *note*.
Histoire des Navigations aux Terres Australes, 1756, De Brosses, 54.
Historical aspect of religion, 12.
— character of the Vedic language, 138.
History among savages, none, 70.
— despised by Hindus, 74.
— of religions, a corruption, 64.
Holidays for pupils learning the Veda, 155.
Homer, never mentions the blue sky, 38.
— on the longing for the gods, 32.
Homonymies, the 56.
Hooker, Dr., in the Himâlayas, 170.
Hottentots, 66.
Hydaspes, river, 194.
Hyettos, statue of Herakles at, 99.
Hylobioi, 339.
Hymn to Indra as a supreme god, 270.
— to Varu*n*a as a supreme god, 273.

IBOS, their name for God, 108.
Idea of deity perfected slowly, 261.
— of the infinite growth of the, 40.
— of law, 226.
Idolatry distinct from fetish worship, 61.
Ife, the seat of the gods, 106.
Ignis, Sk. agnis, fire, 199.
Images of the gods, rough, 99.
Immaterial matter, Robert Mayer's view of, 37.
Immortality, 223.
— of the soul in the Rig-Veda, 78.
Imponderable substances, not admitted by our senses, 37.
Impulse, the first, to the perception of the infinite, 50.
India, Buddhism the barrier between ancient and modern literature in, 129.
— growth of religion in, 127.
Indian tradition, snakes in, 111.
— chief on the blessings of doing nothing, 74.
Indra, 276.
— Agni, and Vish*n*u identical, 280.
— Agni as, 280.
— and Agni, Sûrya identified with. 280.
— as a supreme god, hymn to, 270.
— faith in and doubts about, 289.
— denial of, 133.
— identified with Varu*n*a, 280.
— parent of the sun and the dawn, 252.
— and Pra*g*âpati, 307.
— a supreme god, 270.
— the dog of, Saramâ, 232.
— the rain-giver, 205.
— Jupiter pluvius, 268.
Ind-u, drops of rain, 204.
Inferior spirits, 104.
Infinite, the, Aditi, 218.
— apprehension of, 33.

Infinite, can the finite apprehend the, 28.
— first impulse to the perception of, 50.
— growth of the idea of, 40.
— idea of, a logical necessity, 213.
— idea of the, not ready-made from the beginning, 30.
— Melanesian name for, 51.
— meaning of, 26.
— no finite without an, 43.
— religion as a subjective faculty for the apprehension of the, 21.
— that of which *we* cannot perceive the limits, 173.
— the, in its earliest conception, 217.
— the, an aistheton 45.
— the, a pisteuomenon, 45.
— the, as a negative abstraction, 27.
— the visible, 221.
— there from the first, 42.
— Self the, 47.
Infinitely great, the, 33.
— small, the, 36.
Innate language, no, 248.
— religion, 248.
Inscriptions by Asoka, 130, *note*.
— of the Great Council, 131.
Inspiration, idea of, in India, 134.
Instinct, linguistic, 165.
— religious or superstitious in man, 164.
Instruments never become fetishes, 192, *note*.
Intangible objects, 173.
— objects or deities, 174.
Intelligo, 11, *note*.
Internal revelation, 165.
Invisible, man sees the, 35.
— the, and the visible, 207.
Invocation of natural objects, 193.
— of the rivers of the Penjâb, 194.
Iron, mineral, palustric, or meteoric, 225.
— period, 225.
— poles of the chariot of the setting sun, 221.
Irritus, vain, 239.
Ishira, quick and lively, 191.
— identical with ἱερός, 191, *note*.
Ish*t*is, the fortnightly, 161.
Itihâsas, or legends, 149, *note*.

JADE found in the Swiss lakes, 96.
Jankkupong, word for God and weather in Akvapim, 108.
Jewish monotheism preceded by polytheism, 126.
Jews, never fetish worshipers, 57.
Jongmaa, same as Nyongmo, 106.
Judaism, Zoroastrianism, growth of religious ideas in, 125.
Ju-ju, native word for fetish, 97.
Jumna, river, 194.
Ju-piter, 209.
Jupiter, Dyaush-pitâ, 266.
— pluvius, Indra, the rain-giver, 268.
— Ζεύς, and Dyaush-pitâ in Veda, 138.

KAFFER and Congo races, 66.
Kalidâsa, 140.
Kalpa-sûtras, learnt by the *S*rotriyas, 161.
*K*andragupta, 131.
Kant and Fichte, definitions of religion, 13.
— discussion of the antimonies of human reason, 34.
— on cultus, 17.
— religion is morality, 13.
Kant's Critik der reinen Vernunft, 44.
*K*ârvâka, follower of Br*i*haspati, 135.
Karwar, the Papuan, 12.
Kathenotheism, or henotheism, 261.
*K*aturmâsyas, the, 161.
Kautsa, considers the Veda as meaningless, 134.
*Kh*andas, metre and *scandere*, 142.
— period, 146.
Kingsley, Charles, on the All Father, 208.
Kla, Ashanti word for life, 112.
Know thy Self, 306.
Knowledge, sensuous and conceptual, 30.
Kosmos or Asha, recognized by Zoroaster, 241.
Krama, text of the Rig-Veda, 156, 159, 160.
Kritya, Italian fattura, 60.
Krumu, Kurum, river, 194.
Kubhâ, Kophen, Cabul river, 194.
Kurum, river, 194.

LACTANTIUS, his derivation of religio, 11, *note*.
Language and thought, origin of, 177.
— conscious perception impossible without, 38.
Language, no innate, 248.
— of savages, 67.

Language, origin of, 177.
Languages, from without, language from within, 248.
Law books, Sanskrit, 143.
Law, idea of, 226.
— of inheritance, 336.
— of *Ri*ta, 234.
Lectures on the Veda, native, 154.
Lex, legis, from ligare, 12, *note*.
— old Norse, lög, English law, 12, *note*.
Lictor, a binder, 12, *note*.
Life in the forest, 341.
Life in trees, 169.
Life, little valued by savages, 75.
Likeness, originally conceived as negation, 187.
Limit, the, and what is beyond it, 173.
Linguistic instinct, 165.
Literary nations, study of the religion of, 77.
Literary religions, usefulness of the study of, 124.
Lividus, from fligvidus, 39.
Locke, on faculties, 23, *note*.
Lokâyata, name for unbelievers, 134, *note*, 135.
Lunar mansions, or Nakshatras, 142.
Lyall on Indian religion, 192, *note*.

MADHU, honey, 193.
Mâdhyandinas, how they indicate the accents, 160.
— learning the Veda, 160.
— *s*âkhâ, 157.
Mafoor, Meyer, Über die, 39, *note*.
Mahinda, son of Asoka, 130, *note*.
Maitreyî and Yâ*g*navalka, 316.
Makuas, their word for God and heaven, 108.
Malay, Sanskrit in, 128.
Malevolent spirits, require worship, 104.
Man, religious or superstitious instinct in, 164.
— sees the invisible, 35.
Mana, Melanesian name for the infinite, 51.
Mangaia, Mr. Gill on words for God in, 87.
Manifest, meaning of, 167.
Manifestation of belief, religion as the, 8.
Mantra period, 145.
Manu, laws of, 148.
— Vaivasvata, the poet, 275.
Maori word for shadow, used in Mota for soul, 86.
Mar, rubbing, 177.
— an imperative, 178.
Marâ*th*â country, study of the Veda in the, 156.
Married life, second stage, 333.
Marry, right age for a man to, Manu, 333, *note*.
Mars, represented by a spear, 99.
Marudv*ri*dhâ, river, 194.
Marutas, storm gods, 203.
Mâs, the measurer, 181.
Mater, not a feminine, 182.
Matthews, Hidatsa grammar, 70, *note*.
Mayer, Robert, on immaterial matter, 37.
Medin, a friend, 253, *note*.
Megasthenes, visits to *K*andragupta, 131.
Mehatnu, river, 194.
Meiners, Allgemeine Kritische Geschichte, 58, *note*.
Melanesian name for the infinite, 57.
Melanesians, Mana of the, 51.
Men, as God's children, 355.
Meteoric iron, 225.
Metre (Gâthâ) and prose editions of Buddhist stories, 73, *note*.
— in India, 141.
Metrical and prose extracts from the Purâ*n*a, 149, *note*.
Meyer, Über die Mafoor, 39 *note*; 68 *note*.
Mineral iron, 225.
Missing link, the, 88.
Mithilâ, 343.
Mitra, the sun, 251, 253.
— friend, for Mittra, 253, *note*.
— the bright sun, 205.
— greater than the earth, 259.
— Agni as, 280.
Mitra and Pushan, Savit*ri* identified with, 280.
Moira or fate, Greek, 228.
Mokisso, word for fetish, 97, *note*.
Monarchical polytheism, 263.
Monkeys, as fetish worshipers, 108.
— looked on as men, 110.
Monotheism, 362.
— is it a primitive form of religion, 245.
— Jewish, preceded by polytheism, 126.
— original, 262.
— tendency towards, 282.

Moon, a measurer, 181.
Moors, 66.
Morals among savages, none, 74.
Morning and evening, contrasted colors, 253, *note*.
Moseley, on the inhabitants of the Admiralty Islands, 70, *note*.
Mother, a river as a, 181.
Motogon, the author of good, 16.
Mountains, 169.
— invoked, 193.
Muir's Sanskrit Texts, 81.
Mummifying, without mûm or wax, 250.
Muni, the, 337.
Mythology, ancient, how produced, 186.
— chiefly solar, 200.
— among the Hebrews, Goldziher, 236, *note*.

NAISHTHIKA, students who stay all their lives with their masters, 333.
Nakiketas and Yama, 320.
Nakshatras, or Lunar Mansions, 142.
Naraka, or hell, 230.
National fetishes, 92.
— religions, 125.
— traditions, among the Polynesians, 71.
Natural objects as active, 264.
Nature, but a Deva, 207.
— from, to nature's God, 207.
Neander and Strauss, confounded together, 65.
Neapolitans, whip their saints, 100.
Nec-ligere, 10.
Negation, 187.
— likeness originally conceived as, 187.
Negative abstraction, the infinite as, 27.
Negligo, nec-lego, 11, *note*.
Negro inhabitants of Western Africa, 66.
Negroes, Benin, believe their shadows to be their souls, 85.
Negroes wanting rain, 62.
Neoteric senses, 166.
Neptune, punished by Augustus, 99.
Nero, his belief in Dea Syria, 99.
Neuter forms, 183.
— names, 301.
New Guinea, Capt. Moresby on mistaken accounts in, 92.
New Testament, no mention of the blue sky in, 38.
Newton, 353.
Nihil in fide, nisi quod ante fuerit in sensu, 210, 224.
Nirbhuga or Samhitâ text, 159.
Nir-riti, going away, 230.
No religion consists of fetishism only, 101.
Noiré's philosophy, 177, 179, *note*.
Nomina, 214.
Noumenon, the infinite to Kant a mere, 55.
Not-yet, the, instead of faculty, 23.
Numbers, among savages, 69.
Numerals of savages, 69.
Numina, 214.
Nunneries, 340.

OBJECTS, intangible, 173.
— semi-tangible, 172.
Object of belief, religion as the, 8.
Odjis or Ashantis, their name of the Supreme Being and of created spirits, 104, 105.
Old and new faith, Strauss, 2.
Old Testament, no mention of the blue sky in, 38.
Olorun, Yoruba name for God, 106.
Om or *avam*, 81.
— Herbert Spencer, his remarks on the word, 81.
Om, yes, 154.
Oral tradition, Veda handed down by, 148.
Orchomenos, temple of the Graces, 99.
Ordior, to weave, 238.
Ordo, 238.
Origen and Celsus, Froude on, 196, *note*.
Origin of language and thought, 177.
— of reason, 177, *note*.
— of religion, problem of the, 1.
Origin of the name fetish, 58.
Original form of all religion, fetishism, 53.
— monotheism, 262.
Osiris, Herodotus avoids naming, 82.
"Our Father which art in Heaven," 209.

PADA, text of the Rig-Veda, 156, 158.
Palaioteric senses, 166.
Palladium at Troy, 98.
Palustric iron, 225.
Pânini, 142.

Pâ*n*ini and Yâska, period between, 153.
Pâ*n*ini's Grammar, known by heart, 158.
Pantheon, Vedic, 205.
Papa, Scythian name for God, 175,
Papua, the, worshiping his karwar, 12.
Parâ*s*ara, laws of, 143.
Par*g*anya, indentified with Dyaus, 280.
Parishads, 141.
Parivrâ*g*, the, 337.
Parushnî, Ravi, river, 194.
Pater, not a masculine, 182.
Path of *Ri*ta, 231.
Pausanias, on the rude images of the gods, 98.
Peep of day, Saramâ, 232.
Perception of the infinite, first impulse to, 50.
Percepts and concepts, addition and subtraction of, thinking, 29.
Periods, time of stone, bronze, and iron, 225.
Persian religion, Herodotus on, 175.
— Celsus on, 175.
Personal religions, 125.
Personification, 120, 182.
— of parts of nature, 264.
Phainomenon, the infinite not a, 45.
Pharæ, sacred stones at, 99.
Philosophy and religion, distinction between, 325.
— Noiré's, 177, 179.
— of the Upanishads, 306.
Phonetic type, the root, 179.
Phonetics in India, 141.
— or *S*ikshâ, 151, *note*.
Physiolatry, 61.
Pisteuomenon, the infinite as a, 45.
Plants invoked, 193.
Plato and the Delians, 143, *note*.
Plough as an agent, not an instrument, 180.
— and wolf *v*rika, 180, *note*.
Poets of the Veda, on their own writings, 132.
Polygamy, 74.
Polynesia, first used by De Brosses, 54.
— Sanskrit in, 128.
Polynesian word for God, 86.
Polynesians, Whitmee on, 71.
— national traditions, 71.
— legends in prose and poetry, 72.
Polytheism, 261, 362.
Polytheism, monarchical, 236.
— preceded Jewish monotheism, 126.
Poona, prizes for Sanskrit scholarship, 156.
Portuguese navigators and feitiços, 58.
— sailors on African savages, 55.
Poseidon, water worshiped as, 175.
Positive philosophy, 28.
Power of belief, religion as the, 8.
Pra*g*âpati, 282.
— lord of man, 257.
— and Indra, 307.
— epithet of Savit*ri*, 284.
— father of Agni, Vâyu, Âditya, 286.
— father of Indra, 308.
— fell to pieces, 287.
— half mortal, half immortal, 297.
— the lord of creatures, 284.
Pra*g*âpati's love for his daughter, story of, 286.
Prakriyâ, theoretical knowledge of Sanskrit learning, 156.
Prâ*n*a, breath or spirit, 303.
Pra*s*na, a section, in teaching the Veda, 154.
Pra*s*nas, sixty to a lecture, 154.
Prâti*s*âkhya of the Rig-Veda, 153.
Prat*ri*nna, or Pada text, 159.
Prayogas, or manuals, 161.
Predicate of God, 249.
— God, slowly conquered, 262.
— of God, whence derived, 118.
Predicates, forming names of a class of beings, 262.
Priests, authority of, 90.
Primary form of religion, fetishism not a, 122.
Primeval revelation, 245.
Primitive conceptions, Herbert Spencer on, 63.
P*ri*thivî, the earth, 220.
Private fetishes, 62.
Problem of the origin of religion, 1.
Prodikos on the gods, 175.
Pronominal roots, 178.
Prose and poetry, Polynesian legends in both, 72.
Psycholatry, 112.
Public opinion, influence of, on travelers, 88.
Pugna, a battle, 168.
Punctum, 168.
Purâ*n*a, extracts from, 149, *note*.
Purâ*n*as, 149.

Puranas, to be distinguished from Purâna, 149, *note*.
Pûshan, the sun, 251.
— the sun of shepherds, 254.
— as lord of all that rests and moves, 259.
— conducts souls to the regions of the blest, 259.
— his sister and beloved Sûryâ, 254.
Psychological necessity of fetishism, supposed, 115.

RADJA, speech, 240.
Rain, and the rainer, 204.
— how negroes seek for, 62.
Rainbow, seven colors of, 37.
— tricolored, 37.
— in the Edda, 37.
Rainy season, term for teaching the Veda, 155.
Ram Mohun Roy, 321.
Rasâ, 194.
Râta and *ratus*, 239.
Rathjan, to number, 240.
Rathjo, number, 240.
Ratio, counting, reason, 240.
Ratu, order, he who orders, 238.
— order and orderer, 185, *note*.
Ratus, constant movement of the stars, 238.
Ravi, river, 194.
Reason, altar erected to, 23.
Reason and sense, distinction between, 21.
Reason evolved from what is finite, 31.
Reason, faith, and sense, the three functions of, 24.
Reason, gate of, 212.
Redjon, to speak, 240.
Regard, religio, 10.
Relegere, 10.
Religare, 10.
Religens and *religiosus*, distinction between, 11, *note*.
Religio, 8.
— derivations of, 10, 11, and *note*.
— derived from *religare*, 11, *note*.
— meant attention, regard, 10.
Religion, problem of the origin of, 1.
— etymological meaning of, 10.
— Strauss, have we still any, 2.
— science of, 5.
— the object of belief, 8.
— the power of belief, 8.
— the manifestation of belief, 8.
— used in three senses, 8.
Religion, specific characteristic of, 20.
— retrogression in, frequent, 63.
— universal among savages, 76.
— unwillingness of savages to talk of, 91.
— an universal phenomenon of humanity, 76.
— as a mental faculty, 21.
— as a subjective faculty for the apprehension of the infinite, 21.
— and philosophy, distinction between, 325.
— antiquity of, 3.
— difficulty of defining, 20.
— definitions of, 2, 9.
— definitions of, by Fichte and Kant, 13.
— definition of Schleiermacher (dependence), and of Hegel (freedom), 18.
— is knowledge, Fichte, 14.
— is morality, Kant, 13.
— with or without worship, 15.
— evidence of, never entirely sensuous, 162.
— fetishism, not a primary form of, 122.
— Henotheism the dialectic period of, 275.
— historical aspect of, 12.
— inevitable, if we have our senses, 30.
— innate, 248.
— national and personal, 125.
— book, 125.
— of literary nations, study of, 77.
— literary, usefulness of the study of, 124.
— difficulty of studying it, 83.
— of savages, study of, 65.
— of the Germans, Cæsar on, 175.
— of the Persians, Herodotus on, 175.
— Celsus on, 175.
— in India, growth of, 127.
— of the Upanishads, 325.
Religiosus and *religens*, distinction between, 11, *note*.
Religious ideas in Judaism, Zoroastrianism, growth of, 125.
— ideas in the Veda, 224.
— or superstitious instinct in man, 164.
Renan, on German religious opinion, 3.
Retirement, third stage, 336.

Retrogression in religion, frequent, 64.
— as frequent as progression in the human race, 64.
Revelation and faith, slow but sure growth of the ideas of, 362.
Revelation, external, 163.
— internal, 164.
— primeval, 245.
— idea of, in India, 133.
Right age. for man to marry, according to Manu, 333, *note*.
Rig-Veda, the only real Veda, 146.
— compared with the Atharva-Veda, 147.
— Prâtisâkhya of, 153.
— and the immortality of the soul, 78.
Rig-Veda-sâkhâ, time taken to learn a, 155.
Rishi, subject of the hymn, 189.
*Ri*ta, 228.
— original meaning of, 230.
— the sacrifice, 235.
— development of, 236.
— was it a common Aryan concept, 237.
— in Asha in Zend, 240.
— abode of, the East, 231.
— as the place where they unharness the horses, 231.
— takes the place of Aditi, 231.
— the law of, 234.
— the path of, the right path, 231.
— — gâtu, 234.
Rite, ritus, 238.
Ritual in India, 141.
Ri-tvan, ordo, 238.
Rivers, 170.
— Seneca on, 170.
— invoked, 193.
— of the Penjâb invoked, 194.
Root, the phonetic type, 179.
Roots, pronominal, 178.
Rosaries, 340.
Rousseau's ideas of savages, 88.
Rudra, the thunderer, 202.
Rupi, name for Supreme Being, 106.
Russian peasants and their saints, 100.

SABAOTH, 175.
Sabeism, 56.
Sacramental rites, samskâras, 331.
Sacrifices, daily, 335.
— fortnightly, 335.
— harvest, 335.
— three seasons, 335.
Sacrifices, half-yearly, 335.
— yearly, 335.
— five daily, 334.
— various Vedic, 161.
— Vedic, why offered by men of wisdom, 135.
St. Anthony and Portuguese sailors, 100.
St. Augustine, his derivation of religio, 11, *note*.
Saints, images of, in Roman Catholic countries, 100.
*S*âkhâs or recensions of the Veda, 161.
*S*âkyâdaya*h*, *S*âkyas, Buddhists, 338, *note*.
Salvado, on the natives of Western Australia, 15, *note*.
Samâv*ri*tta, a, 332.
Sa*m*hitâ text of the Rig-Veda, 158.
Sa*m*hitâs, different, 159, *note*.
Sa*m*skâras, twenty-five, 331.
Sandhyâ-vandana, or twilight-prayers, 158.
Sandrocottus, 130.
— or *K*andragupta, 130, *note*.
*S*annyâsin, the fourth stage, 337.
Sanskrit in Malay, 128.
— in Polynesian and Caucasian, 128.
— literature, discovery of 129.
— MSS. in different libraries, 129, *note*.
— scholarships, prizes for, 156.
— no subjunctive mood in, 138.
— 10,000 separate works in, 129.
— and Zend, some technical terms, in both, 240.
Santhals in India, 201.
Saramâ, peep of day, 232.
— story of, 232.
— the dog of Indra, 232.
Sârameya, sons of Saramâ, 232.
— identified with Hermeias or Hermes, 232.
Sarasvatî, Sursûti, river, 194.
Sarit, the runner, 179.
Satya, the true, 233, 258.
Savages, absence of recognized authorities among, 89.
— and children, contrasted, 119, 120.
— difficulty of studying the religion of, 65.
— language of, 67.
— numerals of, 69.
— little value for life, 75.
— morals among, 74.
— no history among, 70.
— religion and language of, 67.

Savages, religion universal among, 76.
— study of the religion of, 83.
— unwillingness to talk of religion, 91.
— tribes, usefulness of the study of, 62.
Savit*ri*, the sun, 251.
— Agni as, 280.
— identified with Mitra and Pûshan, 280.
— is Mitra, 253.
— Pra*g*âpati as epithet for, 284.
Savit*ri*'s golden chariot, 252.
Sâya*n*a Â*k*ârya, 148.
Scent, in animals and man, 167.
Schiller, professed no religion, 13.
Schleiermacher's absolute dependence, 204.
— definition of religion, 2, 18.
Schliemann, his labors, 139.
Schultze, F., on the word fetish, 97, *note*.
Science of religion, 5.
— of language, and the science of religion, 246.
— of religion, and the science of language, 246.
— of religion, right position of the Veda in the, 128.
Scythian name for God, Papa, 175.
Seasons, *ri*tu, 237.
Second stage, married life, 333.
Seleucus Nicator, contemporary of Sandrocottus, 131.
Self, 207, 348.
— annihilation of, 347.
— of the world, 207.
— the shadow or image is, 308.
Semi-deities or semi-tangible objects, 174, 195, 206, 218.
— rise to the rank of supreme gods, 265.
Semi-tangible and tangible, division of sense-objects, 168.
— objects, 172.
— objects, or semi-deities, 174.
— objects among Vedic deities, 19.
Seneca, on rivers, 170.
Senegal and Niger, the negro found between, 66.
Sense and reason, distinction between, 21.
Sense objects, division of, into tangible and semi-tangible, 168.
Sense of duty, 47.
Sense, reason, and faith, three functions of, 24.
Senses, gate of the, 212.
— the, and their evidence, 166.
— neoteric and palaioteric, 166.
Sensuous and conceptual knowledge, 30.
Sensuous perception, never supplies entirely the evidence of religion, 162.
Sentences impossible without the copula, 184.
Serial concepts, 27.
Serpent and tree-worship, 94.
Servetus and Calvin, 295.
Servius, his derivation of religio, 11, *note*.
Seven colors of the rainbow, 37.
Sex, denoting languages, 182.
Shadow and soul, 84, 85.
— and breath, 86.
— dead body casts no, 86.
— or image is Self, 308.
Shankar Pandurang, 151.
Shooting stars as gods in Fiji, 83.
— as departing souls, 84.
Sky, husband of the earth, 279.
Sky, the, as Dyaus or the illuminator, 265.
*S*ikshâ or phonetics, 151, *note*.
Sin and darkness, 222.
Sindhu, Indus, 194.
— the defender, 180.
— the rivers, 220.
Sinlessness, prayer for, 223.
Sisa in Ashanti, 113.
*S*iva and Vish*n*u, 140.
Slavery, excused by American ethnologists, 88.
Sm*r*iti, 134.
Snakes, why worshiped, 110.
— name assumed by many tribes, 111.
— how viewed in India, 111.
— of the Zendavesta, 111.
— of Genesis, 111.
— symbol of eternity, 112.
— naka, a, 332.
— oftes, an atheist, 294.
R.ar mythology, 200.
Solomon, his idolatry, 64.
Soma sacrifices, 161.
Somah, rain, 186, 277.
Soul, meaning of in Fiji, 84.
— Mota word for, 85.
— words for, meant shadow, 85.
Sounds, limited power of distinguishing, 40.
Spencer, Herbert, on primitive conceptions, 63.

Spencer, H., on the word Om, 81.
— on undeveloped grammatical structures, 83.
Spinoza, 307.
Spirits, malevolent, 104.
Spiritual guides or âkâryas, 332.
*S*râddha, 136.
*S*rad-dhâ, credo, 290, *note*.
*S*ramana, ascetic, 342.
*S*rotriyas, oral tradition of, 152.
— or *S*rautîs, 161.
*S*ruti, 134.
— or revelation, Upanishads belong to, 326.
Stages, four, 331.
— first, 331.
— second, 333.
— third, 336.
— fourth, 337.
Stars, constant movement of, ratus, 238.
Steps, the four, 121.
Stone, a cutter, 180.
— period, 225.
— the coronation, 97.
— why worshiped, 96.
Stones, as images of the gods, 99.
Storm gods, Marutas, 203.
Strauss, have we still any religion, 2.
— "old and new faith," 2.
Students, naish*th*ika, who stay all their life at their masters, 333.
Studentship, first stage, 331.
Subjective faculty for the apprehension of the infinite, religion as a, 21.
Subjunctive mood, none in Sanskrit, 138.
*S*uddhâ Sa*m*hitâ, 159, *note*.
*S*ûdras, 331.
— prohibited from knowing the Vedas, 330.
— servants or slaves, 330.
Sulabhâ and *G*anaka, 343.
*S*ulva Sûtras, on square and round altars, 142.
Sun, the, 200.
— and day used synonymously, 253.
— as creator of the world, 255.
— a defender and protector, 255.
— dies, 223.
— a divine being, 255.
— names for, 251.
— maker of all things, 257,
— sees everything, 255.
— knows the thoughts in men, 256.
— settled movement of, 230.
Sun, as supreme in Dahomey, 108.
— the, in his natural aspects, 251.
— as a supernatural power, 255.
— in a secondary position, 260.
— Tyndall's discoveries, 200.
— various names for, 251, 253.
— Xenophon on the, 202, *note*.
Supernatural power, the sun as a, 255.
— predicate of a fetish, whence derived, 117.
Supreme being, meaning of names for the, 105.
— god, Indra as a, 270.
— Varu*n*a, as a, 273.
— semi-deities never become, 265.
Sursuti, river, 194.
Sûrya, god among gods, 258.
— identified with Indra and Agni, 280.
— the creator, 252.
— the sun, 251.
— the son of the sky, 251.
— the sister and beloved of Pûshan, 254.
Sûrya's chariot, 252.
Susartu, river, 194.
Sushomâ, river, 194.
Sutlej, river, 194.
Sûtra period, 140.
Sûtras, philosophy in the, 143.
Sutudri, Sutlej, 194.
*S*vetî, 194.

TACITUS, his views of the Germans, 88.
Tahiti, idleness in, 75.
Tailingana, study of the Veda in, 157.
Tangible and semi-tangible division of sense objects, 168.
— objects among Vedic deities, 191.
— objects and fetishism, 174.
Taplin, "The Narrinyeri," 68, *note*.
Tat tvam, thou art it, 345.
Ten Commandments, place assigned to the prohibition of images, 114.
Teraphim, the, 57.
Thales, declared all things full of the gods, 13.
— why a philosopher, 7.
Theogonic, or god-producing character of stones, shells, etc., 123.
Theogony of the Veda, 216.
— of Hesiod, 190.
Theology, begins with anthropology, 36.
Thespians, their image of Eros, 99.

Thibaut, translation of the *Sulva Sûtras*, 142, *note*.
Thiedos or infidels, name for believers in fetishes, 91.
Thinking, is addition and subtraction of percepts and concepts, 30.
Third faculty needed to account for religion, 31.
— stage, retirement, 336.
— stage abolished, 338.
Thought and language, origin of, 177.
Three debts, 334, *note*.
— functions of sense, reason, and faith, 24.
Three-colored bridge, name for rainbow, 37.
Thunder, 202.
Tiele, religion as an universal phenomenon of humanity, 76.
Tillotson, 296.
Tiu, or Zio, 209.
Tonsure, 340.
Translating, difficulty of, 236.
Travelers, influence of public opinion on, 88.
Tree, life in the, 169.
— and serpent-worship, 94.
Trees, 169.
— invoked, 193.
Tricolored rainbow, 37.
Trish*t*âmâ, 194.
Trish*t*ubh, 142.
Troy, Palladium at, 98.
True story by Celsus, 196, *note*.
Tshuku, word for God among the Ibos, 108.
Tylor, Mr. E., list of contradictory accounts of the same tribe, 88.
Tyndall on the sun, 200.

UBHAYAM - ANTARE*N*A, or Krama text, 159.
Ultra-violet, to the eye utter darkness, 40.
Unborn being, the, 304.
— part, eternal part, the, 78.
Unclean hands, 149.
Unconscious cerebration, 227.
Unity of the Godhead, felt by Abraham, 64.
Universal primeval fetishism, 93.
Unknown God, the, 300.
Upâdhyâyas, teachers, 332.
Upanishads belong to Sruti or revelation, 326.
Upanishads, 143, 144.
— the oldest, 306.
Upanishads, sessions, 306.
— look on the Veda as useless, 134.
— meaning of *deva* in, 196, *note*.
— religion of, 325.
— philosophy of the, 306.
Upasthiti, general knowledge of Sanskrit learning, 156.
Upavîta, or sacred cord, 152.
Urim and Thummim, 57.

VAIDIKAS, the *S*rotriyas are good, 161.
— knowledge of the Veda, 158.
Vala, the robber, 233.
Vânaprastha, a, 336.
Vânaprasthas, or the dwellers in the forest, 144.
Vanini, 295.
Varu*n*a, Greek, 205.
— Agni as, 280.
— 277.
— knows and upholds the order of nature, 277.
— watches over the order of the moral world, 278.
— identified with Indra, 280.
— as a supreme god, 273.
— the law of, 234.
Vas, to dwell, 185.
Vasu, bright, 190.
Vâta, the blast, 203.
Vâyu, the blower, 203.
Veda, certain gods looked on as created beings in the, 82.
— right position of, in the science of religion, 128.
— proclaimed as revealed, 132.
— Buddhists deny its authority, 132.
— claims to be divinely revealed, 132.
— Poets of, on their own writings, 132.
— considered as useless in the Upanishads, 134.
— meaningless by Kautsa, 134.
— untruth, self-contradiction, and tautology of the, 135.
Vedas, authors of, were knaves, buffoons, and demons, 136.
— handed down by old tradition, 148.
— method of teaching the, 154.
— time employed in learning the, 155.
— traveling Brahmans repeating the, 157.
— different forms of, 157.

Vedas, study of, in different parts of India, 157.
— various texts of, 158, 159.
— accents in, 160.
— authority of the, 161.
— testimony of, 175.
— theogony of, 216.
— religious ideas in, 224.
— new materials supplied by, 250.
— student of a Brahma*k*ârin, 332.
Vedas, *S*ûdra caste prohibited from knowing, 330.
— becoming lower knowledge, 344.
Vedânta-sûtras, the Âsramas discussed in the, 334, *note*.
Vedânta, end or highest object of the Veda, 307.
Vedic language, historical character of, 138.
— literature, four strata of, 140.
— tangible objects among, 191.
— semi-tangible objects among, 192.
— deities, audible objects among, 202.
— pantheon, 205.
— religion, evolution in, 327.
Verbs, auxiliary, 184.
Versus, 142.
Vi, a bird, 183.
— arrow, 183.
Viro*k*ana, chief of the Asuras, 307.
— son of Prahrâda and Kayâdhû, 308.
Vish*n*u, 140.
— the sun, 254.
— his three strides, 254.
— supports the worlds, 260.
— Indra and Agni identical, 280.
Visible, the, and invisible, 207.
— infinite, 221.
Visvakarman, maker of all things, the sun as, 257.
— 282.
— the maker of all things. 282.
Visve Devas, All-gods, 281.
Vitastâ, Hydaspes, Behat, 194.
Vocative of Dyaus, accent of, 139.
— of Dyaus and Ζεύς, 140.
V*r*ika, a wolf and plough, 180, *note*.
V*r*itta, metre, 142.

WAITZ on African religion, 102.
— classification of African tribes, 66.
Waitz's Anthropology, 102.
Water invoked, 193.
Water, worshiped as Poseidon, 175.
Watts, 327.
Wax or mûm, 250.
West Africa, Wilson's, 103.
West coast of Africa, home of the negro, 66.
Western Australia, mission in, 15.
White, Ya*g*ur-Veda, 157.
Whitmee, on the Polynesians, 71.
Widah, God only known to the nobility, 90.
Widow-burning, 80.
Wilson's West Africa, 103.
Wine worshiped as Dionysos, 175.
Wind, the, 203.
— high position assigned to the, 203.
Winterbottom, Account of Africans of Sierra Leone, 70, *note*.
Wolf and plough, *v*rika, 180, *note*.
Wolves that devour dead bodies sacred, 110.
Wong, the spirits of the air, 107.
Wongs, of the Gold Coast, 107.
Wordsworth quoted, 42.
Worship, religion with or without, 15.
— tree and serpent, 94.
— required by malevolent spirits, 104.
Wyttenbach on Kant, 29, *note*.

XENOPHANES, 7.
— view of the rainbow, 37.
Xenophon on the sun, 202, *note*.

YÂ*G*NAVALKYA, laws of, 143.
Yâ*g*navalkya and Maitreyî, 316.
Yâ*g*nikas, the, 158.
Yama and Na*k*iketas, 320.
Yamunâ, Jumna river, 194.
Yâshâr, straight, 236, *note*.
Yâska and Pâ*n*ini, period between, 153.
Yati, the, 337.
Yearly sacrifices, 335.
Yebus, their prayers, 105.
Yorubas, name for God, Olorun, 106.
Yudh, a fighter, 183.
— weapon, 183.
— fight, 183.

ZELLER, on the power of personification, 117.
Zend and Sanskrit, same technical terms in both, 240.
Zendavesta, no mention of blue sky in, 38.

Zendavesta, snakes in the, 111.
Ζεὺς πατήρ, 209.
Ζεύς and Dyaus, same accent, 138.
Ζεύς, Dyaus, 265.
Zeus Meilichios, image of, 99.
Zio or Tiu, 209.
Zoölatry, 61, 109.
Zoroaster, his system complete from the first, 126.
— recognized a kosmos or rita, 241.
Zoroastrianism, Judaism, growth of religious ideas in, 125.